About the Author

Suzanne Weixel is a self-employed writer and editor specializing in the technology industry. Her experience with computers began in 1974 when she learned to play football on the Dartmouth Time-Sharing terminal her brother installed in a spare bedroom.

Suzanne has written, edited, and contributed to more books than she can keep track of for Macmillan Computer Publishing, including *Using Windows 3.11*; *Using DOS*; and *Easy PCs, 2nd, 3rd,* and *4th Editions*. She has also written many text books in Que Education and Training's *Essentials* series, including *Word 97 Level III Essentials*; *Excel 97 Essentials*; *Microsoft Office Professional for Windows 95 Essentials*; *Excel for Windows 95 Essentials*; *Lotus SmartSuite for Windows Essentials*; and *Personal Computing Essentials, 1st* and *2nd Editions*. In addition, Suzanne was one of the authors of *Success with WordPerfect 7 for Windows 95*, *Power User's Guide to Windows 95* and *Success with Word for Windows 95*, also published by Que Education and Training. She also likes to write about non-computer-related subjects whenever she has the chance.

Suzanne graduated from Dartmouth College in 1981 with a degree in art history. She currently lives in Marlborough, MA with her husband, Rick, their sons Nathaniel and Evan, and their dog, a Samoyed named Cirrus.

Acknowledgments

Thanks, as always, to Rick, Nathaniel, and Evan for their patience. Thanks also to everyone at Prentice Hall who had a hand in putting this book together during one of the hottest summers on record, and to Susan Hobbs, Development Editor, and Asit J. Patel, Technical Editor, both of whom provided useful comments and suggestions for how best to bring PC Essentials into the 21st century.

Trademark Acknowledgments

Screens reproduced in the book were created using Collage Plus from Inner Media, Inc., Hollis, NH.

Contents at a Glance

essentials

PERSONAL COMPUTING

Third Edition

SUZANNE WEIXEL

Prentice Hall

A division of Pearson Education
Upper Saddle River, NJ 07458

Personal Computing Essentials, 3rd Edition

International Standard Book Number: 0-13-026195-5

Printed in the United States of America

First Printing: November 1999

03 02 01 00 4 3 2 1

Interpretation of the printing code: the rightmost double-digit number is the year of the book's printing; the rightmost single-digit number, the number of the book's printing. For example, a printing code of 00-1 shows that the first printing of the book occurred in 2000.

Library of Congress Cataloging-in-Publication Data

Weixel, Suzanne.
Personal computing essentials / Suzanne Weixel.—3rd ed.
p. cm.
ISBN 0-13-026195-5
1. Microcomputers. I. Title.

QA76.5 W4717 2000
004.165—dc21

99-051341

Editor-in-Chief:
Mickey Cox

Acquisitions Editor:
Alex Von Rosenberg

Development Editor:
S. A. Hobbs

Technical Editor:
Asit J. Patel

Managing Editor:
Susan Rifkin

Editorial Assistant:
Jennifer Surich

Marketing Manager:
Kris King

AVP/Director of Production & Manufacturing:
Michael Weinstein

Production Manager:
Gail Steier de Acevedo

Project Manager:
Tim Tate

Senior Manufacturing and Prepress Manager:
Vincent Scelta

Book Designer:
Louisa Klucznik

Full Service Composition:
Graphic World

Copy Editor:
Nancy E. Sixsmith

Indexer:
Larry Sweazy

Table of Contents

Introduction

Essentials courseware from Prentice Hall is anchored in the practical and professional needs of all types of students. This edition of *Personal Computer Essentials, 3rd Edition* has been completely revamped as the result of painstaking usability research by the publisher, authors, editors, and students. Practically every detail—by way of pedagogy, content, presentation, and design—was the object of continuous online (and offline) discussion among the entire team.

The *Essentials* series has been conceived around a "learning-by-doing" approach that encourages you to grasp application-related concepts as you expand your skills through hands-on tutorials. As such, it consists of modular lessons that are built around a series of numbered, step-by-step procedures that are clear, concise, and easy to review. Explicatory material is interwoven before each lesson and between the steps. Additional features, tips, pitfalls, and other related information are provided at exactly the right place where you would most expect them. They are easily recognizable elements that stand out from the main flow of the tutorial. Likewise, the end-of-chapter exercises have been carefully graded from the routine Checking Concepts and Terms to tasks in the Skill Drill and Challenge sections that gently prod you into extending what you've learned into areas beyond the explicit scope of the lessons proper. Later in this introduction, you'll learn more about the rationale behind each book element and how to use each to your maximum benefit.

How to Use This Book

Typically, each *Essentials* book is divided into seven or eight projects, covering topics such as identifying external components of the system unit to creating program shortcuts. A project covers one area (or a few closely related areas) of application functionality. Each project is divided into several lessons related to that topic. For example, a project on PC data storage is divided into lessons explaining how to identify different types of storage media, preparing a floppy disk for use, viewing the contents of a disk or folder, working with folders, and working with files. Each lesson presents a specific task or closely related set of tasks in a manageable chunk that's easy to assimilate and retain.

Each element in *Personal Computing Essentials, 3rd Edition* is designed to maximize your learning experience. Here's a list of the *Essentials* project elements and a description of how each element can help you:

- **Project Objectives.** Starting with an objective gives you short-term, attainable goals. Using project objectives that closely match the titles of the step-by-step tutorials breaks down the possibly overwhelming prospect of learning about personal computers into small, attainable, bite-sized tasks. Look over the objectives on the opening page of the project before you begin, and review them after completing the project to identify the main goals for each project.
- **Key Terms.** This book includes a limited number of useful vocabulary words and definitions, such as ***cable modem***, ***graphical user interface***, and ***motherboard***. Key terms introduced in each project are listed in alphabetical order immediately after the objectives on the opening page of the project. These key terms are shown in bold italic, and are defined during their first use within the text. Definitions of key terms are also included in the glossary.
- **Why Would I Do This?** You are studying personal computers to accomplish useful tasks in the real world. This brief section tells you why these tasks or procedures are important. What can you do with the knowledge? How can these application features be applied to everyday tasks?

- **Lessons.** Each lesson contains one or more tasks that correspond to an objective on the opening page of the project. A lesson consists of step-by-step tutorials, associated data files, screenshots, and the special notes described below. Though each lesson often builds on the previous one, the lessons (and the exercises) have been made as modular as possible. For example, you can skip tasks that you've already mastered and begin a later lesson.
- **Step-by-Step Tutorial.** The lessons consist of numbered, bolded step-by-step instructions that show you how to perform the procedures in a clear, concise, and direct manner. These hands-on tutorials, which are the "essentials" of each project, let you "learn by doing." Regular paragraphs between the steps clarify the results of each step. Also, screenshots are introduced after key steps for you to check against the results on your monitor. To revise the lesson, you can easily scan the bold, numbered steps. Quick (or impatient!) learners may likewise ignore the intervening paragraphs.
- **Need to Know.** These sidebars provide essential tips for performing the task and using the application more effectively. You can easily recognize them by their distinctive icon and bolded headings. It's well worth the effort to review these crucial notes again after completing the project.
- **Nice to Know.** Nice to Know comments provide extra tips, shortcuts, alternative ways to complete a process, and special hints. You can safely ignore these for the moment to focus on the main task at hand, or you may pause to learn and appreciate these tidbits. Here you'll find neat tricks and special insights that you can use to impress your friends and coworkers!
- **If You Have Problems...** These short troubleshooting notes help you anticipate or solve common problems quickly and effectively. Even if you don't encounter the problem at this time, do make a mental note of it so that you know where to look when you find yourself (or others) having difficulties.
- **Summary.** This section provides a brief recap of the tasks learned in the project. The summary will guide you to places where you can expand your knowledge, which might include references to specific Help topics or the Prentice Hall *Essentials* Web site (http://www.prenhall.com/essentials).
- **Checking Concepts and Terms.** This section offers optional true/false, multiple choice, screen ID, and discussion questions designed to check your comprehension and assess retention. If you need to refresh your memory, the relevant lesson number is provided after each true/false and multiple choice question. For example, [L5] directs you to review Lesson 5 for the answer. Lesson numbers might also be provided for other types of exercises, but only where relevant.
- **Skill Drill Exercises.** This section enables you to check your comprehension, evaluate your progress, and practice what you've learned. The exercises in this section build on and reinforce what you have learned in each project. Generally, the Skill Drill exercises include step-by-step instructions.
- **Challenge Exercises.** This section provides exercises that expand on or relate to the skills practiced in the project. Each exercise provides a brief narrative introduction followed by instructions. Although the instructions are written in a step-by-step format, the steps are not as detailed as those in the Skill Drill section. Providing less specific steps helps you learn to think on your own. These exercises foster "near transfer" of learning.
- **Task Guide.** The Task Guide that follows the last project lists all the procedures and shortcuts you will have learned in the book. It can be used in two complementary ways to enhance your learning experience. You can refer to it while progressing through the book in order to refresh your memory about procedures learned in a previous lesson. Or you can keep it as a handy real-world reference for use during your daily work.

- **Glossary.** Here you'll find the definitions—collected in one place—of all the key terms defined throughout the book and listed in the opening page of each project. Use it to refresh your memory.

Typeface Conventions Used in This Book

We have used the following conventions throughout this book to make it easier for you to understand the material:

- Key terms appear in ***italic and bold*** the first time they are defined in a project.
- Text that you type, as well as text that appears on your computer screen as warnings, confirmations, or general information, appears in a special `monospace` typeface.
- Hotkeys, the underlined keys onscreen that activate commands and options, are also underlained in this book. Hotkeys offer a quick way to bring up frequently used commands.

Project 1

Project 1

Getting Started with Personal Computer Hardware

Objectives

In this project, you learn how to

- **Identify External Components of the System Unit**
- **Identify Internal Components of the System Unit**
- **Identify Input Devices**
- **Identify Output Devices**
- **Identify Storage Devices**

Key terms introduced in this project include

- bit
- bus
- byte
- Central Processing Unit (CPU)
- chip
- compact disc (CD) drives
- controller board
- data
- digital pen
- digital video disc (DVD)
- digitizing tablet
- disk drive
- expansion slots
- file server
- handheld device
- hardware
- inkjet
- input
- joystick
- keyboard
- laser
- laptop
- megahertz (MHz)
- modem
- monitor
- motherboard
- mouse
- network
- on/off switch
- output
- peripheral
- personal computer (PC)
- port
- random access memory (RAM)
- resolution
- scanner
- status lights
- system unit
- tape drive
- toner
- trackball

Why Would I Do This?

A ***personal computer (PC)*** is a stand-alone computer system designed for use by a single person. Most PCs that are available today have the same basic electronic components, which are called ***hardware***. These components include the ***system unit***, or the main case housing the computer components; the display ***monitor***, which is the screen that displays computer data in a format that you can understand; the ***keyboard***, which is an input device used to type characters and enter commands; the ***mouse***, which is another input device used to select commands on a PC monitor; and the ***disk drives***, which are storage devices used to read and write information onto magnetic storage disks. You use the hardware to enter information into the computer; the computer uses hardware to process the information and send it back out to you.

Understanding the different hardware devices that make your personal computer work provides you with more information about your system. If you are purchasing a new computer system, you will benefit from knowing what kinds of hardware are available and what best suits your needs. If you are learning to use a personal computer, you will grasp concepts more quickly if you know the names of the hardware devices, where they are located, and what functions they perform.

In this project, you learn to identify the necessary hardware devices attached to your PC—called ***peripherals***. You also learn about some optional devices that give computers increased capabilities and make them more fun to use. These devices include **modems**, devices used to exchange information with other computers via telephone lines or cables; and **tape drives**, storage devices used to store data on tape cassettes.

Lesson 1: Identifying External Components of the System Unit

Every personal computer has a ***system unit***—the box, or case, that contains the most vital parts of your PC. The outside of the system unit has the buttons, sockets, and lights that enable you to access the electronic components stored inside the system unit.

System units come in different shapes and sizes, so the system unit on your PC may not look the same as the system unit on a friend's PC. The most typical system unit is the desktop model, which is designed to fit easily on a desktop. Other types include a tower model, which usually stands up on the floor; and a portable model (laptop, notebook, or handheld), which you can carry with you.

Try locating the external components of the system unit now.

To Identify External Components of the System Unit

1. **Look at the main case of the computer, and find the computer's on/off switch.**
   Although the electrical power switch used to turn your PC on and off—the ***on/off switch***—may be located in different places on the system unit, all computers have an on/off switch. Look for a push button, a switch that flips up and down like a light switch, or a switch that rocks back and forth. The switch may appear on the front, side, or back of the system unit (see Figure 1.1).

On a PC, the on/off switch works like the on/off switch of any electrical appliance. It connects to the power supply inside the system unit so that when you activate the switch, the PC starts.

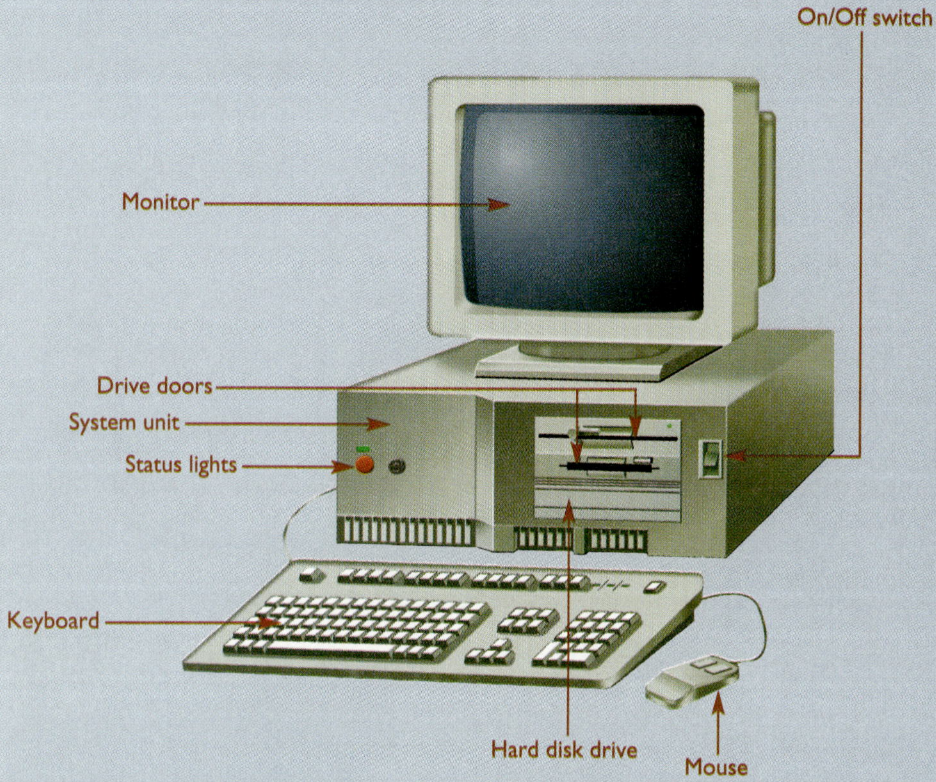

Figure 1.1
All personal computers have these same basic hardware components.

❷ **Look at the front of the system unit and locate the status lights.**
If you turn the PC on, the ***status lights*** may appear red, green, or amber (refer to Figure 1.1). Each status light is a light-emitting diode (LED) that appears illuminated when the device is active and does not appear illuminated when the device is inactive. If your PC is off, then the lights are off. You may be able to identify the lights by their labels. Look for a light marked Power and one marked HDD, for hard disk drive. The power light indicates when the PC is on; the HDD light indicates when the hard disk drive is in use.

❸ **Find the disk drive door(s) on the system unit.**
Most personal computers have three kinds of disk drives: floppy drives, hard drives, and ***compact disc (CD) drives***. CD drives are used to read and sometimes write ***data***—information processed by your computer—to and from ***compact discs (CDs)***. Some PCs have ***digital video disc (DVD)*** drives instead of CD drives. DVD drives are similar to CD drives in that they both store data in digital format. DVD drives, however, use a different encoding method, which makes it faster to read data from the disc and lets you store more data on the disc. DVD drives can read regular CDs as well. Floppy drives have doors that enable you to insert and remove the disks. The drive doors look like mail slots in the system unit (refer to Figure 1.1). CD drives and DVD drives have trays that slide out from the system unit so you can insert a disc and then slide it back in.

continues ▶

To Identify External Components of the System Unit (continued)

4 Look at the back of the system unit for ports.

Ports are sockets on the system unit in which you plug in hardware devices such as the keyboard and printer (see Figure 1.2). When you plug a hardware device into a port, it connects to a ***controller board*** stored inside the system unit. The controller board is a printed circuit board that enables the personal computer to communicate with the hardware device. You may hear controller boards also referred to as controller cards, expansion boards, or expansion cards.

Figure 1.2
The system unit has different kinds of ports where you plug in different hardware devices.

Ports

Different Types of CDs

CD drives read compact discs, just like the CD player you use to play music CDs. In fact, if you have the right software, you can play your music CDs on your PC. Some CDs are CD-ROMs, which stands for compact disc–read only memory. Your PC can read data from a CD-ROM, but it cannot copy data onto a CD-ROM. CD-R discs are CDs that you can write data to one time only. CD-RWs can be written and rewritten as many times as you want. To use CD-Rs and CD-RWs, you need a CD drive that supports writing data onto CDs.

If you have a DVD drive, you can buy or rent movies on disc, and then watch them on your computer.

Lesson 2: Identifying Internal Components of the System Unit

If you could take the top of your system unit off, you would see the most important parts of your personal computer (see Figure 1.3). Inside the case, you would find the electrical components that actually make your PC work—components such as ***chips***, wires, and circuits. Chips are the tiny integrated circuits that control computer functions or store information.

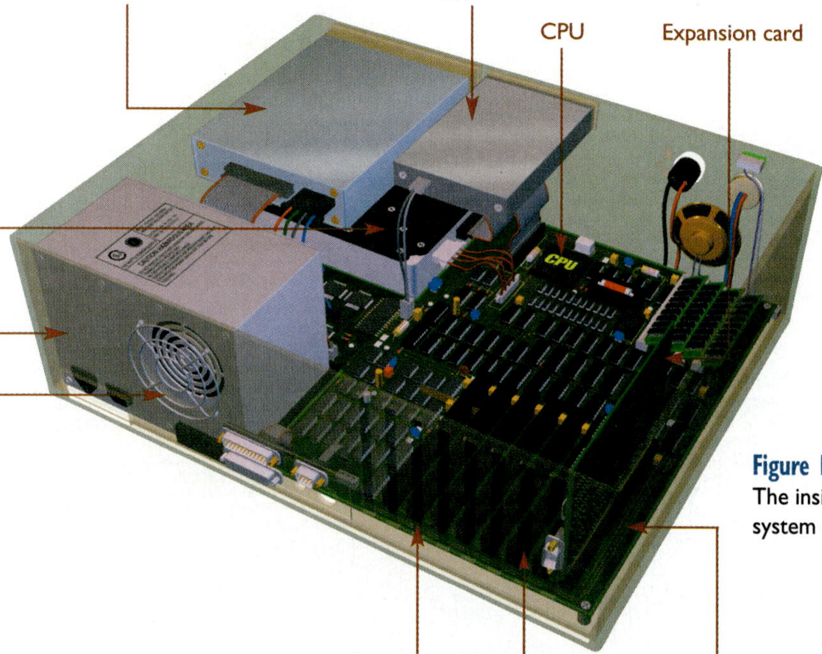

Figure 1.3
The inside of a typical system unit.

You shouldn't actually open your system unit in order to locate the devices in this lesson. The components inside your computer can easily get damaged by dirt, motion, and static electricity. Use the illustrations to help you visualize the location of each part.

To Identify Internal Components of the System Unit

1. **Look for the *motherboard* inside the system unit.**
   The ***motherboard*** is the main circuit board in the system unit (refer to Figure 1.3). The most important electronic components, such as the ***central processing unit (CPU)***, which is the main microprocessor chip controlling your PC; and the ***random access memory (RAM)***, which is the electronic memory where the PC processes data until the data can be used or stored on disk, are located on the motherboard. Other hardware components, such as disk drives, are attached to the motherboard so that every component can exchange information back and forth.

continues ▶

To Identify Internal Components of the System Unit (continued)

Identifying CPUs

CPUs are identified by a designation that includes a name, a version, and a processing speed. The designation is actually stamped right on the chip.

Initially, Intel Corp. was the only manufacturer of PC processors. The earliest Intel processors were called 80286, and each subsequent generation went up by 100: 80386, 80486, and so on. Intel has discontinued using numbers alone to identify its CPUs; now it sells Pentiums and Pentium Pros, and other manufacturers sell their own versions of similar chips.

CPU speed is measured in ***megahertz (MHz)***, or millions of cycles per second. Each microprocessor contains a clock that controls its speed. The faster the clock ticks (or cycles), the faster the computer can process data. Most new PCs today run at a minimum of 100MHz. However, clock speed alone does not determine the real processing speed of a PC. An 80486 running at 200MHz does not outperform a Pentium III running at 100MHz.

Figure 1.4
All hardware devices are attached to the motherboard.

2 Look on the motherboard for the CPU chip (refer to Figure 1.4).
The CPU acts like the computer's brain. It is the microprocessor chip that controls every instruction performed by the PC.

3 Look on the motherboard for the RAM modules.
RAM, the short-term memory in which your PC processes information, is constantly being written to, erased, and written to again like a blackboard.

RAM

RAM is actually a memory chip, which is usually built into a circuit board that attaches to the motherboard (refer to Figure 1.4). There are a few different types of circuit boards that contain the RAM chips. The most common type is called a single in-line memory module (SIMM). Each SIMM holds a group of nine RAM chips. Newer types include dual in-line memory modules (DIMMs), each of which can hold more than twice as much RAM as a SIMM, and synchronous dynamic random access memory (SDRAM), which support higher speeds.

You measure RAM in ***bytes***. One byte equals approximately one character of information. One thousand bytes is called a kilobyte, or KB. One million bytes is called a megabyte, or MB. Most computers come with 96 megabytes of RAM, but you can have much more than that. To learn more about memory, see Project 6, "Learning about PC Memory."

4 **Find the expansion slots and cards on the motherboard.**

The motherboard has sockets, called ***expansion slots***, where you can plug in controller boards—sometimes called circuit boards or expansion cards (refer to Figure 1.4). The way the slots look depends on the type of ***bus*** your system uses. The bus is the set of wires or conductors that expansion cards and peripherals use to communicate with the CPU. The number of expansion slots depends on the size of the system unit. Chances are, your PC has a disk controller card attached to the motherboard to control the disk drives, as well as a video adapter card to control the display monitor. You probably also have an internal modem card and a sound card. You may also have a network card if your PC is part of a ***network***, or group of computers linked together by cable to share data and resources. If you don't have these cards, you may have open slots so that you can add them in the future.

5 **Find the disk drives inside the system unit.**

On the outside of the system unit, you found the disk drive doors and the drive status lights. You would need to look inside the system unit to find the drives themselves (refer to Figure 1.3).

Disk drives are devices that the computer uses to store information that is not currently being used, such as a paper you wrote yesterday or last week's expense report. Floppy drives and hard disk drives read and write information to and from magnetic disks, whereas CD-RW drives read to and write from optical discs. CD-ROMs and DVD drives read information, but can't write on the discs.

The amount of information—or data—that can fit onto a disk is measured in bytes, just like memory. One byte equals about one character. Most hard disks available today have capacities measured in gigabytes! One gigabyte, or GB, equals one billion bytes.

continues ▶

To Identify Internal Components of the System Unit (continued)

6. **Look for your PC's power supply.**
The power supply converts the AC electricity from an outlet in your home or office to the DC electricity that the PC uses (refer to Figure 1.3). If your PC is a portable computer, such as a ***laptop*** that you can carry and use while away from your desk; or a ***handheld device***, which is an even smaller PC designed to be carried in your hand, it may run on a battery.

Lesson 3: Identifying Input Devices

Before you can store or process data with your PC, you must enter the data into the computer. The two most common hardware devices used to enter, or ***input***, data are the keyboard and the mouse, but other types of input devices also exist.

You can have more than one input device attached to your PC. Most PCs, for example, have both a keyboard and a mouse. Some input devices are used for special purposes.

To Identify Input Devices

1. **Find the keyboard attached to your computer.**
You will easily recognize the keyboard because it looks very much like a typewriter. Most keyboards, however, have more keys than a typewriter (see Figure 1.5). Not all keyboards look the same or have the same keys. The 104-key extended keyboard is the most common keyboard for new desktop PCs. Table 1.1 describes the purpose of keys on a PC keyboard. See Figure 1.5 for the location of the keys on a 101-key keyboard.

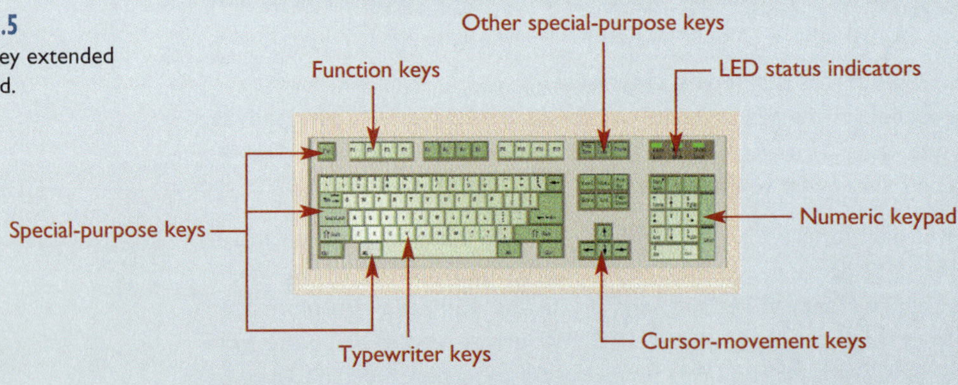

Figure 1.5
A 101-key extended keyboard.

Table 1.1 Keyboard Keys

Keys	Purpose
Typewriter keys	Enable you to type letters, punctuation, and numbers, just as you would on a typewriter.
Function keys	Perform various tasks, depending on the software application you use.
Cursor-movement keys	Enable you to locate a certain spot in a document or file displayed on your monitor.
Numeric keypad keys	Enable you to enter numbers in a calculator-like fashion.
Special-purpose keys	Used for computer functions, such as entering and canceling commands.

2 Locate the mouse attached to your computer.
The mouse, a small device that can fit easily into the palm of your hand, connects to your PC by a cable. Because some of the first users thought this cable looked like a tail, the device became known as a mouse. Most mouse devices have two or three buttons, but some (such as those used for a Mac) have only one button (see Figure 1.6).The Microsoft Intellimouse, designed specifically for use with Microsoft software applications, has a wheel in addition to the buttons.

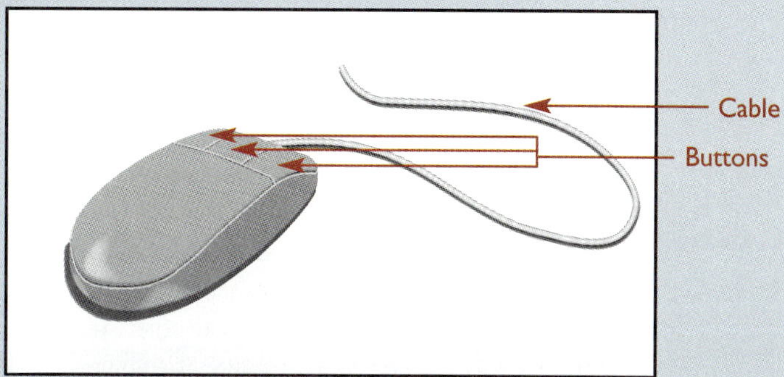

Figure 1.6
A mouse is a common input device.

3 Locate other input devices.
Your computer may have other input devices, such as a ***joystick***, ***trackball***, or ***scanner***. Joysticks, usually used while playing games, connect to a game port on the system unit. Trackballs move a pointer around the screen. Because they don't require a flat area, they are often built into portable PCs in place of a mouse. Scanners are used to input data that has already been printed on paper.

Some computers, particularly handheld devices, can recognize words that are handwritten on a device called a ***digitizing tablet*** with a ***digital pen***. The tablet translates the written data into digital data that the PC can understand.

Lesson 4: Identifying Output Devices

Output devices translate data produced by the computer into a form that you can understand. They enable you to know what the PC is doing and to access data after it has been processed by the PC. The two most common output devices are the video display monitor and the printer.

As with input devices, you can have more than one output device attached to your PC.

To Identify Output Devices

1 Find your display monitor.
The display monitor looks like a TV (see Figure 1.7). It usually sits directly on your desk or on top of the system unit. On the monitor, you can see your input, as well as the output that your computer produces in response to your input.

continues ▶

To Identify Output Devices (continued)

In many ways, your monitor operates like your TV. The screen is measured diagonally, in inches. It has knobs to control brightness, contrast, and the position of information on the screen.

A Word About Thin Monitors
Two other types of monitors that are gaining in popularity are liquid crystal displays (LCD) and flat panel screens. LCDs are currently used in notebook and laptop PCs because they are thin and light. Flat panel displays are sleek, take up much less space on the desktop, and produce a better image because of the lack of curvature. Currently, however, the flatter the screen, the higher the price.

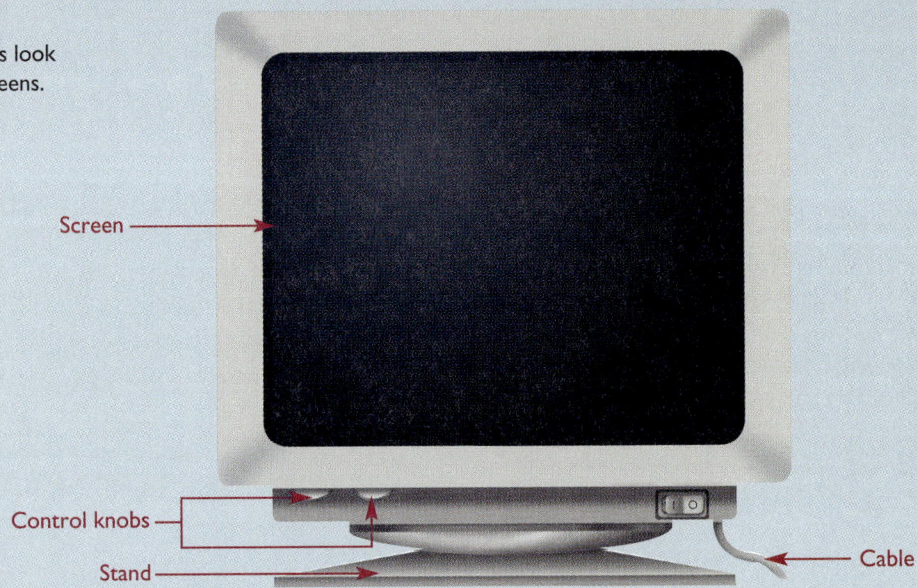

Figure 1.7
Display monitors look a lot like TV screens.

2 Find your printer.
Your printer may be attached directly to your PC by a cable. However, if you are on a network, the printer may be located somewhere else—maybe even in a different room or on a different floor.

Printers let you make hard copies of the information stored on your computer.

3 Determine the type of printer you have.
There are two basic types of PC printers: ***laser*** and ***inkjet***. Inkjet printers produce an image on a page by spraying ink through a matrix. Laser printers use light and ink powder (called ***toner***) to create an image.

4 Locate your computer's speaker(s).
Your computer probably has external speakers attached via cable to the system unit, but it may have a built-in speaker somewhere on the system unit. Built-in speakers have traditionally been used for emitting warning beeps or other sounds. Now that people use computers for applications that involve music and dialog, however, they use external speakers because they provide better quality sound.

5 Locate your computer's modem.

Most modems are built into expansion cards and plug into a slot inside the system unit (see Figure 1.8). Some modems are external devices that attach to the outside of the system unit via cables. Look for a telephone line running from a jack on the wall to a plug on your computer or a cable like those used for cable television.

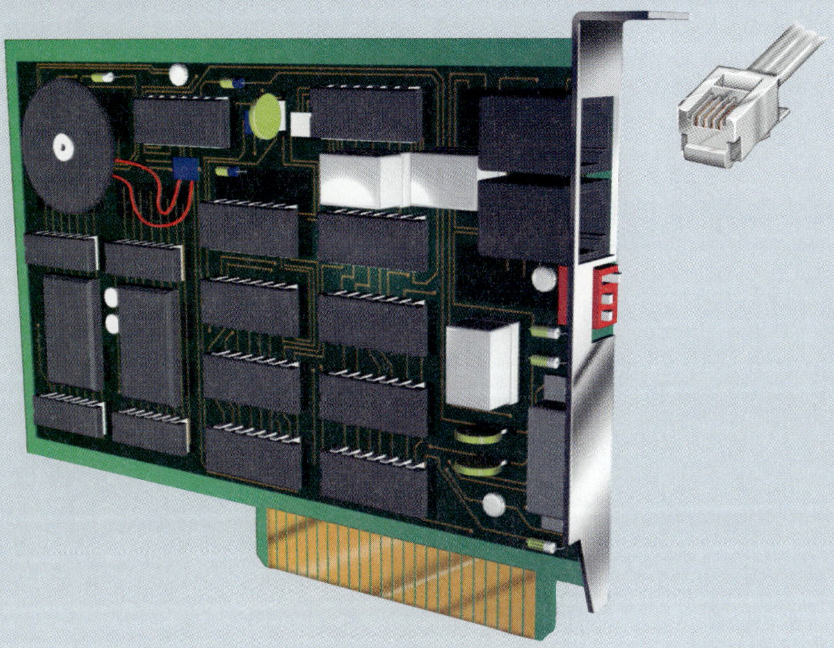

Figure 1.8
An internal modem and standard phone jack.

Monitors and Modems

Monitors come in either monochrome or color, although most are color. Monochrome monitors display a single color on a black background. Color monitors can display anywhere from 16 colors to 16.7 million colors. The quality of the picture on your monitor, however, is determined by the type of video display adapter card you have installed inside your system unit, as well as by the type of ***resolution*** your monitor can achieve. Resolution is the measurement of the sharpness of an image, and it refers to the number of dots (called picture elements, or pixels for short) used to create an image. VGA, SVGA, and XGA are high-quality video display adapters, and there are adapters designed to display 3-D graphics, as well.

Modems are used to connect your PC to standard telephone lines, coaxial cables, or ISDN cables, so you can exchange information with other computers or connect to the Internet and World Wide Web. Some modems have fax capabilities, which means that you can use them to send files from your computer to fax machines and to receive files sent from fax machines. Data transfer via modem is measured in bits per second, with a ***bit*** being the smallest unit of computer data. Effective data transfer rates start at 28.8 thousand (or K) bits per second, but many modems operate at much faster speeds.

Laptops and handheld devices often use PC card modems (formerly known as PCM CIA cards). A PC card slips into a slot on the side of the PC to connect to the motherboard; you connect the cords dangling from the other end of the card to your phone lines.

Lesson 5: Identifying Storage Devices

Without a storage device, your PC has no place to keep data permanently. Data held in RAM is erased whenever the PC is turned off or when something else takes its place. The most common type of storage device is the disk drive.

Most PCs come with at least one hard disk drive and one floppy disk drive. Disk drives store data for future use. Without disk drives, you would have no way to keep data permanently. Many PCs also have CD drives that read or write data to and from compact discs. You have already located the drive doors on your system unit and drives inside the system unit. Now, try to identify the different types of disk drives.

To Identify Storage Devices

1. **Find the 3 1/2-inch floppy disk drive.**
   Most floppy disk drives are designed to hold 3 1/2-inch floppy disks. Disk drives usually have small push buttons or a disk removal button near the drive door. When a drive contains a disk, the push button sticks out. When the drive is empty, the push button does not stick out (see Figure 1.9).

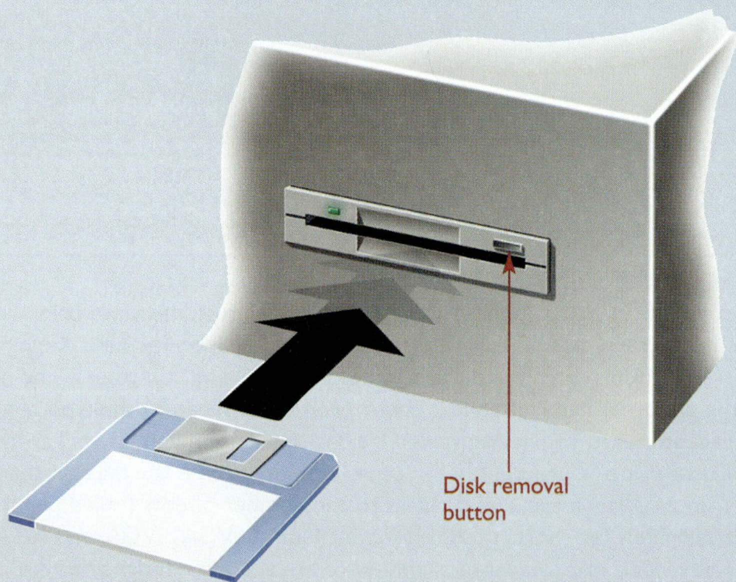

Figure 1.9
A 3 1/2-inch floppy drive door.

2. **Find the hard disk drive.**
   You can't locate a hard disk drive by finding the drive door because hard disk drives don't have drive doors—hard disks are fixed inside the drive. Look for the drive in-use status light on the system unit. Hard disks are actually many disks, stacked one on top of another; they can hold many times more data than floppy disks, and they are less easily damaged.

3 Locate the CD or DVD drive, if applicable.

Most computers have a CD or DVD drive built into the system unit. The drive usually has a button you push to eject the tray used to hold the disc. DVD drives can read standard CDs as well as DVDs, so it is unlikely that your computer has both.

4 Locate any other drives.

If your computer is attached to a network, you may share drives with other computers. These drives are located at a central computer, called a ***file server***, which is used to control files, programs, and access to data on a network.

You might also have a tape drive or a high-capacity disk drive. A tape drive stores data on cassette tape, in a similar manner to a video cassette recorder. Often, tape and high-capacity drives are used for copying large amounts of data for safekeeping—or backing up.

How Much Hard Drive Space Do You Need?
When you buy a hard disk drive, the most important factor to consider is capacity, the amount of storage space on the drive. A good rule of thumb: Always buy twice as much as you think you need. Your storage requirements will probably increase over time, not decrease. Upgrades (improvements to programs) usually get larger, not smaller, and thus occupy more disk space.

Summary

In this lesson, you were introduced to the basic hardware components found in almost all personal computers. You learned the difference between internal and external components, input and output devices, and various types of storage devices.

To expand on your knowledge, take the time to check your knowledge of concepts and terms. Additionally, complete some of the Skill Drill and Challenge exercises.

Checking Concepts and Terms

True/False

For each of the following, check *T* or *F* to indicate whether the statement is true or false.

__T __F **1.** All personal computer systems have two floppy disk drives and one hard disk drive. [L1]

__T __F **2.** The CPU is the most important part of your computer. [L1]

__T __F **3.** A mouse enables you to scan printed material into the computer. [L3]

__T __F **4.** Joysticks are used most often for playing games. [L3]

__T __F **5.** The system unit is so big that it must be kept on its own desk. [L1]

__T __F **6.** If your computer has a DVD drive, it must have a CD drive, too. [L1]

__T __F **7.** Tape drives can read data, but they cannot write data. [L5]

__T __F **8.** Some handheld devices accept input from digital pens. [L3]

__T __F **9.** If you have the right software and hardware, you can play music CDs in your computer's CD drive. [L1]

__T __F **10.** A standard mouse has four buttons. [L3]

Multiple Choice

Circle the letter of the correct answer for each of the following.

1. Which of the following is an input device? [L3]
   a. video adapter card
   b. printer
   c. keyboard
   d. on/off switch

2. A(n) ______________ is an output device. [L4]
   a. video adapter card
   b. printer
   c. keyboard
   d. on/off switch

3. You can find a modem ______________. [L4]
   a. attached to the display monitor
   b. inside a drive door
   c. on a DVD
   d. on an expansion card inside the system unit

4. You can tell whether your computer is on by looking at the ______________. [L1]
   a. power status light
   b. printer
   c. display monitor
   d. CPU

5. CPU stands for ______________. [L1]
   a. computer printer unit
   b. central processing unit
   c. computer processing university
   d. central printers university

6. RAM stands for ______________. [L2]
   a. random action mouse
   b. read all modem
   c. random access memory
   d. random action monitor

7. Which type of drive stores data on a cassette? [L5]
   a. hard disk drive
   b. DVD drive
   c. CD-RW drive
   d. tape drive

8. Which of the following measures the sharpness of a monitor image? [L4]
   a. resolution
   b. RAM
   c. CPU
   d. toner

9. What size disk fits in the most common floppy disk drives? [L5]
   a. 6 1/4-inch
   b. 3 1/2-inch
   c. 7 1/8-inch
   d. 2 1/3-inch

10. What unit is used to measure disk storage space? [L5]
   a. square feet
   b. bits per second
   c. bytes
   d. pixels

Screen ID

Label each of the following elements shown in Figure 1.10

Figure 1.10

A. Status Lights
B. Mouse
C. System unit
D. On/Off switch
E. Drive doors
F. Display monitor
G. Keyboard

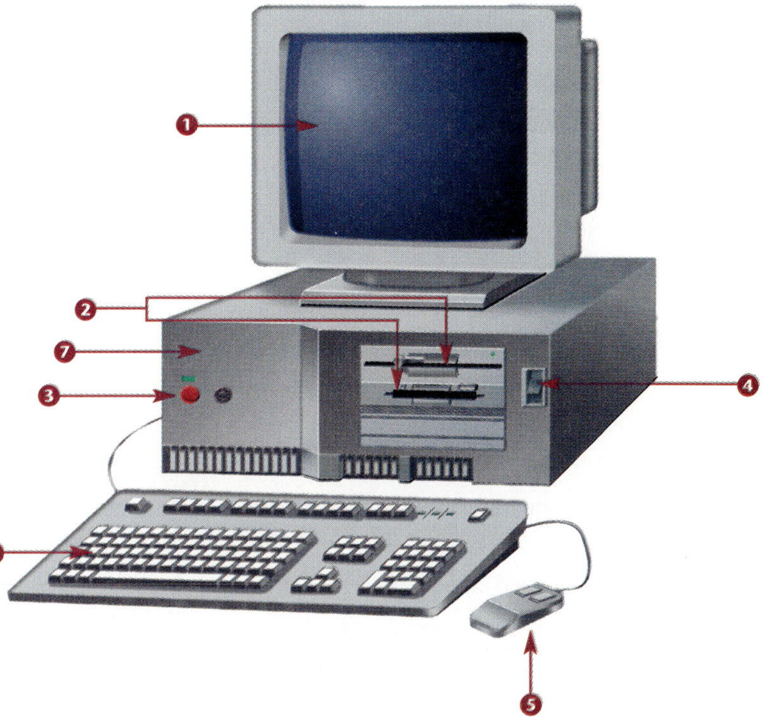

1. ____________
2. ____________
3. ____________
4. ____________
5. ____________
6. ____________
7. ____________

Discussion Questions

1. Describe the different shapes and sizes of PCs that are available. Why might one type be preferable to another?
2. Why do you think some PC components are internal and some are external? List some internal components.
3. Explain the difference between input devices and output devices. Provide at least two examples of each.

Skill Drill

Skill Drill exercises reinforce project skills. Each skill reinforced is the same, or nearly the same, as a skill presented in the project. Detailed instructions are provided in a step-by-step format.

1. Planning a Home Computer System

Now that you are familiar with the basic hardware components that make up a personal computer system, think about the types of components that you would want in a computer system for your home. To plan a home computer system, follow these steps:

1. Make a list of the necessary components you would need to make your computer work.
2. Identify each component as internal or external.
3. Expand the list to include hardware devices that may not be necessary, but that you would like, also marked as internal or external.

2. Familiarize Yourself with Your Computer System

If you already have a computer system, take the time to look at it closely so that you know what components and peripherals you have. If possible, ask the person responsible for the computer to explain it to you.

1. Identify the basic components of your computer system and peripherals.
2. Write down the number and capacity of all disk drives.
3. Write down the brand names of the components, including the monitor, the keyboard, and the system unit.
4. Determine whether you have an impact printer or a nonimpact printer.
5. Draw a diagram of your computer, labeling the essential components.

Challenge

Challenge exercises expand on or are somewhat related to skills presented in the lessons. Each exercise provides a brief narrative introduction, followed by instructions in a numbered-step format that are not as detailed as those in the Skill Drill exercises.

1. Planning a Business Computer System

You are the office manager for a small retail store. You have been authorized to purchase a computer for the business. Before making a purchase, you need to examine the store's computer requirements to make sure that you make a wise decision.

1. Make a list of all the activities you think can be accomplished by using a personal computer.
2. Make a list of the minimum hardware requirements you think you will need.
3. Make a list of additional hardware devices that may be useful.

2. Budgeting for a Computer System

Whether you work for a business or want a PC for home use, your purchasing decisions may be limited by the amount you can spend on computer equipment. Plan a budget for a computer system, and then justify your expenditures.

1. Look through catalogs and magazines and contact computer retailers to find out how much the computer system you want to purchase will cost.
2. Examine your priorities to determine whether or not you can cut back anywhere to save money.
3. List the reasons why the equipment you have decided to purchase is worth the expense.

Project 2

Setting Up a Work Area

Objectives

In this project, you learn how to

- **Plan a Good Work Area**
- **Unpack the Computer**
- **Attach the Cables**
- **Protect Your Computer**
- **Move Your Computer**

Key terms introduced in this project include

- cable modem
- computer virus
- dedicated outlet
- ergonomic
- female connector
- male connector
- parallel
- SCSI (small computer system interface)
- serial
- surge suppressor
- task lighting
- uninterruptible power supply (UPS)
- virus

Why Would I Do This?

A computer is a sophisticated electronic machine. Like other machines you use in your home or office, you get the most efficient use of the computer when you place it in an area best suited to its particular function. You do not install dishwashers in a bedroom nor office copiers in the bathroom; they would be inconvenient and out of place. Likewise, you should set up your computer in an area where it will be convenient and comfortable to use and where it will be out of harm's way.

Creating a good work environment is important for both your health and the health of your PC. You should take into consideration many factors, including the things you need to run your PC, such as electricity; and things that make using your PC easier, such as good lighting. In this project, you learn how to plan, set up, and protect your work area.

Lesson 1: Planning a Good Work Area

You need a location for your computer system that is both convenient and comfortable. Of course, with just those two criteria, you might decide to set up your PC on the dining room table, which would prove awkward at meal times.

Ideally, you want to set up your PC someplace so that you will not have to move it and so that the computer won't be disturbed when you aren't using it.

In this lesson, you learn how to plan a good work area.

To Plan a Good Work Area

1. **Pick a room where you will set up the computer.**
   Find a room that has plenty of space for a desk, bookshelves, and a separate table for a printer. Ideally, the room should be a dedicated office, in which no other activities take place. If you use a playroom or family room, for example, the computer could be damaged by other people in the room.

   Supervising Children
   If the computer will be used by children and young adults, you may want to keep it in a more public place, such as the family room. It is important to provide proper supervision when children play computer games or surf the Web.

2. **Locate the right size desk.**
   You need enough room on the top of your desk to accommodate your computer system. In addition to the monitor and system unit, you need room for the keyboard, the mouse, and other items you use during the day—such as a telephone, pen, pencil, and notebook (see Figure 2.1). If you are setting up a printer, plan to have a separate printer table. Not only do printers take up a great deal of space on the desktop, but they often shake during use, which can damage the internal components of the PC.

3 Check the sturdiness of the desk.

The desk that you use must support the weight of the computer without shaking or collapsing. If you are using a desk with wheels, make certain that the wheels lock in place so your work surface doesn't roll.

4 Find electrical outlets.

The system unit, the monitor, and the printer must all plug into electrical outlets, so you need to place the desk near an outlet. Other peripherals, such as speakers, may need electricity, too. If possible, install a ***dedicated outlet***, which is an electrical outlet used solely for plugging in your PC and PC components (see Figure 2.1).

5 Look for telephone jacks or cable outlets.

If you have a modem, you need access to a telephone line or cable (see Figure 2.1). If you use a telephone jack, you should consider installing a dedicated line because when you have the modem in use, you can't use the telephone line for other calls. Most modems, however, provide jacks for connecting a telephone so that when you aren't using the modem, you can make and receive calls.

6 Make sure you have adequate lighting.

You need to consider two types of lighting when planning a work area: ***task lighting*** for illuminating work on your desktop, and general lighting for the whole room. You want to see your screen clearly, without any glare. Because bright sunlight can block out almost everything on your monitor, make sure that you have shades or curtains if the room has windows. To light the materials on your desk, you need a lamp or a well-placed overhead light (see Figure 2.1).

Figure 2.1
The necessary ingredients for a well-planned workspace.

continues ▶

To Plan a Good Work Area (continued)

Sunlight Can Damage Computers
Don't place your computer system in direct sunlight. The heat will damage the components.

7. **Make sure that the room has plenty of ventilation.**
The room must have space for air to circulate around your PC components so that they don't overheat. Keep about three inches of open space around your system unit and display monitor so that air can move freely around the devices. Be careful not to block the fan at the back of the system unit.

Computer Desks
You can purchase a desk designed specifically for a computer system. Such desks have a drawer where the keyboard sits; shelves for the monitor and system unit; strategically placed holes for cables, cords, and wiring to pass through; and side tables for printers. Some even provide CD storage units.

In addition to providing space for all the components, these desks are usually ***ergonomic*** (this is a fancy way of saying that they take into consideration the way you physically use the equipment, so as not to add stress to your body.) The keyboard is at the right height and the monitor is at eye level, which helps avoid strain on your wrists and neck.

Lesson 2: Unpacking the Computer

Depending on how many components you have purchased, computer systems usually come in many cartons, with boxes for the system unit, the monitor, the keyboard, and the printer. If you have other components, such as speakers or an external high-capacity drive, you have boxes for those items as well.

Now that you have a work area defined, you need to unpack the boxes and arrange the components so that they are ready to be attached. In this lesson, you learn how to unpack the computer.

To Unpack the Computer

1. **Find your order slip or invoice.**
You should compare the items that you ordered with the items you received to make sure that the dealer gave you the correct system. Be prepared to compare the items on your order slip with the items on the packing slips; also compare the items on the order slip to the items themselves.

2. **Identify the boxes.**
Look on the outside of the cartons to identify which component is in which box; then place the carton near where you plan to set up the component that the carton contains. For example, put the carton containing the printer near the printer table. Because components are well-protected inside the cartons, you should move them before unpacking them.

3. **Open the boxes.**
Use a small knife, a letter opener, or a key to cut the tape sealing the boxes. Be very careful not to damage the components inside the box.

4. **Find all packing slips, warranty cards, and other documentation.**
In every box, you should find instructions that will help you identify the items in the box and figure out how to set up the system.

5. **Unpack the system unit.**
Lift the system unit gently out of the box and place it on the desk or shelf where it will remain. Make sure that you have access to the ports. Look inside the box to find the cables, screws, and electrical cords. If the device is covered in plastic or Styrofoam, remove the wrapping and put it back into the carton.

6. **Unpack the other components.**
Repeat the procedure for all the other components.

7. **Make sure that you got what you paid for.**
As you unpack the cartons, compare the information on the packing slip and your order slip with the items you received. Also, look at warranty cards and documentation booklets for the product name and number. Checking the packing slip and the warranty cards is a good way to make sure that you got what you paid for, especially for internal components that you can't see, such as RAM, CPU, and add-on cards.

Keep the Packing Materials!
Don't throw away the boxes, Styrofoam, and other packing materials! If you have to return a component, you usually have to repack it in the original carton. If you ever move the computer, you should pack it in the original carton.

Also, be sure to store the packing slips and invoices in a safe place. In the future, you may need them to look up delivery dates, order numbers, serial numbers, or precise product names.

Lesson 3: Attaching the Cables

Every external device attaches to the system unit via cables. Many devices also plug into electrical outlets, which can mean lots of cables and cords that you must connect correctly if you want your PC to work.

You can't attach devices to just any port that happens to be available. The port on the system unit and the plug on the cable must be compatible, which means that both the size and type must match. Also, connections are always made between a ***male connector*** and a ***female connector***. Male connectors have pins sticking out, whereas female connectors have sockets sticking in. You can't plug a male cable into a male port or a female cable into a female port.

Making these connections is not difficult because you can't physically attach a cable to the wrong port. If you don't find the right match at first, just try another port.

Making the Plug Fit
Most of the connectors between the PC and peripheral devices are "D" shaped, which means that one side is longer than the other (see Figure 2.3). Before trying to plug in a device, make sure that the longer side of the plug is aligned with the longer side of the socket.

Also, never try to force a connector into a socket! If it doesn't fit—it doesn't fit. Don't run the risk of breaking or bending the pins needed to make the connection.

In this lesson, you learn to match socket to port and to make the connections.

To Attach the Cables

1. **Find the necessary tools.**
   Although you may not need any tools at all, have on hand a small Phillips-head screwdriver and a small standard-head screwdriver, just in case.

2. **Attach the keyboard.**
   The cable from the keyboard has a small round connector on it that attaches to a small round port on the system unit. On some units, the keyboard port is on front of the system unit, but on most systems, the port is on the back (see Figure 2.2). Align the pins on the connector with the sockets on the port; then gently insert the connector. Most keyboard connectors must be aligned exactly or they won't fit, so you may have to twist the connector to line it up with the port.

   How to Run the Cables
   Before you attach the cables, make sure that they are in position to run behind the desk, safely out of the way. Make use of the holes provided in your desk! For example, if the keyboard or mouse will stay in a keyboard drawer in your desk, make sure that the cord runs through the back of the drawer before you attach it. If cables run across the middle of the room, there's a risk that they might be kicked or pulled on by accident, or that you'll trip on them.

Figure 2.2
The round keyboard connector plugs into a round keyboard port.

If your system unit has two small round ports, one is for a mouse. Look for a picture above the port to identify which connects to the keyboard and which connects to the mouse.

3 Attach the mouse.

Find the port that corresponds to your mouse cable, and make the connection. If screws appear on either side of the connector, screw them in firmly to secure the cable. Some mouse devices connect to a nine-pin ***serial*** port. Serial connections send data through one wire and are commonly used for attaching serial printers, modems, and mice. Serial connectors have nine pins in two rows (see Figure 2.3).

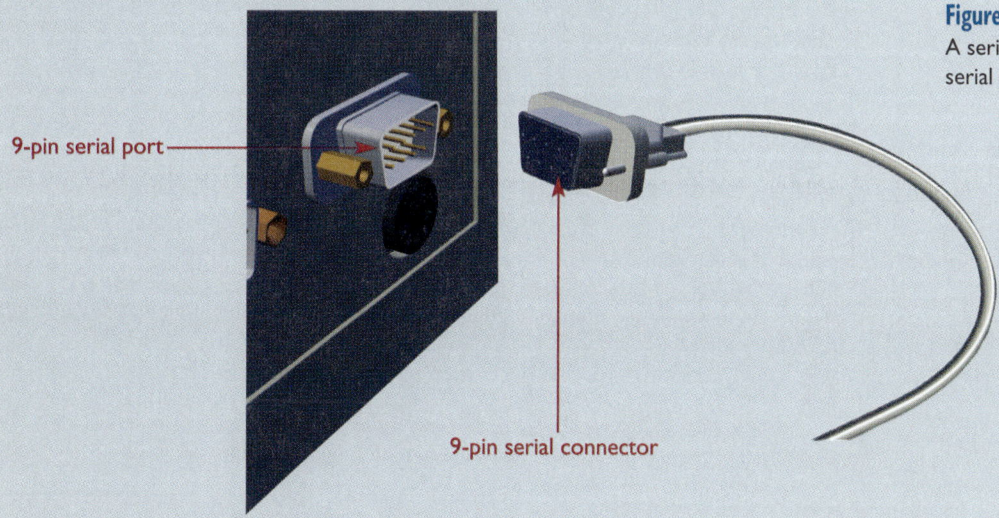

Figure 2.3
A serial connector and a serial port.

continues ▶

To Attach the Cables (continued)

Plug Adapters
Some devices, such as serial mouse devices, come with plug adapters that allow them to fit in other ports.

4 Attach the monitor.
The monitor cable plugs into the video adapter port, which usually has 15 holes in three rows (see Figure 2.4). Locate the port, and then firmly attach the cable to it. If you see screws on either side of the connector, screw them in to secure the cable.

Figure 2.4
The display monitor cable plugs into the video adapter port.

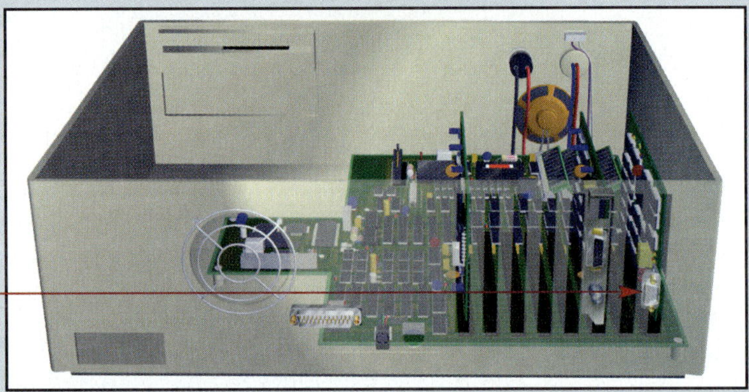

5 Attach any other devices.
If you have other external devices, attach them to the correct ports on the system unit. For example, a joystick attaches to a game port, which has 15 holes in two rows. Speakers plug into ports on a sound card that probably also has ports for a microphone (see Figure 2.5). External devices such as printers, CD drives, tape drives, and external hard disk drives may attach to either a ***SCSI (small computer system interface)*** port, such as the one shown in Figure 2.6, or a USB (universal serial bus) port. Both SCSI (pronounced "scuzzy") and USB are data transfer standards.

6 Attach phone lines.
If you have an internal modem, connect the phone lines. One jack on the system unit is labeled *To Phone* and one is labeled *To Line*. If you have one cord, attach one end to the *To Line* jack on the system unit and one end to the jack in the wall. If you have two cords, attach the second cord to the *To Phone* jack in the system unit and the other end to a telephone.

Connecting a Cable Modem
If you have a ***cable modem***, which is a modem that transfers data over cable instead of over telephone lines, you need to have your cable service provider connect your computer system to the cable system.

Figure 2.5
Speakers attach to ports, which connect to a sound card inside the system unit.

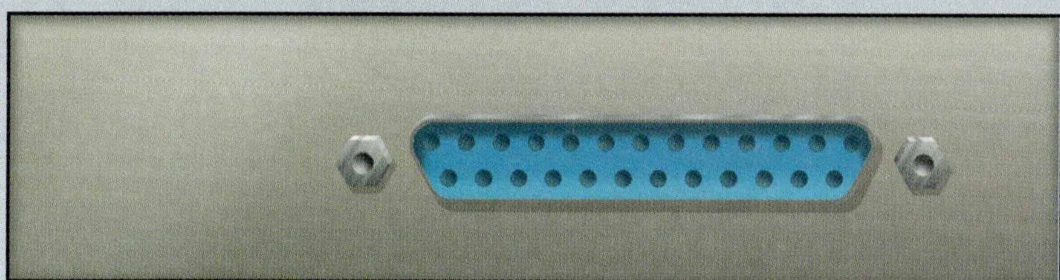

Figure 2.6
CD drives often attach to SCSI ports like this one.

7 Plug in all the power cords.

The system unit, the monitor, and the printer all have electrical cords. Make sure that one end is attached to the device; then plug the socket into the electrical outlet on the wall or into a power protection device, such as a ***surge suppressor*** or ***uninterruptible power source (UPS)***. Surge suppressors moderate the flow of electricity in order to eliminate sudden surges that might damage the PC, whereas a UPS actually provides a backup power source to keep your PC running during a power failure. If you have other devices with electrical cords, plug them in as well.

Attaching Your Printer

When setting up a new computer system for the first time, wait to attach the printer until after you start the computer and set up your operating environment. Then, attach the printer.

Most printers—usually dot-matrix printers, inkjet printers, and some of the newer laser printers—have double-ended cables. Attach one end securely to the printer. If you see screws or clips that secure the cable in place, tighten them. Some printers have cables already attached to the printer itself. With both types of printers, you attach the other end of the cable to the 25-pin ***parallel port*** on the system unit (see Figure 2.7). A parallel connection sends data through eight wires simultaneously. Again, if you see screws or clips, tighten them to secure the cable in place.

continues ▶

To Attach the Cables (continued)

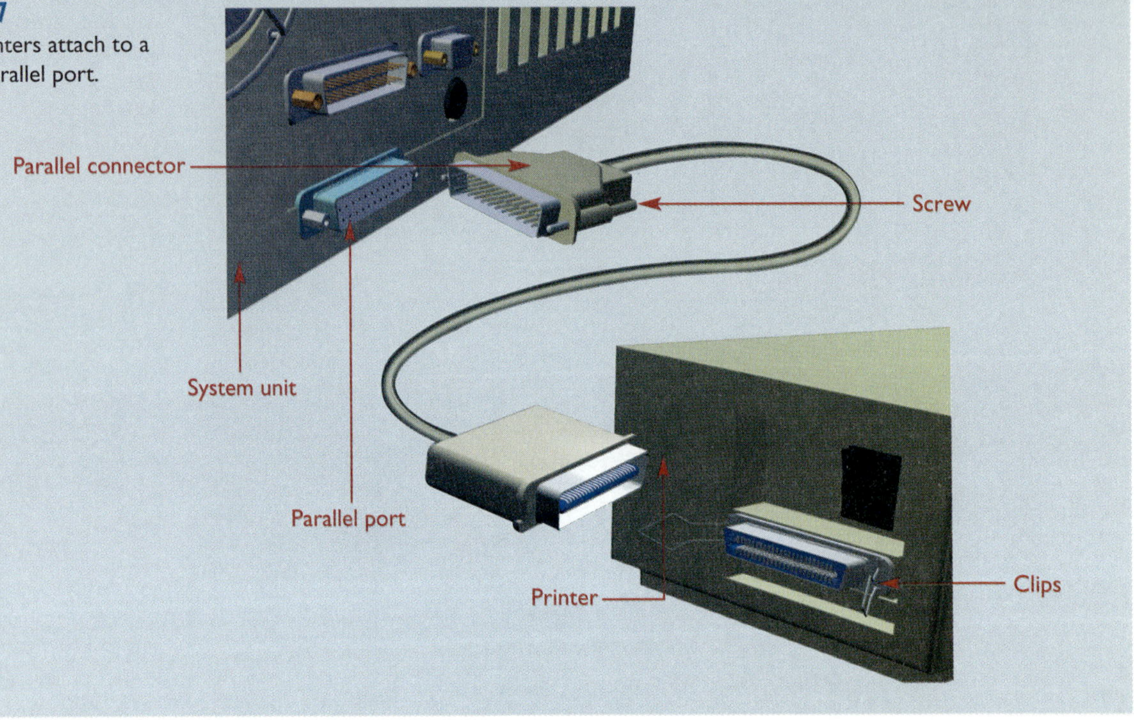

Figure 2.7
Most printers attach to a 25-pin parallel port.

If the printer cables are not long enough, you can buy longer ones.

Identifying Ports
One way to tell which port plugs into which cable is by counting the number of connectors, or pins, that the port has. Look on the system unit for a port that is the same shape and size and has the same number of pins as the connector on the end of the cable. Don't panic, however, if it looks as if some of the pins on the cable connector are missing. Manufacturers may only include the pins required to make the device work.

Lesson 4: Protecting Your Computer

A computer represents a significant investment, which you should not treat casually. With a little care and common sense, you can ensure that your computer will last a long time and that your data will be kept safe.

In this lesson, you learn some of the ways you can protect your computer.

To Protect Your Computer

1 Attach a power-protection device.

Computers are highly sensitive to changes in the electrical current. Power surges, fluctuations, and outages can damage the hardware components and your data. Instead of plugging cords directly into wall outlets, plug them into a surge suppressor or an uninterruptible power supply (UPS), as shown in Figure 2.8. A UPS contains a backup power supply, such as a battery, so that your PC can continue to operate long enough for you to save and power down safely in the event of a power failure. When devices are not in use, unplug them.

More About Power-Protection Devices

An added benefit is that power-protection devices usually provide extra outlets, which come in handy if you have many devices to plug in; these devices also have a built-in on/off switch, which you can use to start your computer instead of flipping a switch on every single component.

When looking into buying a UPS, check how long the backup power supply will last Fifteen minutes is typical, but more expensive devices may provide more time.

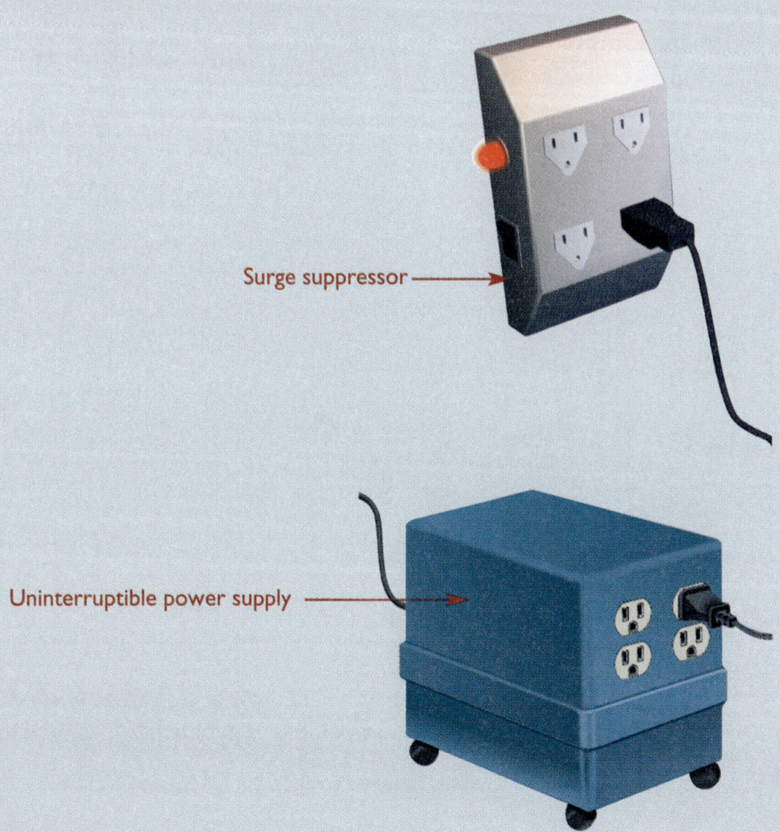

Figure 2.8
Always use a power-protection device.

continues ▶

To Protect Your Computer (continued)

2. **Send in the registration cards.**
   All of your computer components came with registration cards or warranty cards. After you ensure that each product is in good working order, fill out its card and send it to the manufacturer. Some warranties may not be valid unless you send in the cards. Also, when you register the device, the manufacturer can send you product information and update you on technical support phone lines and the like.

   Register Online
   Many companies let you register online. The first time you start your computer, you may be prompted to connect to the Internet in order to register.

3. **Clean the PC.**
   Dust and dirt can damage the computer components. Use a cover to help keep dust from building up inside the system unit and the peripherals. When the computer is off, you can gently vacuum the keyboard and other external devices with a small handheld vacuum cleaner, and you can use a clean cloth and glass cleaner on exterior surfaces, such as the monitor screen.

4. **Store important information in a safe location.**
   Keep records of the serial number, purchase date, and dealer where you purchased your components, including the software. Invest in a fireproof safe or a safety deposit box in which you can keep information that can't be replaced, including important software and data on disks.

5. **Purchase insurance.**
   Most homeowner's or renter's insurance policies do not automatically cover computer equipment. Check your policy and add a rider, if necessary.

6. **Install virus-protection software.**
   A computer ***virus*** is an insidious software program designed to harm your hardware or software. Viruses are spread through files that are passed along on disks, downloaded from the Internet, or sent via email. Virus-protection software locates viruses that make their way into your computer system and deactivates them. It is an absolute must for protecting your computer.

Don't Do Lunch with Your PC
Don't eat or drink while using your PC. Any liquid can severely damage the equipment, not to mention cause electrical problems. Crumbs can also damage a keyboard or disk drives.

Lesson 5: Moving Your Computer

Someday, you may have to move the computer to another location. Whether you move it across the room or across the country, you must take care to protect the components from damage.

In Lesson 2, you learned the importance of saving the original packing materials. Now, you will use them to repack the hardware. In this lesson, you learn how to safely move your computer.

To Move Your Computer

1. **Turn everything off.**
   Make sure that you turn the power off on every device, including the system unit. If you have a power-protection device, turn it off.

2. **Unplug all power cords.**
   Disconnect all power cords from the electrical outlets.

3. **Disconnect all cables.**
   Disconnect the cables connecting all devices to the system unit. When necessary, loosen the screws securing the cables, and make sure that you put the screws in a safe place, where you will be able to find them.

4. **Secure disk drives.**
   Insert a cardboard disk or an old floppy disk into the floppy drives to protect the drives. Most hard disk drives lock into a safe position when you turn the computer off.

5. **Repack the devices.**
   One by one, repack the hardware components in their original boxes so that they won't move around. Keep cables and power cords with their components. Secure the boxes with packing tape, and label the boxes if they don't already have labels.

Code Your Cables
When you disconnect cables, code the port and socket with masking tape to make it easier to reconnect them when you are setting up the computer again.

Summary

In this lesson, you learned about creating an effective work environment. You also learned how to unpack and set up a new computer so that it will work correctly the first time you turn it on. You also learned how to protect your computer from damage.

To expand on your knowledge, spend a few minutes checking your understanding of concepts and terms. Additionally, complete some of the Skill Drill and Challenge exercises.

Checking Concepts and Terms

True/False

For each of the following, check *T* or *F* to indicate whether the statement is true or false.

__T __F **1.** It's a good idea to place a computer directly in front of a window. [L1]

__T __F **2.** You should never place a computer on a table that has wheels that don't lock. [L1]

__T __F **3.** You can connect a mouse to any port on the back of your computer. [L3]

__T __F **4.** It's OK to throw away the registration and warranty cards that come with your computer. [L2]

__T __F **5.** Always unplug your computer before you attach or unattach peripheral devices. [L3]

__T __F **6.** Computer viruses can be downloaded from the Internet. [L4]

__T __F **7.** You should attach your printer to your computer before you start your computer the first time. [L3]

__T __F **8.** All printer cables are the same length. [L3]

__T __F **9.** Most computer systems are delivered in one big box. [L2]

__T __F **10.** Female connectors always attach to other female connectors. [L3]

Multiple Choice

Circle the letter of the correct answer for each of the following.

1. What type of port transmits data through one wire? [L3]

a. SCSI

b. serial

c. unilateral

d. parallel

2. Most printers attach to a ______________ port. [L3]

a. mouse

b. parallel

c. COM

d. video

3. You use a(n) ______________ to protect computers from electrical currents. [L4]

a. surge suppressor

b. extension cord

c. tongue depressor

d. power cord

4. To verify that you received all the components you ordered, ______________. [L2]

a. call the computer dealer while you unpack the boxes

b. compare the items you received to the packing slip and the order slip or invoice

c. see whether there are any parts left over after the system is set up

d. see whether there are any open ports after the system is set up

5. Which of the following is not a good way to protect your computer? [L4]

a. Buy insurance.

b. Send in registration cards.

c. Install a computer alarm system.

d. Store important information in a fireproof safe.

6. What type of modem does not require a telephone line? [L3]

a. fax/modem

b. cable modem

c. cellular modem

d. parallel modem

7. What is the best method of protecting your computer from viruses? [L4]
   a. Do not use the Internet.
   b. Do not use floppy disks.
   c. Install virus-protection software.
   d. Lock your keyboard.

8. Which type of lighting is necessary for illuminating papers on your desk? [L1]
   a. overhead
   b. fluorescent
   c. natural
   d. task

9. Which type of connector has pins sticking out? [L3]
   a. female
   b. male
   c. parallel
   d. serial

10. Which type of connector has sockets sticking in? [L3]
   a. female
   b. male
   c. parallel
   d. serial

Screen ID

Label each of the following elements shown in Figure 2.9.

Figure 2.9

A. Phone jacks for modem and network access
B. Ergonomic keyboard and mouse trays
C. Task Lighting
D. Surge suppressor
E. Adjustable seating
F. Dedicated electrical outlets

1. ____________________ **3.** ____________________ **5.** ____________________

2. ____________________ **4.** ____________________ **6.** ____________________

Discussion Questions

1. What are the characteristics of a good working environment? Include things you can do to make sure your working environment is comfortable.
2. Why is it important to protect your computer? Explain some of the things you can do to ensure that your computer lasts a long time.
3. What are the different types of ports you might find on your computer, and how can you tell them apart? Name a device that might attach to each type of port.

Skill Drill

Skill Drill exercises reinforce project skills. Each skill reinforced is the same, or nearly the same, as a skill presented in the project. Detailed instructions are provided in a step-by-step format.

1. Evaluating Your Current Workspace

Take a good look at your current workspace and decide whether it is really suitable. Make a list of the pros and cons of your current workspace. To evaluate your current workspace, follow these steps:

1. List the pros and cons of the location of the desk or table where the PC resides.
2. List the pros and cons of the size of the desk.
3. List the pros and cons of the quality of lighting and ventilation.
4. List the pros and cons of access to electrical outlets and to phone cords.
5. Based on the information you gathered in Steps 1 through 4, decide whether or not your current workspace is suitable.
6. If you need to improve your workspace, list some of the ways to do so.

2. Plan a New Workspace

If you do not have a current workspace or if your current workspace is less than suitable, look around your home or office to find a place to create a workspace. To plan a new workspace, follow these steps:

1. Find a safe quiet area.
2. Measure the area to see whether there is enough room for a good-sized desk, as well as tables for peripherals, bookshelves, and cabinets.
3. Determine whether you need additional electrical outlets or phone jacks. If so, decide where.
4. Calculate how much money it will cost to set up a new work environment. Include the cost of furniture, wiring, and time.

Challenge

Challenge exercises expand on or are somewhat related to skills presented in the lessons. Each exercise provides a brief narrative introduction, followed by instructions in a numbered-step format. The steps are not as detailed as those in the Skill Drill section.

1. Planning a Business Computer Work Area

As the office manager of a small retail store, you are responsible for setting up the computer. You want to make sure that you have a comfortable work area.

1. Make a list of the criteria you must consider for your work area. Take into consideration the number of people who may need access to the computer equipment.
2. Consult a computer catalog or visit a store to find out what types of furniture are available and how much they cost.
3. Draw a diagram of the work area.

2. Budgeting for a Workspace

Creating a suitable work environment can end up costing you money. Planning ahead and budgeting are important parts of setting up your workspace.

1. Make a list of all the items you need in your new workspace, including furniture, lighting, electrical lines, and phone lines.
2. Research and write down the approximate costs of all the items.
3. Determine whether there is any way to cut costs and still create a suitable environment.

Project 3

Starting the PC

Objectives

In this project, you learn how to

- **Turn on the Computer**
- **Become Familiar with the Startup Routine**
- **Solve Problems During Startup**
- **Restart the Computer**
- **Shut Down the Computer**

Key terms introduced in this project include

- boot
- cold boot
- default
- dialog box
- key combinations
- log off
- log on
- operating system
- power-on self test (POST)
- prompt
- sleep mode
- standby mode
- warm boot
- Windows desktop

Why Would I Do This?

You can't use your computer until you turn on your system. Without power, your computer is just a collection of plastic, metal, and wiring—nothing more. Once you start, or ***boot***, your PC, however, it comes to life, enabling you to process information quickly and easily.

During startup, the PC runs a series of diagnostic tests called the ***power-on self-test (POST)*** to make sure that all the internal and external components are in working order. If a component is not working correctly, your computer displays information about the problem onscreen so that you can try to solve the problem yourself or get help.

When it completes the POST, the computer loads the ***operating system*** into memory so that you can start working. The operating system is a collection of software programs that controls the input and output of data, manages the way files are stored and retrieved, and processes commands that you enter. Most PCs run a version of Windows—either Windows 95, Windows 98, or Windows NT. Handheld devices run Windows CE.

If you won't be using your computer for a long time, you should turn it off to conserve energy and protect your equipment.

In this project, you learn how to start, restart, and turn off your computer. You also learn how to troubleshoot common startup problems.

Lesson 1: Turning on the Computer

When you get ready to start your computer, you should first check that all components are attached correctly (as described in Lesson 2) and that all power cords are plugged into an electrical source. Try turning on your computer now.

To Turn On the Computer

1. **Locate the power (on/off) switch on your system unit.**
   In Project 1, "Getting Started with Personal Computer Hardware," you learned how to find the power switch on the system unit. Look for it now to refresh your memory.

2. **Locate the power switch on your display monitor.**
   On most computers, the display monitor has its own power switch (see Figure 3.1). If you don't turn on the monitor, you can't see the computer output.

3. **Remove the disk from the floppy disk drive, if necessary.**
   Your computer won't start correctly if you have a disk in your floppy disk drive. To remove a disk from a 3 1/2-inch drive, push the eject button to release the disk; then, carefully take out the disk.

4. **Turn on the monitor.**
   Press the monitor's power switch into the On position (refer to Figure 3.1). Turn the monitor on first so you can see the information that your computer displays when you start the system unit.

Figure 3.1
Most monitors have their own power switches, as well as brightness and contrast controls.

5 Check the monitor's brightness and contrast controls (refer to Figure 3.1).
Monitors have brightness and contrast controls similar to those on a television. If you set the controls too high or too low, you can't see information on the monitor screen. Adjust the controls so that they are somewhere in the middle—after something displays onscreen, you can fine-tune the control adjustments.

6 Turn on the system unit.
Press the computer's power switch into the On position (refer to Figure 3.1). You will hear noises and see the drive in-use lights come on as the computer starts. On the display monitor, you will also see information about your computer system as your PC checks to see whether the attached devices are working properly (see Figure 3.2).

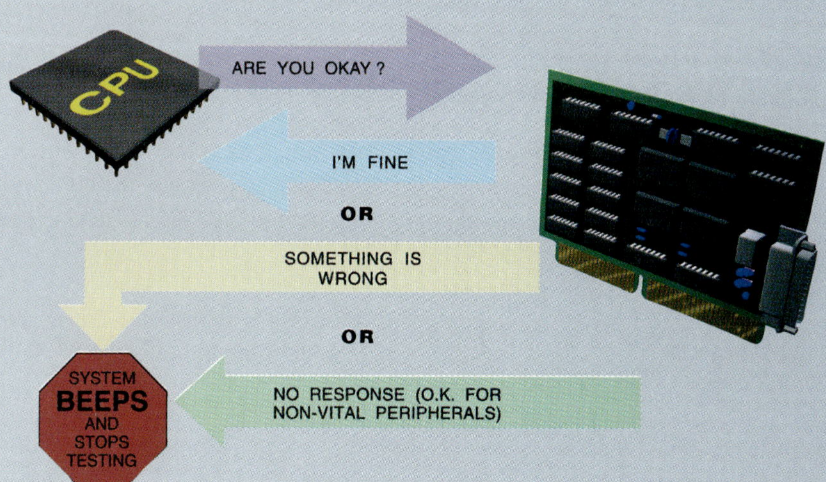

Figure 3.2
During the POST, your CPU checks to see that each component is in working order.

continues ▶

To Turn On the Computer (continued)

What Displays Onscreen During Startup?
The information you see displayed when you start your PC is the output of a series of programs that check to determine what components make up the system and whether or not they are working properly. For example, you might see a list of disk drives and the amount of memory installed. For more information on the startup routine, see Lesson 2.

7. **Turn on the other peripherals.**
You can turn on the other peripherals at any time by gently pressing their power switches into the On position. If you don't plan to use a peripheral, you don't have to follow this step.

If you can't locate the on/off switches, refer to Project 1.

Using a Power Device
If all your system components are connected to a single power device, all you have to do to turn on the computer is turn on that power device.

Lesson 2: Becoming Familiar with the Startup Routine

As soon as the power is on, the PC begins a startup routine. This routine begins with the power-on self-test (POST) that the PC uses to make sure that all components are in working order. When the POST is complete, the PC locates and starts the operating system so that you can start working.

During startup, you hear noises, and see lights on the system unit and messages on the display monitor. These help you identify what the computer is doing. If the computer finds a problem, you can use this information to diagnose and troubleshoot the startup routine.

In this lesson, you learn what to expect during startup.

To Become Familiar with the Startup Routine

1. **Listen as the computer starts checking the system components.**
You hear hums, clicks, and whirs as the fan starts and the CPU counts the memory and checks components, such as the disk drives, to make sure that they work.

2 As the computer checks the system components, watch the lights on the system unit and the messages on your monitor.

You see the status lights on the system unit and monitor go on as the computer starts. On your monitor screen, you see information about the type of computer system you have, including how much memory is installed and what type of CPU you have. If the POST turns up a problem, the computer displays an error message. For example, if the keyboard is not working correctly, a message appears, telling you to check the keyboard.

3 Watch as the computer locates the operating system.

If everything is working correctly, the PC looks for the operating system. First, it looks on your floppy drive. You see the in-use light go on. If that drive is empty, it looks on your hard drive. You see the hard disk in-use light go on. Onscreen, you see a message similar to `Starting Windows 98 . . .`, indicating that your computer is loading the operating system into memory (see Figure 3.3).

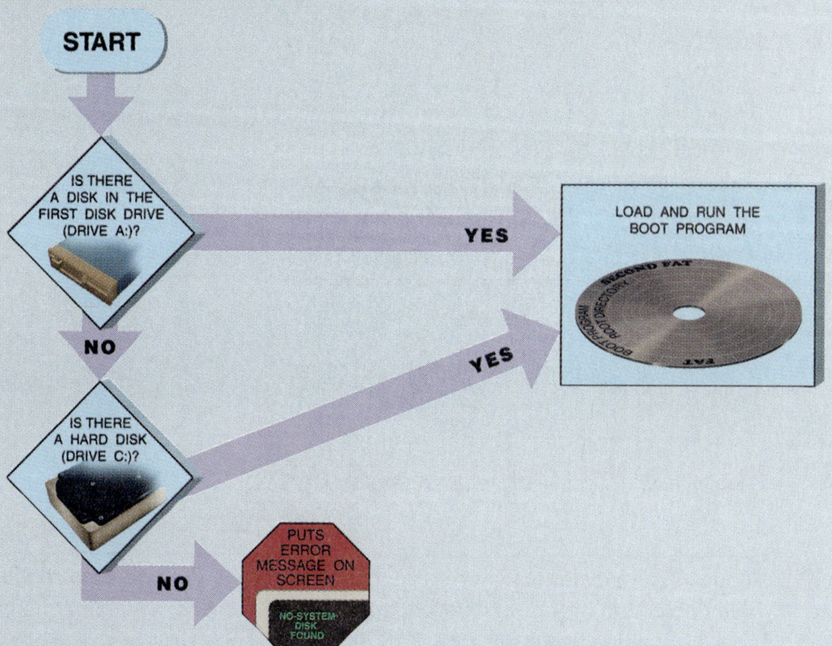

Figure 3.3
When it is sure all components are working, your computer looks for and loads the operating system.

If you see the message `Non-system disk or disk error`, it means you left a floppy disk in drive A. Your computer looks for the operating system in drive A first. If you have a disk in drive A, the computer reads that disk, expecting to find the operating system files. If the operating system files aren't on the disk, you see the non-system disk message. Remove the disk and press any key to continue.

continues ▶

To Become Familiar with the Startup Routine (continued)

4 Wait while the computer loads and processes the Windows startup files.

While the computer starts Windows, it displays the Windows title screen on your monitor. After all startup files have been processed and Windows is loaded into memory, the ***Windows desktop*** is displayed on your screen (see Figure 3.4). The Windows desktop is the main screen of the Windows operating system. It displays when you first start Windows and when no other programs are open on your screen. When the desktop is displayed, your computer is ready to accept commands.

Figure 3.4 The Windows desktop is displayed when Windows is ready for you to enter commands.

Your Windows desktop might not look exactly like the one used to illustrate this book. You may have different applications installed; and someone may have customized your desktop with different colors, toolbars, or icons. It works the same way, however.

If your screen looks very different from the Windows desktop shown in Figure 3.4, however, your computer may have been set up to start a different program. See your instructor for more information.

What's Behind the Windows Title Screen?

During startup, the Windows title screen keeps you from seeing the technical information your computer is processing. If you want to see each startup file as it is processed, press F8 as soon as you see the `Starting Windows` message on your screen. Windows will ask you to confirm each command one-by-one. Press Y to process the command or N to skip it.

Entering a Password
You may have to enter an ID or password before the Windows desktop will appear. If you see a message asking for either of these items, contact your instructor.

Starting Your New Computer for the First Time
The very first time you start your computer, Windows will set up your operating environment for use. That means it will locate and set up each device attached to the system unit, and may process some software application files. This will take a bit longer than a normal startup, and may require that you shut down and restart your computer. If necessary, Windows will display a ***prompt***, which is an onscreen message that tells you what to do to continue. Follow the instructions; ultimately, the Windows desktop displays with a Welcome to Windows window open. To close the window and see just the desktop, click the X—called the Close button—in the upper-right corner of the window.

Lesson 3: Solving Problems During Startup

Sometimes, your computer will find problems during the startup routine. It may beep, display an error message, or give you no response at all.

You will be able to diagnose and solve some problems easily. Other problems may require the attention of a qualified technician. Keep in mind that the most common problems are caused by loose connections between components or between components and the power source.

In this lesson, you learn how to troubleshoot the startup routine.

To Solve Problems During Startup

1. **Listen for sounds from the system unit.**
During startup, you should hear whirs from the fan and the disk drives, as well as clicks and beeps from other components. If you don't hear the fan, it could be a problem with the power supply. If you don't hear anything, it could be a problem with the electrical outlet or the power cord. If you hear incessant beeping, you probably have a problem with a particular peripheral device, such as the keyboard.

2. **Watch the lights.**
As soon as you turn on the computer, the status lights go on. If these lights don't go on, it could mean a problem with the electrical outlet or the power cord.

The disk in-use lights should go on during the POST and also while the computer looks for the operating system. If a drive light does not go on, a problem may exist with the drive. Likewise, watch the status lights on the peripherals. If your keyboard's online light does not go on, there is a problem with the keyboard. Make sure that the cord is attached securely.

continues ▶

To Solve Problems During Startup (continued)

3 Watch the monitor screen.

If the monitor screen is blank, the monitor may be broken. Chances are, however, you forgot to turn it on, the cord came unplugged, or the brightness and contrast controls just need adjusting.

4 Write down error messages.

When the computer encounters a problem, it usually displays an error message on your screen. If an error message appears, write down the message so that you can look for it in a user's manual or ask a technician what it means. Sometimes, the error message tells you exactly what you need to do to solve the problem. For example, if you see the following message, you have a disk in drive A that needs to be removed:

```
Non-system disk or disk error
Replace and strike any key when ready.
```

If you see a message telling you that the computer has no operating system, contact a qualified technician or your computer dealer immediately.

5 Check the connections.

You can easily solve most startup problems by making sure that all connections are secure. Make sure that all components are connected firmly to the correct ports. Make sure that all components are connected to a power source. Make sure that the power source is turned on. Make sure that all components are turned on.

Troubleshooting Peripherals

You can use these same steps to troubleshoot problems with peripheral devices. Because the most common problems have to do with faulty connections, shut off the power; then, check the cables and power cords to make sure that they are attached securely and correctly.

Lesson 4: Restarting the Computer

If your computer won't respond to the keyboard or the mouse, you must restart it. You have two ways to restart the computer. You use a ***cold boot*** when your computer is already off or when you want the computer to run through the whole startup routine from the beginning. You use a ***warm boot*** when your computer is running and you want to start it again without running the POST.

Keep in mind that you should only use these steps to restart your computer when the computer will not respond to commands from the keyboard or the mouse because no matter which method of rebooting you use, all information you have entered that has not yet been stored on a disk is lost. You learn how to shut down the computer in normal operating conditions in the next lesson. Try restarting your computer now.

To Restart the Computer

1. **Press and hold down Ctrl, Alt, and Del on your keyboard.**
   You must press and hold down all three keys at the same time.

2. **Release the three keys at the same time.**
   The Windows Close Program ***dialog box*** is displayed. A dialog box is an on-screen window in which you must make a choice or enter additional information to complete a command.

3. **Repeat Steps 1 and 2.**
   Your computer should then restart. If the computer does not restart, try it again. If the computer still does not restart, continue with Step 4.

4. **Press the Reset button on the front of your PC.**
   Many computers have a Reset button, which lets you quickly restart your PC (see Figure 3.5).

Figure 3.5
Many computers have a Reset button on the front of the system unit.

If Ctrl+Alt+Del does not work, and your computer does not have a Reset button, you can use the on/off switch. Just turn the computer off, wait a minute, and then turn it back it on.

Using Key Combinations
When you press more than one key on your keyboard at the same time, you use ***key combinations***. Key combinations usually combine one of the special-purpose keys on the keyboard and one or two other keys. They are used most often as shortcuts for commands in Windows application programs. When you see a key combination written in a manual, plus signs (+) or hyphens (-) usually appear between the key names, indicating that they should be pressed at the same time (Ctrl+Alt+Del, for example).

ScanDisk
If you shut down or restart your computer without closing Windows first, Windows will run ScanDisk the next time you boot. ScanDisk is a utility program that checks your hard disk(s) for problems. It will take a few minutes to complete the scan, depending on the size of your hard disk(s). Follow the prompts that Windows displays in order to continue.

Lesson 5: Shutting Down the Computer

How often you shut down your computer will depend on your work habits, as well as office policies that may affect you. Some people like to shut down every day, whereas others leave their computers on for days at a time.

Before you shut down your computer, you should make sure that you have closed all programs that you had in use, including Windows. Try shutting down your computer now.

To Shut Down the Computer

1. **Move your mouse so that the mouse pointer is touching the Start button on the Windows taskbar at the bottom of the screen, and then click the left mouse button.**
When you click the Start button, the Start menu appears on the desktop, as shown in Figure 3.6.

If you have never used a mouse before, you may want to skip this lesson for now, or ask your instructor for assistance. Using a mouse is covered in Project 4, "Getting to Know Your Operating System."

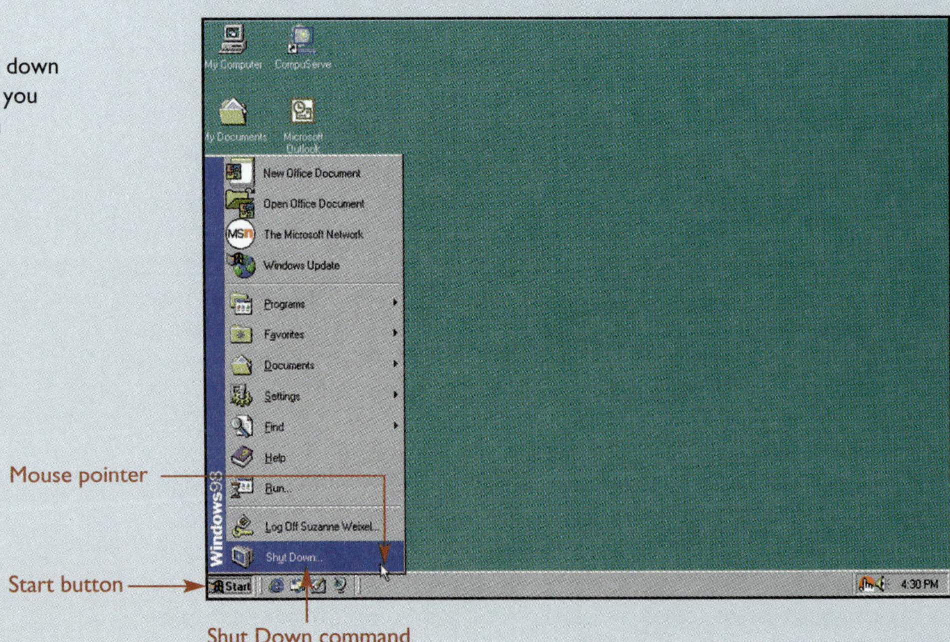

Figure 3.6
Before you shut down your computer, you must shut down Windows.

2 Move your mouse so that the mouse pointer is touching the Shut Down command at the bottom of the Start menu, and then click the left mouse button.

The Shut Down Windows dialog box appears, as shown in Figure 3.7. The ***default*** (preset) option in the dialog box is to shut down the computer. Default means the way an option is set before you change it or customize it.

Shutdown Options

On some computers, there are additional options in the Windows Shut Down dialog box. For example, some might have an option for putting the system into ***sleep mode*** or ***standby mode***, which is a setting used to save energy while you are not using your computer. Some might have an option to ***log off***, or disconnect from, a network in order to ***log on***—sign in to use a network—as someone else. If more than one person share the computer, it may be necessary to log on and off.

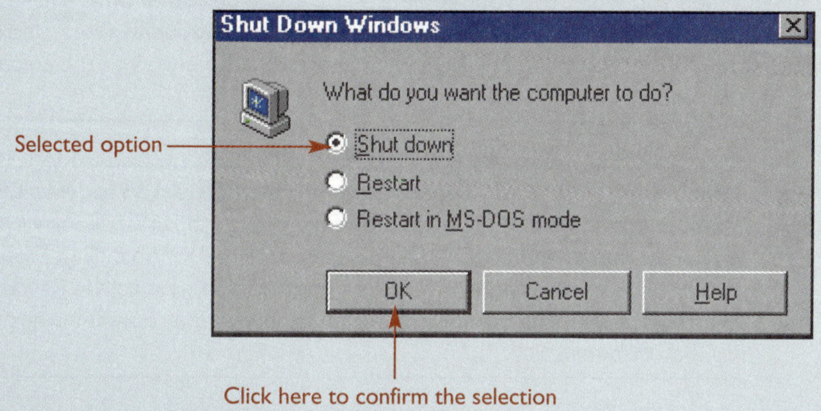

Figure 3.7
The Shut Down Windows dialog box.

3 Move your mouse pointer so that it is touching the OK button in the Shut Down Windows dialog box, and then click the left mouse button.

This confirms that you want to shut down the computer. You see a message on your screen, asking you to wait while Windows performs some shutdown routines to make sure that all files are saved and closed before you turn off the computer. Finally, a message appears, telling you it is safe to turn off the computer.

Automatic Shutdown

Some newer PCs will automatically shut down as soon as Windows has shut down. If your PC turns itself off, all you have to do is turn off the monitor and any other peripherals that may remain on. If you continue with step 4, you'll end up turning your PC back on again! To see if your PC has turned itself off automatically, check the power status light—if it is lit, the PC is still on.

4 Locate the power switch on the system unit.

You use the same switch to turn the computer off that you used in Lesson 1 to turn on the computer.

continues ▶

To Shut Down the Computer (continued)

5. **Press the power switch into the Off position.**
   The computer shuts down immediately.

6. **Shut off all peripheral devices.**
   Shut off the monitor, the printer, and any other peripheral devices you had in use.

Using a Power Device to Shut Down Your Computer
If you have your components plugged into a single power device, you can leave the power switches of each component in the On position and just turn off the power device.

Leaving Your Computer for a Long Time
When you won't use your computer for a long period of time, such as when you go on vacation, it is a good idea to unplug components from electrical outlets. This action protects the equipment from problems with the electrical source.

Restarting Your Computer from the Shut Down Windows Dialog Box
You can use the Shut Down Windows dialog box to restart your system if your computer is responding to your mouse commands. Choose Shut Down from the Start menu, and then click in the option button next to the Restart option and choose OK. This comes in handy if an application program is not responding, but Windows is.

Summary

In this lesson, you finally started your computer and used some commands. You learned two of the most basic and important tasks—starting and shutting off your computer, and you got your first look at the Windows desktop.

Take a few minutes to check your skills and to complete some of the Skill Drill and Challenge exercises.

Checking Concepts and Terms

True/False

For each of the following, check *T* or *F* to indicate whether the statement is true or false.

__T __F **1.** Most computer systems have more than one on/off switch. [L1]

__T __F **2.** During startup, your computer looks for the operating system on drive A, and then looks on drive B. [L2]

__T __F **3.** During startup, your computer runs a test to make sure that all components are working. [L3]

__T __F **4.** The only way to restart a computer is to turn it off and then turn it back on. [L4]

__T __F **5.** It is a good idea to leave your computer running when you go away for a two-week vacation. [L5]

__T __F **6.** Your Windows desktop may not look the same as the one in the illustrations of this book. [L2]

__T __F **7.** During startup, you hear noises, see lights on the system unit, and see messages on the display monitor. [L2]

__T __F **8.** Most startup problems require a certified technician to repair. [L3]

__T __F **9.** Pressing the reset button is one way to perform a warm boot. [L4]

__T __F **10.** You must have a mouse to restart your computer. [L4]

Multiple Choice

Circle the letter of the correct answer for each of the following.

1. When starting your computer, you should turn on the ______________ first. [L1]

a. printer

b. monitor

c. system unit

d. it doesn't matter

2. What is the most common reason for problems during startup? [L3]

a. The operating system is not installed.

b. The connections between components and the power source are not secure.

c. The printer is broken.

d. The system unit is upside down.

3. To quickly restart your computer, press ______________. [L4]

a. F8

b. the Turbo button

c. Ctrl

d. the Reset button

4. During startup, you should hear the whir of the ______________. [L2]

a. fan

b. CPU

c. modem

d. math coprocessor

5. To process the startup file commands one-by-one, you press ______________. [L3]

a. F8

b. the Turbo button

c. Ctrl

d. the Reset button

6. When the operating system is correctly loaded, you see the Windows ______________ onscreen. [L1]

a. Start menu

b. desktop

c. dialog box

d. prompt

7. What type of boot should you use to restart your computer when it is already running? [L4]

a. warm boot

b. cold boot

c. cool boot

d. hot boot

8. You will see an error message if you leave a disk in which drive? [L5]

a. CD-RW

b. DVD

c. floppy drive A

d. hard drive C

9. What is the term for pressing more than one keyboard key at a time? [L4]
   a. key selection
   b. key combination
   c. key triangulation
   d. key indentation

10. What is the energy-saving mode called? [L5]
    a. snooze mode
    b. boot mode
    c. rest mode
    d. sleep mode

Discussion Questions

1. What are the different ways to start and restart a computer? Discuss scenarios in which it would be appropriate to use each different way.
2. What are some of the things that could go wrong during startup? What can you do to prevent or repair the problems?
3. Is it important to be a computer technician if you are going to use a PC? Why or why not?

Skill Drill

Skill Drill exercises reinforce project skills. Each skill reinforced is the same, or nearly the same, as a skill presented in the project. Detailed instructions are provided in a step-by-step format.

1. Practicing Cold Boots

To practice a cold boot, follow these steps:

1. Turn on your computer system.
2. Watch for problems and write down any error messages that appear.
3. Using your mouse, click the Start button on the Windows Taskbar.
4. Click the Shut Down command on the Start menu.
5. Click the Shut down option.
6. Click OK.
7. Shut off your computer.
8. Start your computer again using a cold boot.
9. Repeat Steps 3 through 7 to shut down your computer again.

2. Practicing Warm Boots

To practice a warm boot, follow these steps:

1. Turn on your computer system.
2. Watch for problems and write down any error messages that appear.
3. Press Ctrl+Alt+Del.
4. Press Ctrl+Alt+Del again.
5. When the Windows desktop displays, press the Restart button.
6. When the Windows desktop displays, click the Start button.
7. Click the Shut Down command on the Start menu.
8. Click the Restart option in the Shut Down Windows dialog box.
9. Click OK.
10. When the Windows desktop displays, click the Start button on the Windows Taskbar.
11. Click the Shut Down command on the Start menu.
12. Click the Shut Down option.
13. Click OK.
14. Shut off your computer.

Challenge

Challenge exercises expand on or are somewhat related to skills presented in the lessons. Each exercise provides a brief narrative introduction, followed by instructions in a numbered-step format. The steps are not as detailed as those in the Skill Drill section.

1. Plan Ahead to Avoid Startup Problems

Now that you have planned the type of computer system you want for a small business and you know where you want to set it up, you can get to work. You need to understand, however, some of the problems you may encounter when you first start your computer. If you can't solve the problems yourself, you may have to return the equipment or have it repaired. Follow these steps:

1. Make a list of things that could go wrong with each component.
2. Create a reference of where to go for service and support for each component.
3. Write down a list of ways to avoid problems.

2. Troubleshooting Startup

During startup, be aware of possible problems and watch your system for warning signs. Try creating a few harmless problems to see how your computer reacts.

1. Insert a non-system disk in drive A and start your system.
2. Write down the error message that appears and respond to the problem.
3. Loosen the connection between your keyboard and your PC, and then perform a cold boot.
4. Write down the error message that appears, and then respond to the problem.
5. Use F8 to step through the startup command files.
6. When you finish, shut down your computer system.

Project 4

Project 4

Getting to Know Your Operating System

Objectives

In this project, you learn how to

- **Identify Elements of Windows 98**
- **Use a Mouse in Windows**
- **Change the System Date and Time**
- **Change the Appearance of the Desktop**
- **Get Help in Windows**

Key terms introduced in this project include

- applications
- check boxes
- click
- color palette
- command-line interface
- commands
- context-sensitive
- Control Panel
- double-click
- dragging
- drops
- drop-down arrow
- files
- folder
- graphical user interface (GUI)
- hotkey
- hyperlinks
- icons
- increment arrows
- intuitive
- list boxes
- maximizing
- menu
- menu bar
- minimizing
- nested menus
- option buttons
- pointing
- properties
- restoring
- right-clicking
- screen saver
- ScreenTip
- scrollbar
- shortcut menu
- Systray
- taskbar
- text box
- tiled
- title bar
- toolbars
- wallpaper
- windows

Why Would I Do This?

To communicate with your personal computer, you must understand how to use the PC's operating system (OS). The operating system makes sure that all parts of the PC work together to get the job done, according to the specifications you enter as ***commands***. Commands are the instructions given to the PC by the user or by a software program. The operating system controls the flow of data in and out of the computer, and it calls in the hardware and software to perform the necessary services at the right time. Without an operating system, you would not be able to communicate with your computer, and your computer would not know how to communicate with you.

DOS (pronounced as one word: "DOS," which rhymes with "floss") used to be the most common PC operating system. It uses a ***command-line interface,*** which means you have to type DOS commands one by one in order to communicate with your PC. DOS can be confusing and difficult to use. Now, PCs come with the Microsoft Windows operating system, which has a ***graphical user interface (GUI)***. Using a GUI (pronounced "gooey"), you enter commands and control your PC by using a mouse or the keyboard to choose buttons or items from a ***menu***, or list of commands and options. Windows uses simple English and pictures (***icons***) to explain the actions and commands you should use.

Different Versions of Windows
The steps and illustrations in this book are based on the Windows 98 operating system. If you have a different version of Windows, such as Windows 95 or Windows NT, you might notice some small differences in the way your display looks or your system operates. If necessary, ask your instructor for more information.

In this project, you learn some basic information about using Windows to control your PC.

Lesson 1: Identifying Elements of Windows 98

Windows 98 is based on the idea that the monitor screen is just like the top of your desk. In fact the screen is called the desktop in Windows. On the Windows desktop, the tools you need are displayed as icons (small pictures), or in rectangular areas called ***windows*** (hence, the name Windows). All windows have the same set of elements, such as a ***title bar*** (a row across the top of a window that displays the name of the window) and a ***menu bar***, which displays a row of menu names. If you have more than one window open, they may overlap on the desktop, just as papers on your desk can be stacked on top of each other.

In this lesson, you learn to identify the common elements of the Windows desktop. Use Figure 4.1 to help you locate each element. Use Table 4.1 to find out the purpose of the different elements.

Even if you use Windows 98, your desktop may not look exactly like the one used in this book. Don't worry, though—it works the same way.

To Identify Windows 98 Elements

1 Start your computer.

The computer runs through its POST and loads the Windows 98 operating system. While Windows is loading, you see the Windows logo over a background of clouds floating across a blue sky. When Windows is loaded, the Windows 98 desktop displays (see Figure 4.1).

The Welcome to Windows Window

The Welcome to Windows window may be displayed when you start Windows (see Figure 4.2). If it is, leave it open to use in the rest of this exercise. If not, refer to Figure 4.2 to complete the exercise.

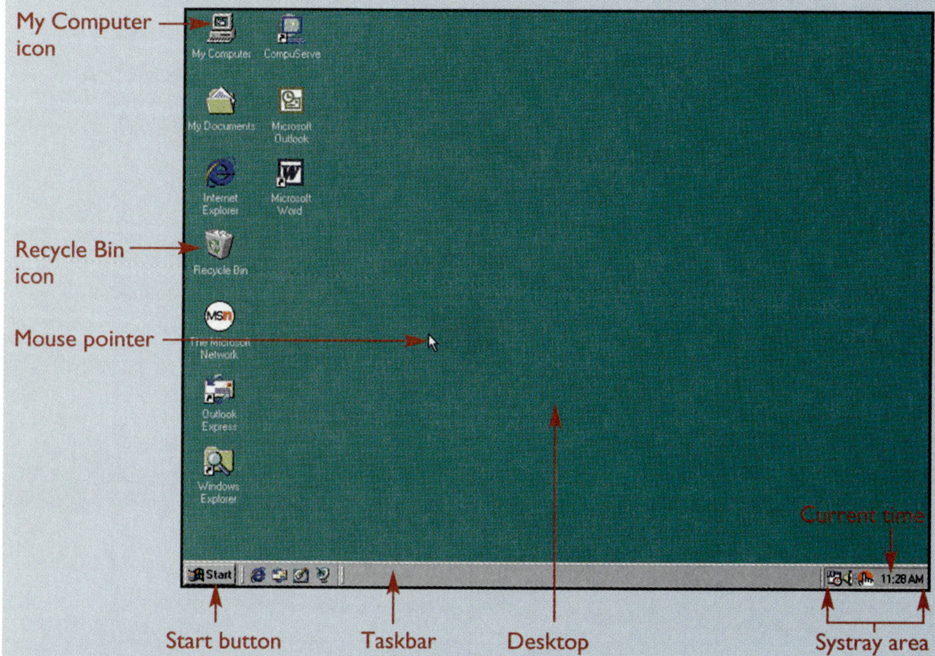

Figure 4.1
The Windows 98 desktop.

2 Locate the taskbar at the bottom of the desktop.

While you are running Windows 98, the taskbar is displayed onscreen. The ***taskbar*** is a Windows element that displays buttons representing open application programs or tools. ***Applications*** are software programs that are designed for a specific purpose, such as word processing. In Figure 4.1, you can see the Start button and the ***Systray*** (short for system tray) area, in which the time is displayed, along with icons for other system tools.

3 Locate the Start button on the taskbar.

The Start button displays at the left end of the taskbar. In Windows, buttons are used to choose actions or commands. When you ***click*** (press and release the left mouse button) on the Start button, a menu opens that you can use to start programs, change settings, shut down Windows, find ***files*** (which are the data you enter and save using an application program), and get help. Windows 98 is a very ***intuitive*** software program, meaning that it works the way you think it should work. If something in Windows 98 says `Start`, it's probably a good place to get started.

continues ▶

To Identify Windows 98 Elements (continued)

4 Locate the Welcome to Windows window. The window may open when you start your computer (see Figure 4.2).

When you open an application, a dialog box, a group of related files called a ***folder***, or a file, is displayed in a rectangular window on the screen. These windows share many common elements, including title bars and command buttons. Some also have menu bars and control buttons for ***maximizing***, ***minimizing***, ***restoring***, or closing the window. Maximizing means to increase the size of a window so that it fills the desktop. Minimizing means reducing a window to a button on the taskbar or to an icon. Restoring means to return a window to its previous size and position on the desktop.

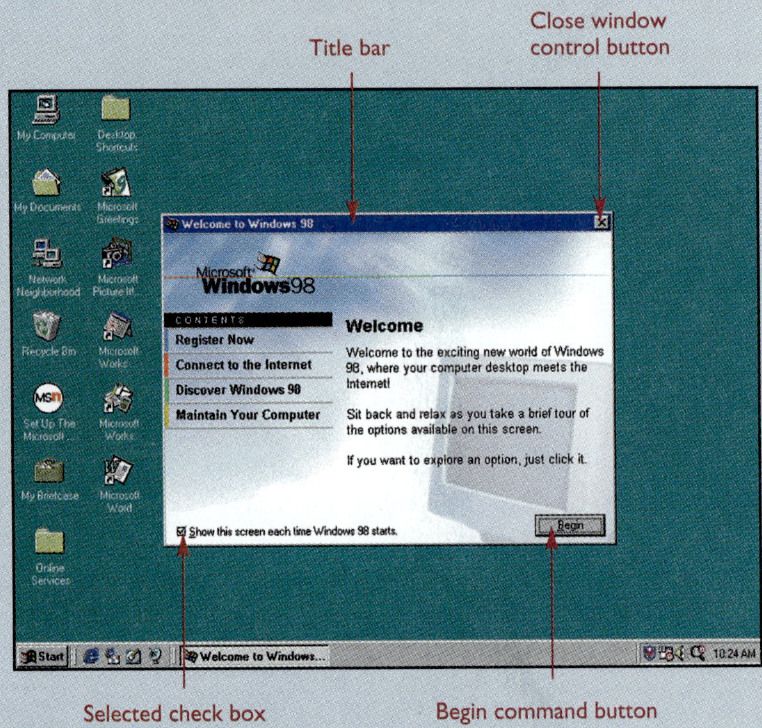

Figure 4.2
The Welcome to Windows 98 window.

5 In the Welcome window (refer to Figure 4.2), locate the Begin command button.

Command buttons are used to choose actions and commands. To choose the command, click on the button with the mouse, or you can press the underlined letter in the command name on your keyboard. Most windows have a Close or Cancel button that closes the window without making any changes, as well as a Yes or OK button, which accepts changes and closes the window. Another way to close a window is to click the Close button at the right end of the title bar—the button with the X on it.

The Welcome to Windows window is different in different versions of Windows. If the one on your screen is different from the one in Figure 4.2, refer to Figure 4.2 to complete the exercise.

6 Locate the Recycle Bin icon on the desktop.

Icons are pictures that represent files, folders, or applications. The Recycle Bin icon represents the folder in which deleted files are stored. When you click an icon, you select the item that it represents. When you ***double-click*** (click the left mouse button twice in rapid succession) an icon, you activate the item that it represents.

Table 4.1 summarizes the purposes of a few commonly used Windows items.

Table 4.1 Windows 98 Desktop Elements

Element	Purpose
Taskbar	A line near the bottom of the Windows 98 desktop that displays buttons for each active application, as well as the Start button and the Systray area. It may also display one or more ***toolbars***, which are rows of buttons used to perform common tasks.
Command buttons	In windows and dialog boxes, command buttons are small rectangular areas that let you choose actions or execute commands.
Start button	A command button on the taskbar that opens the Start menu.
Shortcuts	Icons on the desktop that allow you to quickly access certain applications, files, or folders.
Recycle Bin	A folder in which deleted files are stored until you either restore them to their original locations or empty the Recycle Bin.

In Lesson 2, you learn how to use a mouse in Windows.

Similarities Among Windows Applications

One of the primary benefits of Windows is that all Windows applications use similar elements. For example, all Windows programs run in application windows that have title bars, as well as Minimize and Maximize buttons. Most Windows programs have similar menu commands, including File menus, Edit menus, and Help menus. For this reason, learning to use Windows 98 makes it easy for you to learn to use other Windows applications.

Lesson 2: Using a Mouse in Windows

Windows is designed for use with a mouse. Although you can get by with just a keyboard, using a mouse is much easier. This book assumes that you use a mouse when you work in Windows and Windows programs.

To use a mouse, you move the mouse on your desktop, which in turn moves the mouse pointer on your Windows desktop. To make a selection, you press a button on the mouse.

In this lesson, you learn to use four basic mouse actions. Try using your mouse now.

To Use a Mouse in Windows

1 Move the mouse pointer to the Start button on the taskbar (see Figure 4.3).

This action is called ***pointing*** to the Start button. After a second or two, notice that a ***ScreenTip*** displays beside the Start button, telling you what the button is for. ScreenTips are lines of text that identify the button or object to which the mouse is currently pointing. In Windows 98 and most Windows 98 applications, tips such as this one appear when the mouse pointer rests on a button, helping you figure out what buttons are used for without having to refer to a manual.

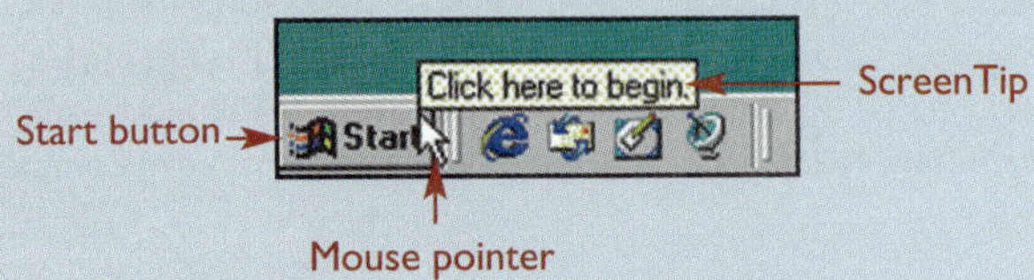

Figure 4.3
Use the mouse to point at items you want to choose or select.

If you have trouble moving the mouse pointer to the location you want, keep your eyes on the mouse pointer, not on the mouse (it's like driving a car—you watch the road, not the steering wheel!). Then try these four steps: move the mouse to the left to move the mouse pointer to the left; move the mouse to the right to move the mouse pointer to the right; move the mouse forward to move the mouse pointer toward the top of your screen; and move the mouse toward you to move the mouse pointer toward the bottom of your screen.

Moving the Mouse
To move the mouse without moving the mouse pointer, pick the mouse up.

2 Click the left mouse button.

The Start menu opens on the desktop (see Figure 4.4). You click the mouse button to open menus, choose menu commands or buttons, and select items. Some mouse devices have only one button, but most have two or three.

3 Slide the mouse pointer up on the Start menu so that it points at the Programs folder command.

The Programs menu opens beside the Start menu, as shown in Figure 4.4. On a menu, items that open in these ***nested menus*** have arrowheads beside them. To open a nested menu, you simply use the mouse to point at the item name. Items that open dialog boxes have ellipses (. . .) beside them. To open a dialog box, you click on the item name.

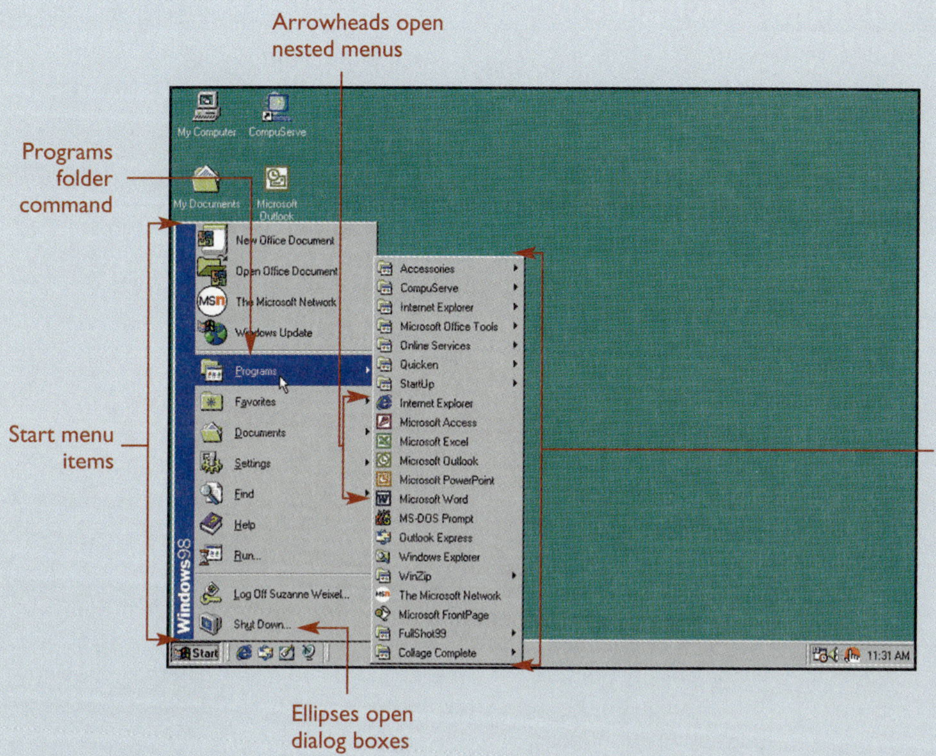

Figure 4.4
Click an item to select it.

4 Point to the Start button again, and click the left mouse button.
The Start menu closes. To open a menu, you click the menu name. To close the menu, you click the menu name again.

Closing Menus
You can also close a menu by clicking anywhere outside of it, or by pressing Escape twice—once to close the menu and again to deselect the menu name.

---

5 Move the mouse pointer to the Close control button in the upper-right corner of the Welcome window and click the left mouse button.
The Welcome screen window closes. You click a button to select the option or activate the command that it represents.

6 Point to the Recycle Bin icon on the desktop.
The Recycle Bin icon represents the folder that contains deleted files. It is created when you first install Windows.

7 Press and hold down the left mouse button.
You performed the first step of ***dragging***, a mouse action used to move and copy Windows elements on the desktop by pressing and holding the left mouse button when moving the mouse pointer to a different location.

continues ▶

To Use a Mouse in Windows (continued)

8 Without releasing the mouse button, move the mouse to the right so that the mouse pointer moves to the right.

The Recycle Bin icon is dragged along with the mouse pointer.

> If the icon doesn't move with the pointer, you aren't holding down the mouse button, or you don't have the mouse pointer touching the icon. Move the mouse pointer to the icon, press and hold down the mouse button, and try dragging the icon again.

9 Release the left mouse button.

Releasing the mouse button ***drops*** the icon in the new location, as shown in Figure 4.5. You have just dragged and dropped the Recycle Bin icon in a different location on the desktop. This does not affect the contents of the Recycle Bin folder or the way it works; it just changes the appearance of the desktop.

> If the icon "snaps" back into its original location, the AutoArrange feature is selected. Point at a blank area of the desktop, click the right mouse button, point at the Arrange Icons command, and then click AutoArrange on the nested menu that is displayed. Repeat Steps 6–9 to drag and drop the icon.

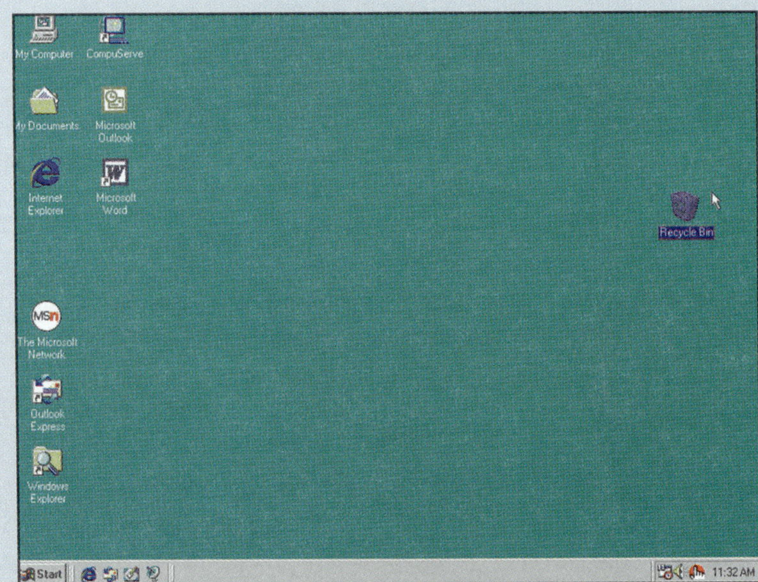

Figure 4.5
You can move items around the desktop by dragging.

⑩ Point to the My Computer icon on the desktop, and double-click the left mouse button.

The My Computer window opens on the desktop, as shown in Figure 4.6. You can use double-clicking to open windows and to start applications. The My Computer window contains icons and folders representing the contents of your computer system.

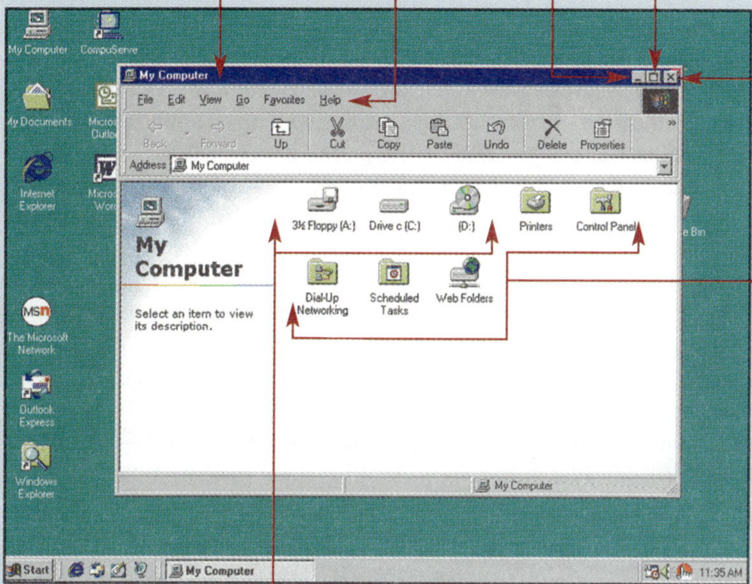

Figure 4.6
The My Computer window is open on the desktop.

If nothing happens when you double-click, you are not clicking fast enough. Try again.

---

⑪ Point to the My Computer window title bar and click the right mouse button.

A ***shortcut menu*** drops down into the window (see Figure 4.7). Shortcut menus display a short list of commonly used commands. Clicking the right mouse button is called ***right-clicking***. Almost every element in Windows 98 has a shortcut menu you can use to quickly choose commands. Right-click the element to open the shortcut menu for it.

Figure 4.7
Right-click elements to open a shortcut menu.

continues ▶

To Use a Mouse in Windows (continued)

12 Click the Close command on the shortcut menu.
The My Computer window closes. Every window has a Close command on its shortcut menu, as well as on its File menu. In the next lesson, you learn how to change some system settings by using Windows 98 and your mouse.

Using the Keyboard in Windows
You don't have to choose between using a mouse and using a keyboard in Windows. You can use a combination of the two. For example, to select a menu topic in a window, press Alt, and then type the underlined letter—called a ***hotkey***—in the menu name. To choose a command from a menu, type the underlined letter in the command name. To close an open window with the keyboard, press Alt+F4. To move from one option to another in a dialog box, press Tab. To open the start menu, press Ctrl+Esc. To close a menu or dialog box without making any selections, press Esc.

Using a Mouse Pad
You can move the mouse more easily if you have a mouse pad—a rubberized or plastic pad that provides a smooth surface for the mouse to move across.

Lesson 3: Changing the System Date and Time

Windows 98 controls many aspects of the way your computer functions. For example, it controls the way mouse clicks and keyboard selections are translated into commands, it controls which ports are used for peripherals, and it controls the current date and time settings. Although most settings are entered by default when you install Windows 98, you can change these settings at any time.

In this lesson, you learn how to set the system date and time in Windows 98.

To Change the System Date and Time

1 In Windows 98, click the Start button on the taskbar.
The Start menu opens.

2 Slide the mouse pointer so that it is pointing to the Settings command on the Start menu.
The nested Settings menu opens, as shown in Figure 4.8. From the Settings menu you can choose the type of system settings you want to change.

3 Click the Control Panel folder on the Settings menu.
The ***Control Panel*** folder window opens on the desktop, as shown in Figure 4.9. The Control Panel is a Windows system folder that contains icons representing the utility programs that control your system settings.

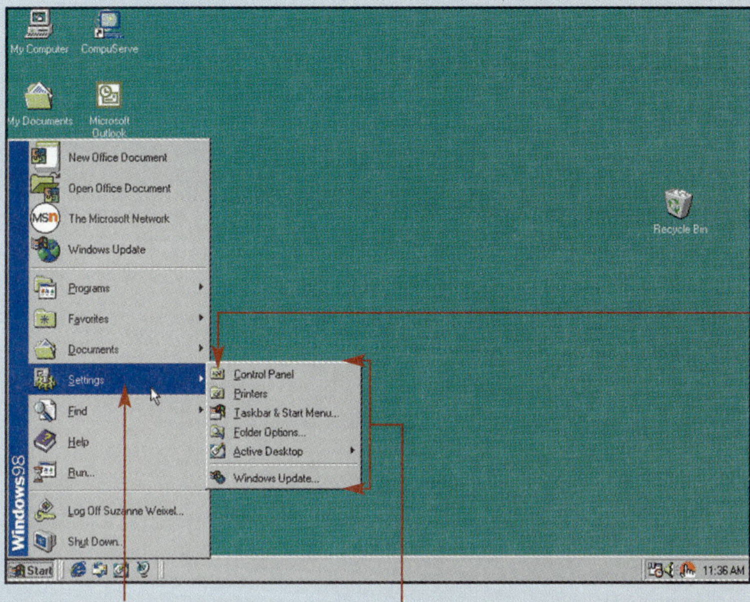

Figure 4.8
Use the Settings menu to open the folder that contains the settings you want to change.

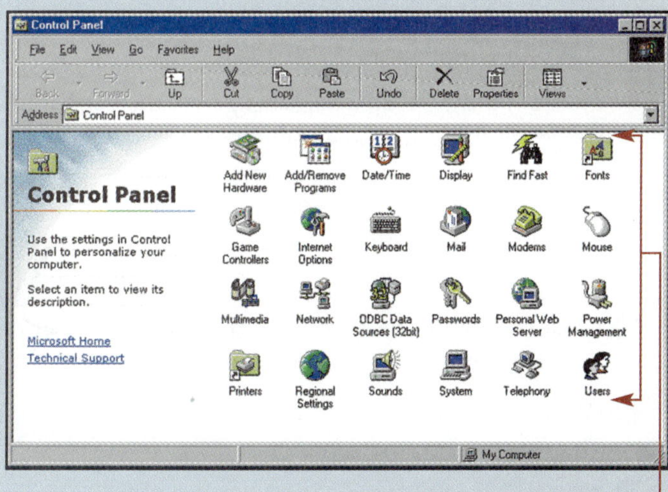

Figure 4.9
Use the programs in the Control Panel to change system settings.

4 Double-click the Date/Time icon in the Control Panel window.

The Date/Time Properties dialog box opens, as shown in Figure 4.10. ***Properties*** are the settings that control the way a Windows element functions. In the Date/Time Properties dialog box, you can change the settings that control the computer's internal clock/calendar. Windows uses these settings to display the time on the taskbar, as well as to mark the files you create and edit. You can change the current date and time, and you can change the time zone. You can even select whether or not you want the clock calendar to automatically adjust the time for Daylight Savings.

continues ▶

To Change the System Date and Time (continued)

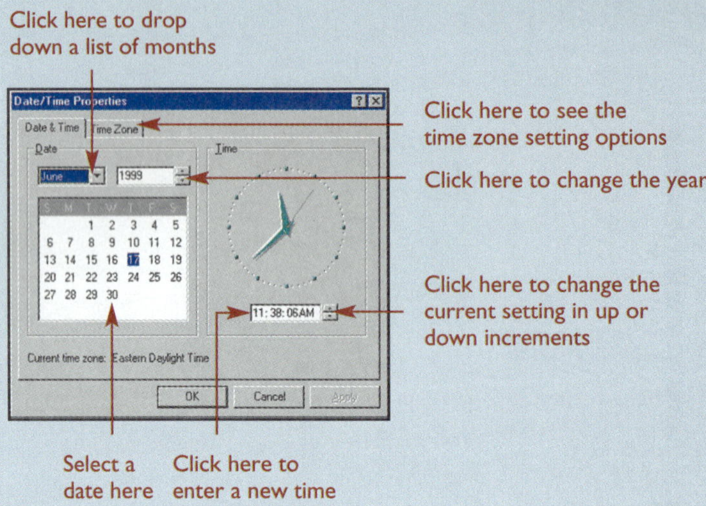

Figure 4.10
The Date/Time Properties dialog box.

5 Click the drop-down arrow next to the current month.
A list of months drops down into the dialog box. A ***drop-down arrow*** is an element used for opening a list from which you can make a selection. It looks like an arrowhead pointing down, and it is usually found next to a button on a toolbar or in a dialog box. In this case, you can select a different month from the list. To change the date, simply click the date on the calendar. To change the year, use the up and down ***increment arrows*** to advance or decrease the year. Increment arrows are also elements used to change a current setting. They are small arrowheads pointing up and down, and they are used to change a number setting in increments. For example, increment arrows can be used to set a size value, change the date, or select a percentage.

6 Click the drop-down arrow next to the current month again.
The month drop-down list closes without a change.

7 Click the down increment arrow next to the current time.
This changes the time from AM to PM or from PM to AM.

8 Click the Apply command button.
This changes the setting on the clock/calendar, leaving the dialog box open. Notice that the current time on the taskbar has changed from AM to PM or from PM to AM.

9 Click the down increment arrow next to the current time to change back to the original settings.
If your original settings were correct, you should change back. You want the clock/calendar to stay accurate. If you need to change the time, simply click inside the time ***text box***, press the Del or ←Backspace key to delete the current time, and type the new time. A text box is a common feature used for entering data in a dialog box or on a toolbar. It is called a text box because it is an area where you type text.

10 Click the Time Zone tab at the top of the dialog box.
The Time Zone settings options are displayed in the dialog box, as shown in Figure 4.11. In many Windows dialog boxes, there is more than one page of options. You click a tab to change the page and display other options.

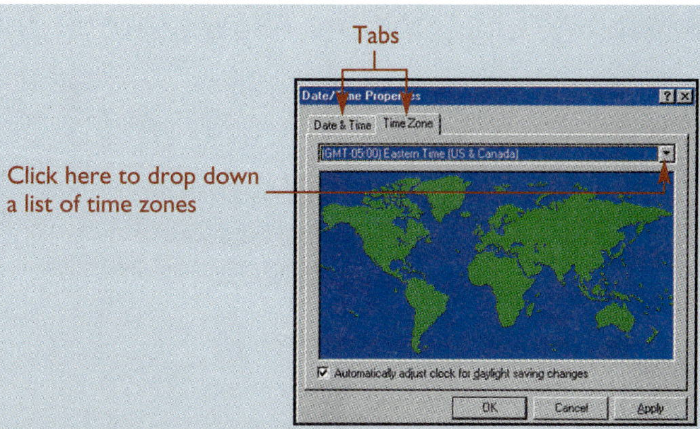

Figure 4.11
The Time Zone settings options.

⑪ **Click the drop-down arrow next to the time zone text box.**
A list of time zones opens. You can choose any time zone from the list.

⑫ **Click the OK command button.**
This accepts the changes you have made and closes the dialog box. The Control Panel window is still open on the desktop. Look at the Date/Time button on the taskbar to see whether the time is correct. Move the mouse pointer to the button to display the date ScreenTip. If necessary, repeat the steps in this lesson to correctly set the date and time.

Leave the Control Panel window open. In the next lesson, you learn how to change the settings that control the appearance of the desktop.

Dialog Box Options
In dialog boxes, there are many different ways to enter commands. You have already used command buttons, such as Close, OK, and Cancel. In this lesson, you were introduced to text boxes, drop-down arrows, and increment arrows. In future lessons, you will use ***option buttons***, ***check boxes***, and ***list boxes***. Option buttons are round buttons that you click to select or deselect an option. The selected option button has a dot in it. A check box is a square box that you click to select or deselect a setting. A selected check box has a check mark or X in it. A list box is a list of options. You click an option in the list to select it. All these items are simply methods for choosing the commands you want

Options for Opening
To quickly open the Date/Time Properties dialog box, double-click the Date/Time button in the Systray on the taskbar, or right-click it and choose Adjust Date/Time from the shortcut menu.

You can also open the Control Panel folder window from the My Computer window. Double-click the My Computer icon on the desktop, and then double-click the Control Panel folder in the My Computer window.

Lesson 4: Changing the Appearance of the Desktop

One of the settings you can easily change using Windows 98 is the appearance of your desktop display. Because you spend a lot of time looking at the desktop, you want a display that you find appealing. You can change the background by adding a pattern or decorative image called ***wallpaper***, you can change the desktop color as well as the color of window elements, and you can choose a ***screen saver***, which is a program that moves images across your display screen when the computer is idle for a predetermined amount of time.

In this lesson, you use the Display Properties dialog box to change the appearance of your desktop.

To Change the Appearance of the Desktop

1 In the Control Panel window, double-click the Display icon.

The Display Properties dialog box opens, as shown in Figure 4.12. Notice that there are six pages of options in this dialog box: Background, Screen Saver, Appearance, Effects, Web, and Settings. Depending on the type of monitor you have, there may more or fewer pages of options. By default, the Background options are displayed. On this page of the dialog box, you can choose a wallpaper pattern for your desktop and view a sample of how the desktop will look with your selection.

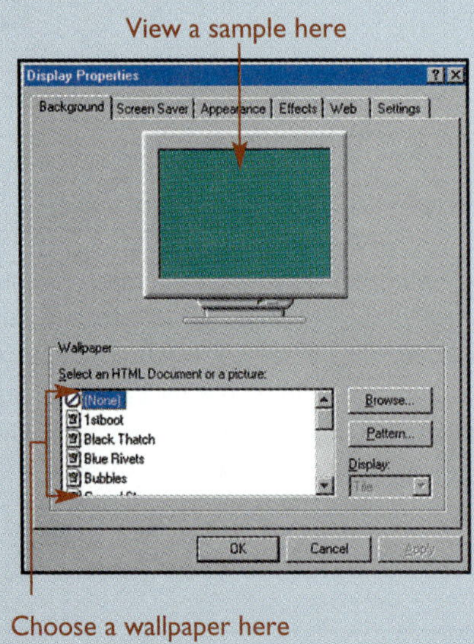

Figure 4.12
The Background options in the Display Properties dialog box.

If the Control Panel window is not open, click the Start button on the taskbar, use the mouse pointer to point at the Settings command, and choose Control Panel from the nested Settings menu.

2 Click Bubbles in the Wallpaper list.

The sample display changes to show you how the desktop will look with the Bubbles wallpaper (see Figure 4.13). You can choose any wallpaper to see how it will look. The wallpaper is not applied to your display until you choose the Apply button or the OK button. By default, the wallpaper image is ***tiled*** to fill the desktop, which means it is repeated side by side; however, you can center a single image on the desktop or stretch the image to enlarge it.

Applying wallpaper to the desktop uses a lot of memory and can be distracting. For now, change back to no wallpaper, and try changing the screen colors only.

Wallpaper tiled on the sample display

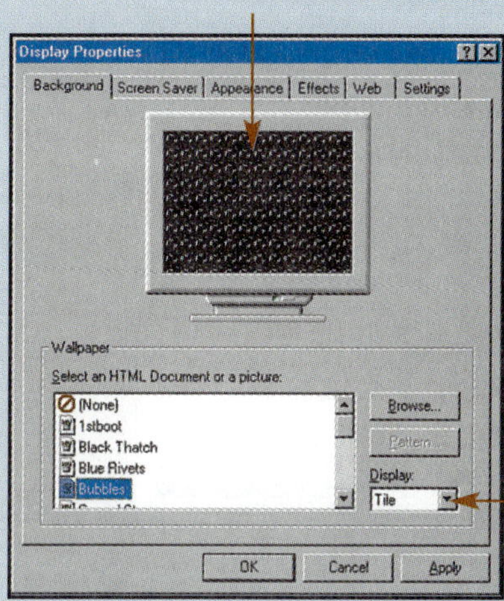

Choose to Center or Stretch the wallpaper image here

Figure 4.13
In the sample area, you can see how the Bubbles wallpaper looks tiled on the desktop.

3 Click (None) in the Wallpaper list.
This removes the wallpaper from the sample desktop.

4 Click the Appearance tab at the top of the dialog box.
The Appearance options display (refer to Figure 4.14). You can choose a preset (default) color scheme or you can choose a color for each Windows element. You can preview your changes in the top half of the dialog box. First, try a preset color scheme.

5 Click the drop-down arrow next to the Scheme text box.
An alphabetical list of available color schemes displays, as shown in Figure 4.14, with the current scheme selected. Notice the vertical ***scrollbar*** on the right edge of the list. A scrollbar is an element used to shift the current display up and down (vertical scrollbar) or left and right (horizontal scrollbar). In this case, there are too many options in the list to be displayed at one time, so you must scroll through the list to find the one you want. To see the items above the ones currently displayed, click the arrow at the top of the scrollbar; to see the items below the ones currently displayed, click the arrow at the bottom of the scrollbar.

6 Click the arrow at the top of the scrollbar repeatedly until you see the Desert color scheme in the list, and then choose Desert from the list.
The preview display changes to show you the colors for the Desert color scheme, as shown in Figure 4.15.

continues ▶

To Change the Appearance of the Desktop (continued)

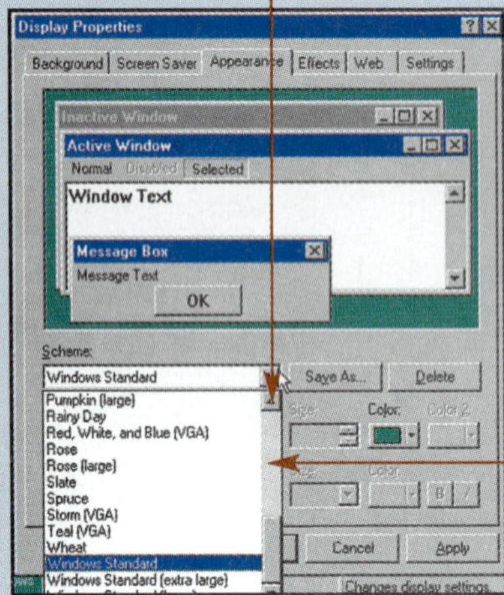

Figure 4.14
Scroll through the list of color schemes to find the one you want.

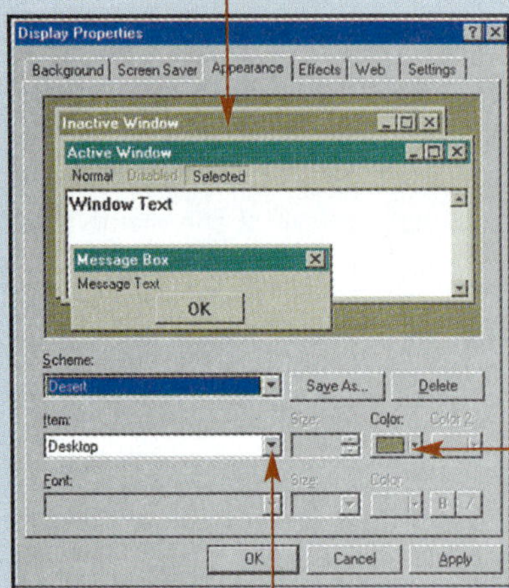

Figure 4.15
The Desert color scheme is displayed in the sample area.

7. **Click the drop-down arrow next to the Scheme text box again, scroll to the bottom of the list and choose Windows Standard.**
The preview display changes to show you the colors for the Windows standard color scheme. You can choose any color scheme you want or use the Item drop-down list to change a color for just the selected element, such as the desktop or the ScreenTips. As with the background options, no changes are applied to the display until you choose the Apply or OK command button.

8. **Click the drop-down arrow next to the Item text box, and choose Desktop.**
This selects the desktop as the Windows element you want to change. If Desktop is already displayed in the Item text box, you can skip this step.

9 Click the drop-down arrow next to the Color text box to the right of the Item text box (refer to Figure 4.16).

A ***color palette,*** or the selection of available colors, opens, as shown in Figure 4.16.

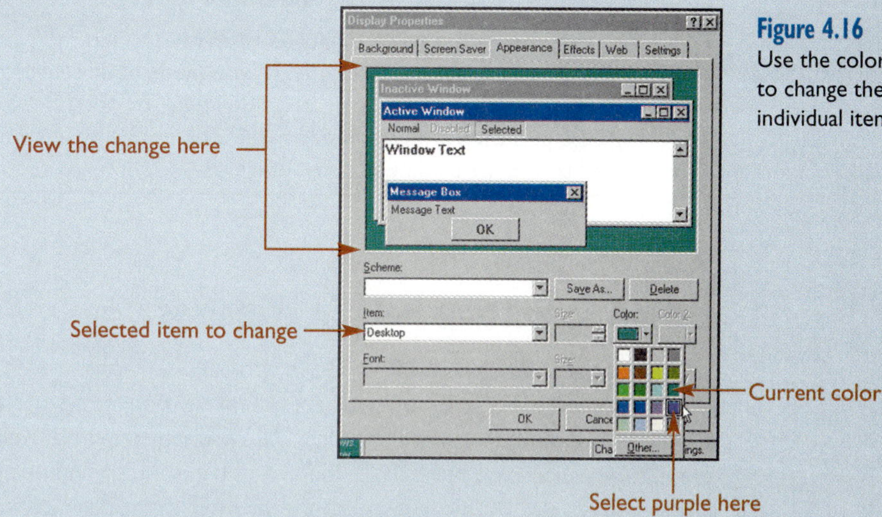

Figure 4.16
Use the color palette to change the color of individual items.

10 Click the purple color directly below the current desktop color.

This changes the desktop to purple.

11 Click the OK command button.

This accepts the changes and closes the dialog box. Your display settings were changed according to the options you selected in the Display Properties dialog box.

12 Click the Close button at the right end of the Control Panel window title bar.

This closes the Control Panel window and returns you to the desktop. Your desktop should look similar to the one in Figure 4.17. In the next lesson, you learn how to start the Windows 98 Help program to get additional information about how to use Windows.

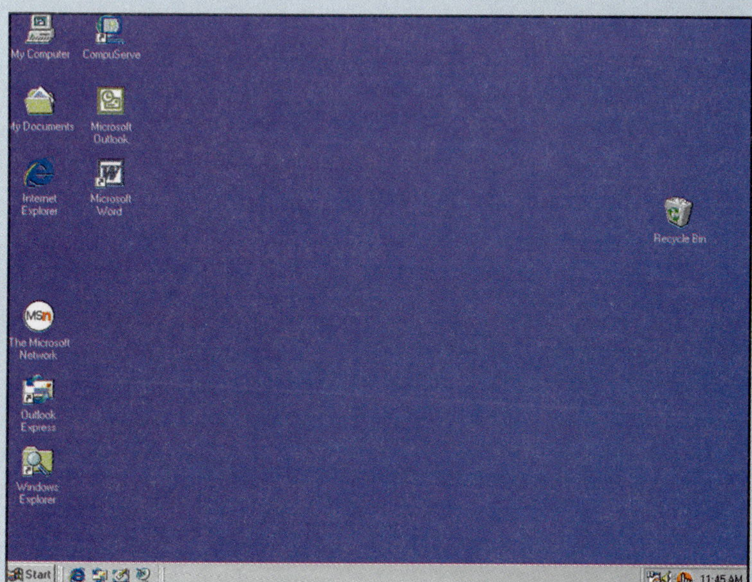

Figure 4.17
The desktop is now purple.

continues ▶

More About Display Properties

To quickly open the Display Properties dialog box, right-click anywhere on the desktop and choose Properties from the shortcut menu.

If you decide you don't like the changes you made to the display, open the Display Properties dialog box, and change back.

You can change the color of individual elements, and then save the colors together as a new color scheme. After you made your selections, click the Save As button next to the Scheme drop-down list to open the Save Scheme As dialog box, and then type a name for your color scheme and choose OK. It will be added to the list of schemes for future use.

Lesson 5: Getting Help in Windows

When you use Windows and Windows applications, help is never more than a mouse click away. Windows comes with an extensive ***context-sensitive*** Help program. Context-sensitive means that the program is designed to provide you with immediate answers to questions you have about the task at hand and to find helpful information about any Windows task. You can also use the Internet to locate Help information. Using the Internet is covered in Project 8, "Getting Started with the Internet."

In this lesson, you learn how to use the Windows Help program to get help on getting help, as well as on changing the appearance of the desktop. Try using the Help program now.

To Get Help in Windows

1. **In Windows, click the Start button on the taskbar.**
   The Start menu opens. Help is one of the commands on the Start menu.

2. **Click the Help command on the Start menu.**
   The Help program starts. The Help window is split into two frames, as shown in Figure 4.18. The left frame displays three page tabs: Contents, Index, and Search, with the Contents tab active by default. You select a Help topic in the left frame. The right frame displays the selected Help topic. Use the Contents page to browse through topics for information; use the Index page to find the specific item you need help for; use Search to search through the entire Help program for a word or phrase.

3. **On the Contents tab in the Help Topics dialog box, move the mouse pointer to touch the topic Introducing Windows 98.**
   Notice that the topic text changes color and becomes underlined, and that the mouse pointer changes to a hand with a pointing finger (see Figure 4.19). That's because the topics in Windows Help are ***hyperlinks***. Hyperlinks are text or graphics linked to related information in the same program, in a different program, or on the Internet. When you click a hyperlink, related information is displayed.

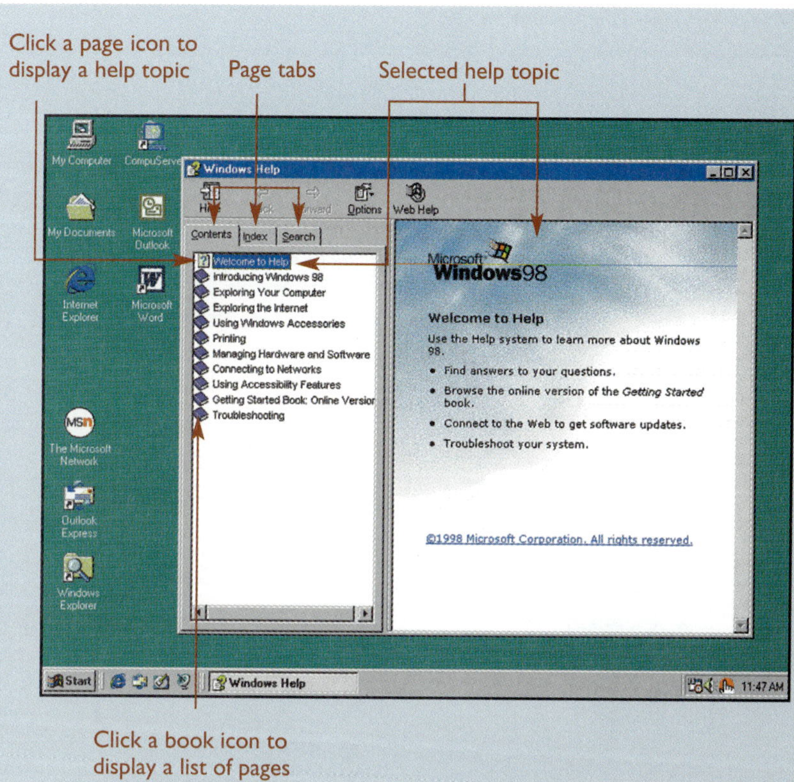

Figure 4.18
Use the Help Topics dialog box to locate the information you need.

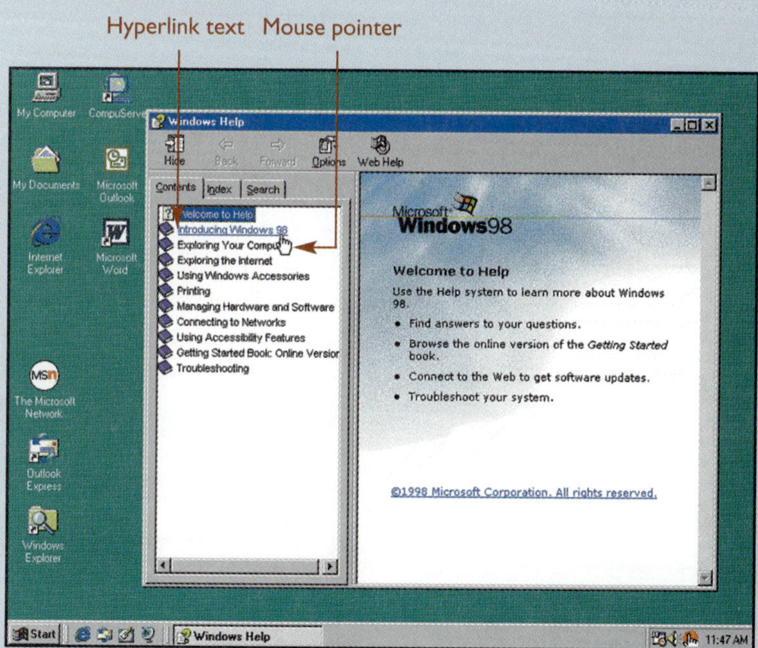

Figure 4.19
Windows 98 Help topics are formatted as hyperlinks so you can quickly access the information you need.

4 Click the topic `Introducing Windows 98`.
A list of subtopics opens. When a Help topic has a book icon beside it, it means the topic contains subtopics. When the icon next to a Help topic resembles a page with a question mark, it opens directly to the Help information.

5 Click the topic `How to Use Help`.
Another list of subtopics opens.

continues ▶

To Get Help in Windows (continued)

6 Click the topic `Find a Topic`.
The topic displays in the right frame (see Figure 4.20).

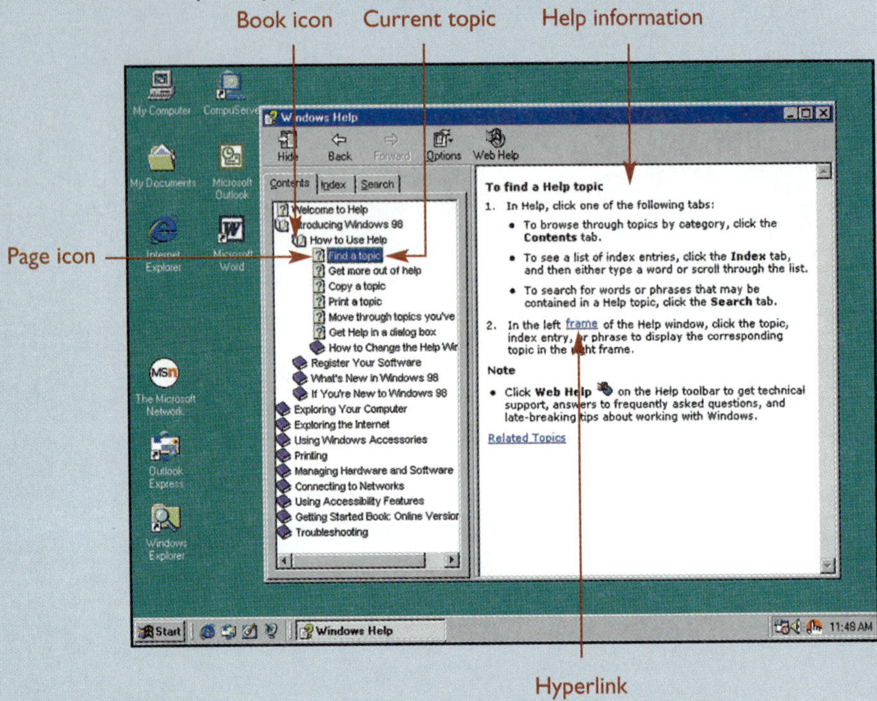

Figure 4.20
Help information is displayed in the right frame of the Help window.

7 Click the hyperlinked word `Frame` in the right frame of the window.
An explanantion of the term is displayed in a ScreenTip.

8 Click anywhere in the Help window that is not a hyperlink to clear the ScreenTip from the screen, and then click the Related Topics hyperlink at the bottom of the right frame.
Windows uses the Help Index to compile a list of related topics, and displays the topics as a shortcut menu (refer to Figure 4.21). Whenever you click the words `Related Topics`, a shortcut menu of topics displays.

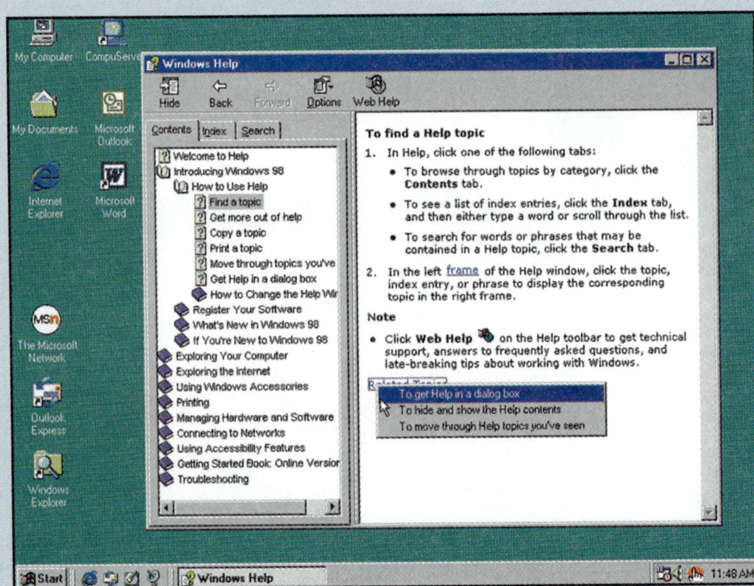

Figure 4.21
You can display a shortcut menu of related topics.

9 Click To get Help in a dialog box on the shortcut menu.
The new help topic replaces the previous topic in the right frame.

10 Click the Back button at the top of the left frame.
The previous topic is displayed again. Click the Back button to move back through topics that have been displayed; click the Forward button after you have clicked the Back button to move forward through the topics again.

11 Click the Index tab at the top of the left frame.
The Index page is displayed. All topics for which Help is available are listed alphabetically in the Help Index. To find a topic, you can scroll through the list or you can type the topic in the text box at the top of the left frame.

12 Type `Settings` in the text box at the top of the screen.
The settings topic is highlighted in the index, as shown in Figure 4.22. Notice the subtopics that display. Notice also that Windows doesn't wait for you to finish typing before it highlights a topic. As you type, Windows automatically scrolls through the Index to the topics that begin with the letters you are typing.

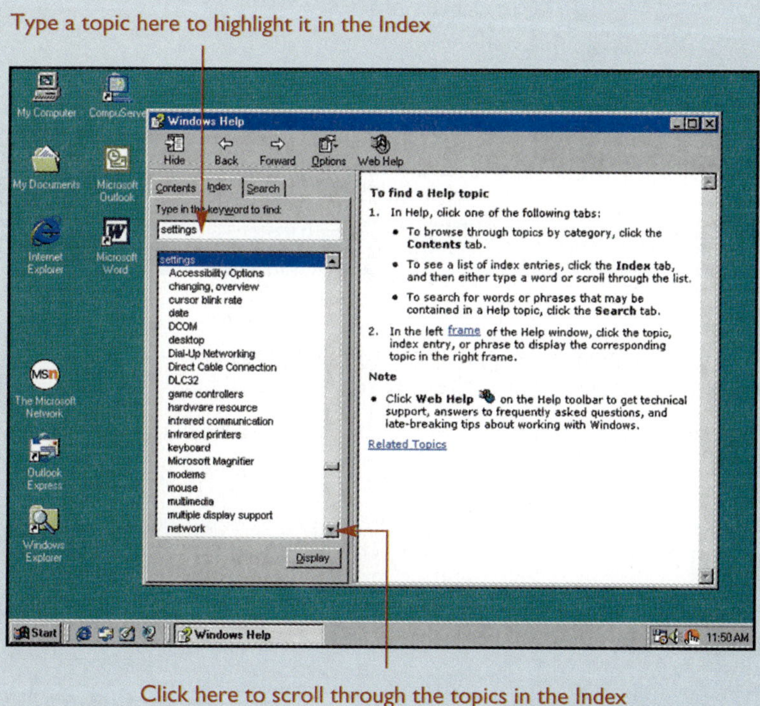

Figure 4.22
You can find any topic in the Help Index.

13 Double-click the topic `Desktop`.
A Topics Found dialog box displays, listing all the topics in the selected category.

14 Double-click the topic `To change the background of the desktop`.
The Help topic is displayed in the right frame.

15 Click the Web Help button at the top of the Window.
Information about getting Help on the Internet displays in the right frame. If the topic you need help for is not in the Help program, you can find information online if you have access to the Internet. (See Project 8 for information about using the Internet.)

continues ▶

To Get Help in Windows (continued)

16 Click the Close button on the Help window title bar.

The Help program closes.

What Does this Do?
To display an explanation of an item in a dialog box, right-click the item, and then choose What's This from the shortcut menu.

Summary

In this project, you had an opportunity to use your mouse to explore Windows. You learned how to identify Windows elements onscreen, and how to change some Windows properties. Finally, you learned how to access the Windows Help program to get more information.

To expand on your knowledge, spend a few minutes checking your understanding of concepts and terms. Additionally, complete some of the Skill Drill and Challenge exercises.

Checking Concepts and Terms ✓

True/False

For each of the following, check *T* or *F* to indicate whether the statement is true or false.

__T __F **1.** Microsoft Windows 98 is a graphical user operating system. [Intro]

__T __F **2.** Once an icon displays on the desktop, it can't be moved. [L2]

__T __F **3.** The Start button displays on the Programs menu. [L1]

__T __F **4.** In Windows, you can use both a mouse and a keyboard. [L2]

__T __F **5.** You double-click an icon to open a window. [L1]

__T __F **6.** You can get help using Windows on the Internet. [L5]

__T __F **7.** Clicking the right mouse button produces an error message. [L2]

__T __F **8.** Select Wallpaper to conserve system memory. [L4]

__T __F **9.** Press Esc to close a menu without making a selection. [L2]

__T __F **10.** After you set the system date and time, you cannot change them. [L3]

Multiple Choice

Circle the letter of the correct answer for each of the following.

1. Which action moves an element on the Windows desktop? [L2]

a. clicking

b. double-clicking

c. pointing

d. dragging

2. What displays when you use the mouse pointer to point at an icon on the desktop? [L2]

a. toolbar

b. ScreenTip

c. Help window

d. dialog box

3. Most system settings can be changed using programs in what folder? [L3]

a. Printer

b. Taskbar

c. Control Panel

d. My Computer

4. Which element(s) of the desktop can you change? [L4]

a. pattern

b. wallpaper

c. color

d. all of the above

5. Which page of the Help Topics dialog box can you use to browse though Help Topics? [L5]

a. Index

b. Topics

c. Contents

d. Search

6. What is the name of the underlined letter in a menu name? [L2]

a. namekey

b. commandkey

c. hotkey

d. selectkey

7. What option do you select when you want a single image displayed on the desktop as wallpaper? [L4]

a. Center

b. Tile

c. Stretch

d. Shrink

8. Which element lets you shift the display up and down or left to right? [L4]

a. Shift

b. scrollbar

c. taskbar

d. title bar

9. What is the name of the area where the date/time is displayed? [L1]

a. Clock/Calendar

b. System dialog box

c. Control Pane folder

d. Systray

10. Which of the following elements can be found in most dialog boxes? [L1]

a. wallpaper

b. hyperlink

c. command button

d. taskbar

Screen ID

Figure 4.23
Label each of the following elements shown in Figure 4.23.

A. Taskbar
B. Desktop
C. Mouse pointer
D. Systray area
E. Start Button
F. My Computer icon
G. Recycle Bin icon

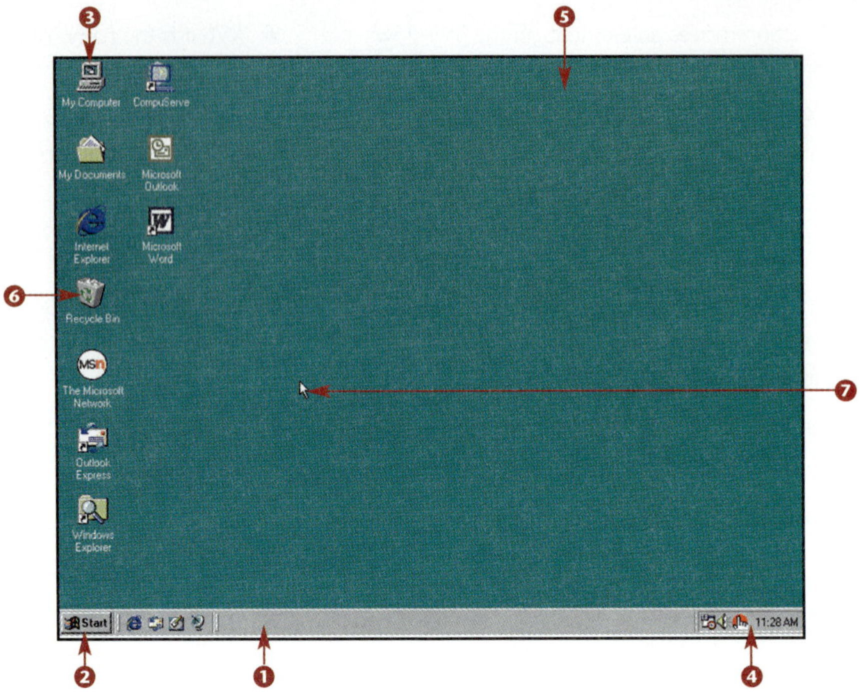

1. ____________________ **4.** ____________________ **6.** ____________________

2. ____________________ **5.** ____________________ **7.** ____________________

3. ____________________

Discussion Questions

1. Why is an operating system important? Discuss some of the tasks that an operating system completes every time you use your PC.
2. List some of the common Windows elements. Explain why it makes sense to have common elements.
3. Does customizing the appearance of Windows affect the way you use your PC? Think about ways you can change Windows, and whether the changes would make you more productive.

Skill Drill

Skill Drill exercises reinforce project skills. Each skill reinforced is the same, or nearly the same, as a skill presented in the project. Detailed instructions are provided in a step-by-step format.

1. Becoming Familiar with Windows

The more comfortable you are using Windows, the easier it will be to control your PC and use applications. To become familiar with Windows, follow these steps:

1. Turn on your computer system.
2. If the Welcome screen opens, click the Close control button to close it.
3. Move the My Computer icon from the left side of the desktop to the right side of the desktop.
4. Move the Recycle Bin icon next to the My Computer icon.

5. Right-click a blank area of the desktop.
6. Move the mouse pointer to point at Arrange Icons on the shortcut menu.
7. Click By Name on the nested menu.
8. Click the Start button on the taskbar to open the Start menu.
9. Use the mouse pointer to point at each command on the Start menu to see if a nested menu is displayed.
10. Click the Help command on the Start menu.
11. Click the Contents page tab.
12. Click the topic `Exploring Your Computer.`
13. Click the topic `Keyboard Shortcuts.`
14. Click the topic `For dialog boxes.`
15. Scroll through the topic in the right frame.
16. Click the Index tab in the left frame.
17. Start typing the word `arrange`. Stop typing when the topic `arranging icons` is highlighted.
18. Click the Display command button.
19. Read the topic in the right frame.
20. Click the Help window Close control button.
21. Click the Start button.
22. Click the Shut Down command.
23. Shut down windows and turn off your computer.

2. Changing System Settings

You can change system settings to customize Windows for your own use. To practice changing system settings, follow these steps:

1. Start Windows.
2. Right-click the time in the Systray on the taskbar.
3. Click Adjust Date/Time to open the Date/Time Properties dialog box.
4. Set the date to `March 10, 1998`.
5. Set the time to `9:50 a.m.`
6. Apply the changes.
7. Change the data and time back so that they are correct.
8. Close the Date/Time Properties dialog box.
9. Click the Start button.
10. Highlight Settings; then click Contol Panel on the Settings nested menu.
11. Double-click the Mouse icon to open the Mouse Properties dialog box.
12. If you are left-handed, click the Left-handed option button to switch the left and right mouse buttons so that you can use the mouse more easily in your left hand.
13. Drag the lever on the Double-click speed scale toward Slow to adjust the double-click speed so that you don't have to click as quickly to register a double-click.
14. Double-click on the box icon in the test area to test the speed.
15. Apply the changes and close the dialog box.
16. Click the Start button.
17. Click the Shut Down command.
18. Shut down windows and turn off your computer.

Challenge

Challenge exercises expand on or are somewhat related to skills presented in the lessons. Each exercise provides a brief narrative introduction, followed by instructions in a numbered-step format. The steps are not as detailed as those in the Skill Drill section.

1. Evaluate an Operating System

You are the office manager for a small retail store. Most PCs come with Windows installed, but there are other operating systems available. Consider the pros and cons of using Windows 98. Make a list of the ways Windows 98 will help your business.

1. Use magazines or newspapers to find out what types of computers use Windows 98 as an operating system, and whether or not the system you selected in earlier projects can use Windows 98.
2. Make a list of the types of applications that work with Windows 98.
3. If Windows 98 is not already installed on your computer system, find out how much it costs and whether your computer has enough memory and storage space to run it.

2. Choosing a Corporate Color Scheme

As you learned, you can customize certain Windows settings for your own use. In this exercise, customize the colors of the Windows elements to create a desktop color scheme for your retail store.

1. Start Windows.
2. Open the Control Panel.
3. Open the Display Properties dialog box.
4. Change to the Appearance page.
5. Try out some of the preset color schemes to see if you like the way they look. If you find one that is close to what you want, you can use it as the basis for your custom color scheme.
6. Try changing the color of just the Active title bar.
7. Try changing the color of the Inactive title bar.
8. Try changing any of the other elements.
9. If you apply colors and then decide you don't like the way they look, change back to one of the preset color schemes.
10. Shut down Windows.

Project 5

Learning About PC Data Storage

Objectives

In this project, you learn how to

- **Identify Types of Storage Media and Drives**
- **Prepare a Floppy Disk for Use**
- **View the Contents of a Disk or Folder**
- **Work with Folders**
- **Work with Files**

Key terms introduced in this project include

- active
- back up
- disk capacity
- disk density
- file types
- filename extension
- format
- label
- Rename mode
- shortcut
- subfolder
- Windows Clipboard

Why Would I Do This?

One of the most important things you do with a personal computer is store data so that you can use it again and again. While you work with data, it is stored in the PC's RAM, but as soon as you turn off your computer, or change application programs, the data in RAM disappears. To keep data safe for future use, you must tell your PC to store it on a disk.

Your PC uses a very strict filing system—but it doesn't do it all by itself. You must know the correct commands to enter to tell your PC what data to store and where to store it. Then, both you and your PC can find the data when you need it.

In this project, you learn about the different types of personal computer storage disks, as well as how to use them. You also learn how your PC keeps data organized on a disk, and how to store and retrieve data from a disk.

Lesson 1: Identifying Types of Storage Media and Drives

The most common type of storage device is a magnetic disk, either hard or floppy. CDs, high-capacity disks such as Iomega Zip disks, and magnetic tape cartridges are also used with PCs.

Storage devices that can be removed from your PC are important and handy because you can use them to ***back up*** data to keep it safe, and for transporting data to another location. Backing up means copying data from one storage location to another, ensuring a spare in case something happens to the original. Removable devices include floppy disks, CDs, high-capacity disks such as Iomega Zip disks, and tape cartridges. Knowing how to use and handle removable devices is a vital part of using a computer.

In Project 1, "Getting Started with Personal Computer Hardware," you learned to identify and locate different disk drives on your PC. In this lesson, you learn how to identify the removable devices used in each type of drive, and how to decide which ones you should buy.

To Identify Types of Storage Media and Drives

1. **Locate the floppy disk drive on your PC.**
   Most PCs today have one 3 1/2-inch floppy drive. (For more information, refer to Project 1.)

   > **5 1/4-inch Floppy Drives**
   > Older computers may have a 5 1/4-inch floppy drive, as well as a 3 1/2-inch drive. 5 1/4-inch disks were the original floppy disks. However, they were large, easily damaged, and unable to store much data. They have since been replaced by smaller devices with larger capacities.

2. **Find a disk that fits into your floppy disk drive.**
   Although a 3 1/2-inch disk is encased in a protective rigid cover, inside the cover is a floppy piece of celluloid (see Figures 5.1 and 5.2).

Figure 5.1
3 1/2-inch disks have a protective plastic-and-metal cover.

Figure 5.2
The back of a 3 1/2-inch disk.

3 Read the label on the floppy disk or disk box.

Disks and disk drives come in two densities—double-density and high-density. The ***disk density*** refers to how tightly packed the data can be on the disk, so it determines the amount of information you can store on it—in other words, the ***disk capacity***. Disk capacity refers to the amount of data you can store on the disk. Most floppy drives today use high-density disks that store 1.44MB of data.

continues ▶

To Identify Types of Storage Media and Drives (continued)

It is almost impossible to tell what the density of a disk is just by looking at it—you must check the label or the disk box. Table 5.1 describes some of the information you find on a floppy disk or CD label.

Table 5.1 Deciphering Disk Labels

Designation	Meaning
DD	Double-density
HD	High-density
2 or DS	Double-sided
1 or SS	Single-sided
Preformatted IBM	Ready to use in an IBM-compatible PC
Preformatted Apple	Ready to use in an Apple personal computer
Microfloppy	3 1/2-inch disk
CD-ROM	A read-only CD
CD-R	A write-once CD
CD-RW	A CD that can be written on and updated, just like a floppy
DVD	A digital variable disc used in a DVD drive

4. **Locate the CD drive on your computer.**
You may have a CD-ROM drive, a CD-R, a CD-RW drive, or a DVD drive. The drive may have a simple slot in which you insert the disc, or it may have a sliding tray you use to insert the disc.

5. **Locate a CD that fits in your CD drive.**
Computer CDs look just like music CDs (see Figure 5.3). There is usually a label on one side, whereas the other side is shiny. When you insert a CD in a drive, the shiny side goes down. If you are using a writable disc, the tinted side goes down.

Figure 5.3
Computer CDs look like music CDs.

6. **Locate other drives for removable media devices.**
You may have a tape drive or a high-capacity drive such as a Zip drive in your PC. The devices may be built into the PC or attached via cables.

7. **Locate the media for the other drives.**
Tape cartridges are generally about three inches by two inches, and look like miniature versions of the cassettes you use in a tape player or large versions of the cassettes you use in an answering machine. Zip disks look similar to 3 1/2-inch floppies (see Figure 5.4).

Figure 5.4
A high-capacity Zip disk looks a lot like a 3 1/2-inch floppy disk.

Naming Disk Drives
Disk drives on a PC are identified by letters of the alphabet, followed by a colon. If you have only one floppy disk drive, it is called drive A:. If you have another floppy disk drive, it is called drive B:. The first hard drive is called drive C:. If there is another hard drive, it is drive D:; otherwise, the CD drive is drive D:, and so on.

Lesson 2: Preparing Floppy Disks for Use

Before you can store data on a floppy disk, you must ***format*** the disk. Until a disk is formatted, it is completely blank, similar to a blank piece of paper. When you format a disk, your operating system draws electronic lines on the disk to divide it into sectors, just as you might draw real lines on paper. The operating system then uses the "lines" and sectors to keep track of where information is stored. Although most disks come preformatted (check the box label or look on the metal shutter of the disk itself to find out if it is already formatted), it is a good idea to know how to format a floppy disk.

Once a disk is formatted, you should ***label*** it so that you know what data it contains. A label can be either (or both) of the following: electronic, an eleven character name written on the disk by the disk drive; or manual, written by the user with a soft-tip pen on a label attached to the outside of the disk.

In this lesson, you learn how to use the Windows 98 operating system to format a disk in drive A.

To Prepare Floppy Disks for Use

1 Turn on your computer.

When you turn on your computer, the Windows 98 opening screen displays on your monitor. If you need information about starting your computer, refer to Project 3, "Starting the PC". If you need information about Windows 98, refer to Project 4, "Getting to Know Your Operating System."

2 Double-click the My Computer icon on the desktop.

The My Computer window opens. In this window, you see icons representing the storage components of your PC.

3 Click the 3 1/2 Floppy [A:] icon in the My Computer window.

This selects drive A, as shown in Figure 5.5. Drive A is now ***active***, which means that any actions you perform affect drive A.

> Don't worry about the whirring sounds you hear as your PC accesses drive A. It is looking to see whether there is a disk in it.

Figure 5.5
The drive A icon is in the My Computer window.

My Computer window

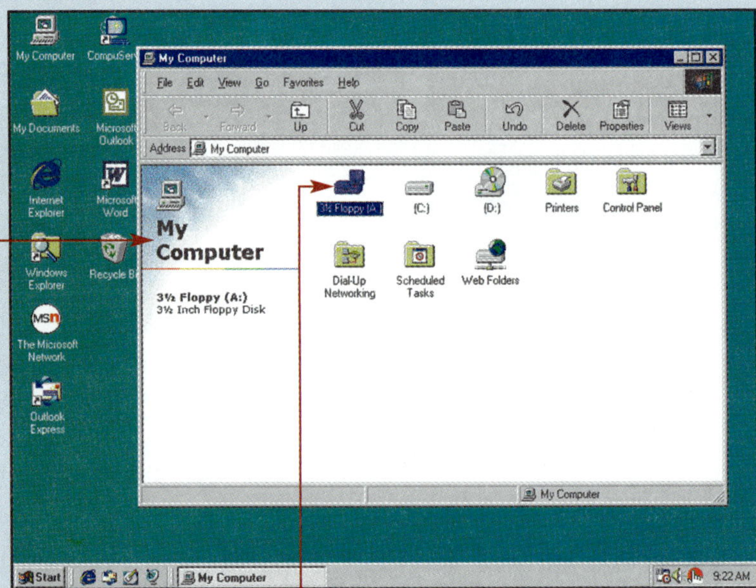

Drive A icon

4 Insert a new blank disk into drive A.

This is the disk you are going to format. Formatting deletes all data already on the disk, so you should use a blank disk unless you are certain that you don't need the old data any more.

5 Click the File menu command in the My Computer window, and choose the Format command from the File menu.

The Format–3 1/2 Floppy [A:] dialog box opens, as shown in Figure 5.6. In this dialog box, you choose the options for formatting a disk in drive A. In this case, the default options are correct for performing a full format on a high-density, 3 1/2-inch disk. You also want to enter an electronic disk label. Note that your default options might show a different capacity than the capacity shown in this figure.

Click here to choose a different capacity

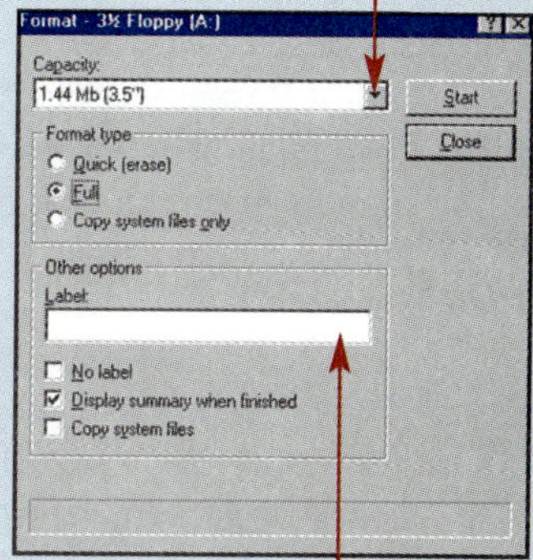

Type a disk label here, if desired

Figure 5.6
The Format–3 1/2 Floppy [A:] dialog box.

6 Click in the Label text box.
This moves the insertion point to the Label text box so that you can type a disk label.

7 Type `Data Disk`.
This is the label you want to assign to the disk. Your operating system will write the label in a hidden place on the disk during formatting. You are now ready to format the disk.

8 Click the Start button in the Format–3 1/2 Floppy [A:] dialog box.
This starts the formatting process. A status bar at the bottom of the Format–3 1/2 Floppy [A:] dialog box displays the progression of the format. When the formatting is complete, Windows 98 displays the Format Results–3 1/2 Floppy [A:] dialog box, showing you the capacity of the newly formatted disk (see Figure 5.7).

Disk capacity

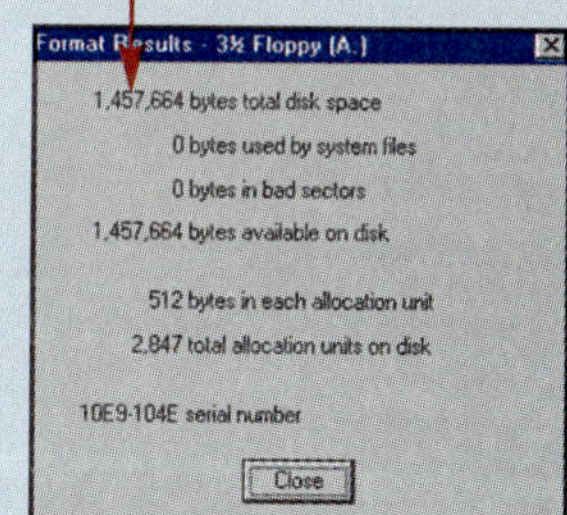

Figure 5.7
The Format Results–3 1/2 Floppy [A:] dialog box.

9 Click Close.
This closes the Format Results dialog box, leaving the Format–3 1/2 Floppy [A:] dialog box open onscreen. You can continue to format more disks in drive A by repeating the procedure or you can close the dialog box.

10 Click Close.
This closes the Format–3 1/2 Floppy [A:] dialog box, leaving the My Computer window open onscreen. The disk in drive A is now ready to store data. Leave the disk in the drive to use in Lesson 3, in which you learn how to see what's on a disk or in a folder.

Never try to format your hard drive (drive C:)! You will erase everything on your disk, including Windows, and you will not be able to use your computer.

Using Paper Labels
Put a paper label on your disk as soon as it is formatted. When you store something on the disk, you can write it on the paper label with a felt-tip pen. That way, you always know what is stored on your disks.

Reformatting a Disk
You can reformat old disks if you are certain that you don't need the data that is already stored on them. Just choose the Quick (erase) option button in the Format–3 1/2 Floppy [A:] dialog box. Quick Formatting is much faster than regular formatting.

Lesson 3: Viewing the Contents of a Disk or Folder

As mentioned earlier, your computer and operating system use a very strict filing system to keep track of information stored on a disk. After you understand the rules of the filing system, you can easily organize and manage it.

The easiest way to find out what is on a disk or in a folder is to open that disk's or folder's window. You can use the icons in the My Computer window to open windows for each of the disks in your PC. When you double-click a disk icon, a window opens, showing you the files and folders stored on that disk. You can double-click folder icons to open additional windows to show the contents of each folder.

In this lesson, you learn how to open a folder to see what is stored in it, and how to see what is stored on a disk. The My Computer window should still be open on your screen from Lesson 2, and the newly formatted disk should still be in drive A.

To View the Contents of a Disk or Folder

1. **Double-click the drive [C:] icon in the My Computer window**
The [C:] window opens, as shown in Figure 5.8. This window displays the contents of your hard drive C. By default, the window displays large icons to represent folders and files. Try changing the way the icons are displayed.

If there are too many items in a window to see all at once, click the scroll arrows to move down or to the right, or maximize the window. Also, keep in mind that the contents of drive C: on your computer may be different than the contents of drive C: on the computer used for the figures in this book.

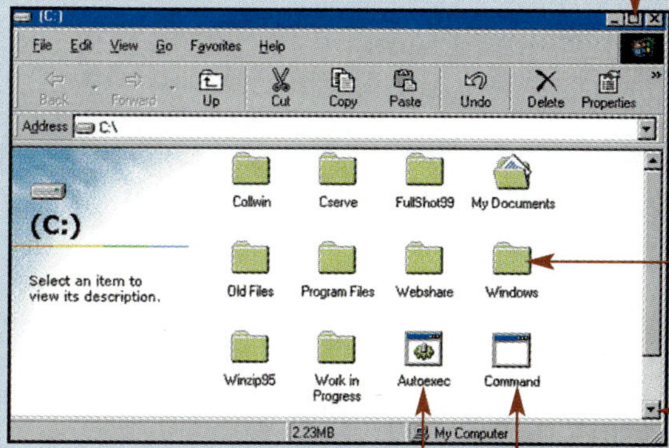

Figure 5.8
The [C:] window displays the contents of your hard drive C.

2 Click View on the menu bar in the [C:] window.
The View menu drops into the window. You can use the commands on the View menu to change the way the contents of the window are displayed.

3 Click Small icons on the View menu.
The window changes to show the files and folders as small icons, as shown in Figure 5.9. You can use a different view in each window. If you have many items in a window, it may be easier to see them all if the icons are small. If you want to see information about the files and folders, such as when they were created, you can use the Details view.

View as Web Page
Windows 98 introduced a new default view option, called View as Web page. Windows displayed as Web pages have more graphics elements than classic windows used in earlier versions of the Windows operating system, and a description of the selected item is displayed on the left side. To revert to a classic display, click View; then click as Web page to deselect the option. If the option is not selected, click View, as Web page to select it. A check mark next to the command on the menu indicates that it is selected.

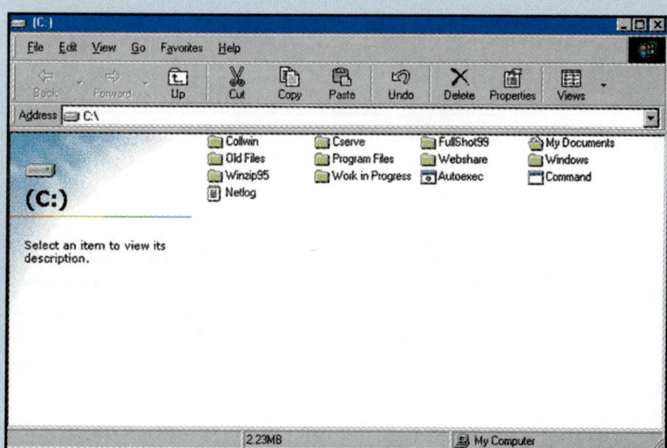

Figure 5.9
You can change the way files and folders are listed in a window.

continues ▶

To View the Contents of a Disk or Folder (continued)

4 Open the View menu again and choose Large Icons.

This changes back to the large icon display. Now, open a folder.

5 Double-click the Windows folder icon.

The Windows folder window opens, as shown in Figure 5.10. This folder contains the components of Windows 98. You can view the contents of any folder by double-clicking its icon to open a window. Notice that the [C:] window and the My Computer window are still open, although they may be hidden behind the active window. In Project 7, "Working with Windows Applications," you learn more about working with multiple windows.

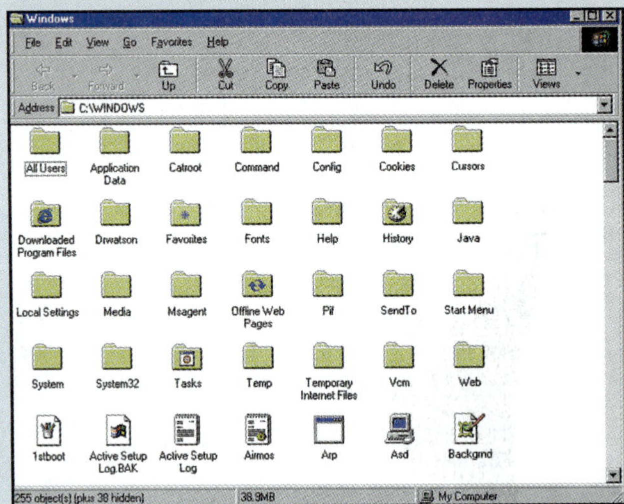

Figure 5.10
The Windows folder window.

6 Click the Close button on the right end of the Windows window title bar.

The Windows window closes.

7 Right-click the drive [C:] icon at the left end of the [C:] window title bar.

A shortcut menu appears. The menu lists commands that you can use to affect drive C. You can open a shortcut menu for any window by right-clicking the window icon on the title bar.

> If the Properties command is not displayed on the shortcut menu, you are probably right-clicking the title bar, not the drive icon. Try again.

8 Click Properties on the shortcut menu.

The [C:] Properties dialog box opens, as shown in Figure 5.11. This dialog box shows you the properties associated with drive C. You can see how much disk space is used and how much is available, and you can access disk-management programs that come with Windows. As you learned in Project 4, most elements in Windows have properties that you can view and change when necessary.

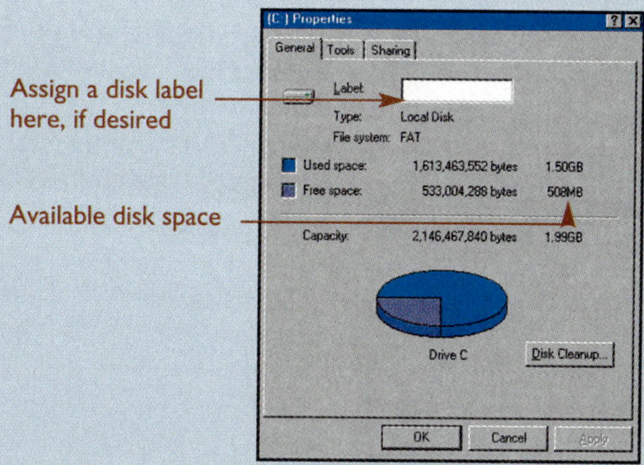

Figure 5.11
The drive [C:] Properties dialog box displays information about your hard disk, drive C.

9 Click the Cancel button in the [C:] Properties dialog box.
This closes the [C:] Properties dialog box without making any changes.

10 Click the Close button in the [C:] window.
This closes the [C:] window. The My Computer window is still open. Now, take a look at what's stored on the disk in drive A.

11 Double-click the 3 1/2 Floppy [A:] icon in the My Computer window.
The drive [A:] window opens, as shown in Figure 5.12. Because this is the disk you formatted in Lesson 2, there is nothing stored on it yet. Leave the drive [A:] window open to use in Lesson 4, in which you learn how to create a new folder.

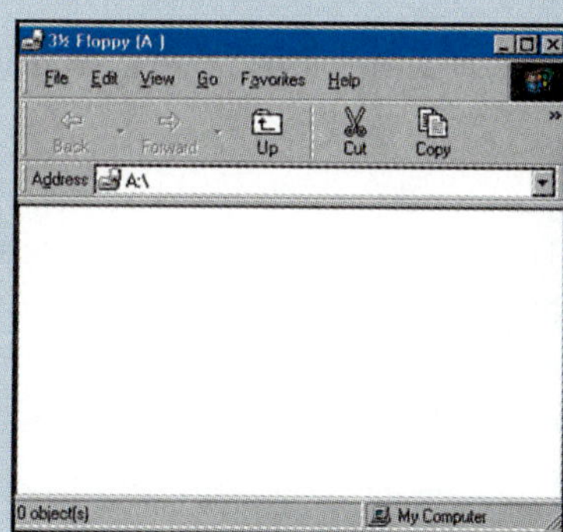

Figure 5.12
Nothing is stored on drive A yet.

Other Ways to Open Folders
Another way to open a folder is to select it, and then choose Open from the File menu. Yet another way is to use the shortcut menu.

Opening Multiple Folders

You can open as many folder windows at one time as you want, or as your computer memory allows. For example, to open a window for drive A while you look at the contents of drive C, double-click the drive A icon, switch back to the My Computer window, and then double-click the drive C icon. To switch to an open window, click its button on the Taskbar.

If you don't like to have so many separate windows opening on the desktop, you can set Windows so that each folder you open replaces the previous folder in the same window. To do this, click the Start button, highlight Settings, and click Folder Options on the Settings nested menu. Click the Settings button next to the Custom option near the bottom of the Folder Options dialog box. In the Browse folders as follows area, select the Open each folder in the same window check box, click OK, then click Close.

Using Windows Explorer

You can also use the Windows Explorer program to see what's on a disk or in a folder. Windows Explorer is a program that comes with Windows. It displays a hierarchical list of the contents of your computer system. To start Windows Explorer, click the Start button on the Taskbar, move the mouse pointer to Programs, and then click the Windows Explorer command. Alternatively, you can choose Explore from any window's shortcut menu. You may find Windows Explorer useful if you have used Windows 3.1 and are familiar with the File Manager program.

Lesson 4: Working with Folders

If you just stored all your data on a disk in one big lump or threw all your personal papers into a single box, it would be very difficult to find the information you need to use it again. That's why you create files, both electronic on a disk as well as files in your file cabinet. To help make it even easier to keep data organized, you can group related files together into folders. A folder on a disk is like a folder in a file cabinet. You can keep all your letter files in one folder and all your report files in another folder.

In this lesson, you learn how to create and name folders on a disk in drive A. You also learn how to move folders and how to delete them.

To Work with Folders

1. **In the drive [A:] window, open the File menu and move the mouse pointer to the New command.**

   The nested New menu appears, as shown in Figure 5.13. You can use the commands on this menu to create a new folder or a new program ***shortcut***, or new files of various types. A shortcut is an icon that directly accesses the file for starting a program or opening a folder or file.

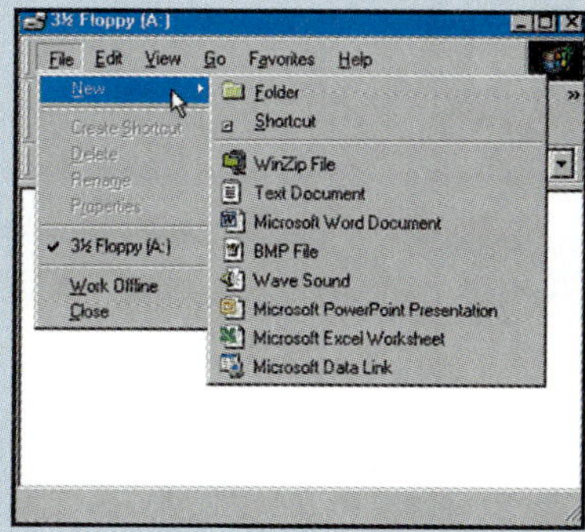

Figure 5.13
The New nested menu.

2 Click Folder on the New menu.

Windows creates a new folder in the drive [A:] window, as shown in Figure 5.14. By default, the folder name is in ***Rename mode***, which means that you can change the name by typing. Whenever you create a new folder in Windows 98, it is called `New Folder` until you change the name.

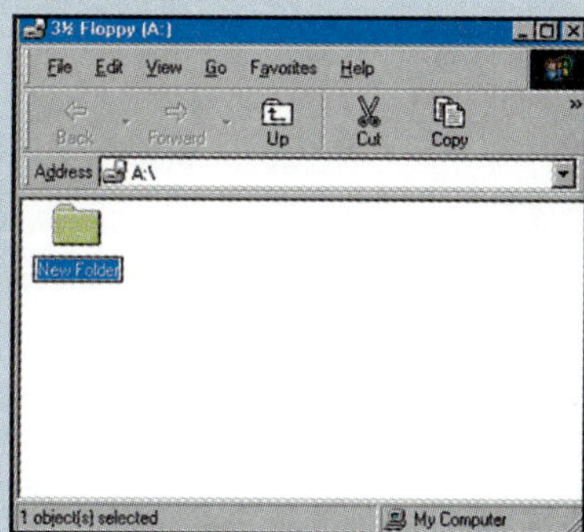

Figure 5.14
The new folder in drive A.

3 Type `First Folder` and press Enter.

This text replaces the default folder name. The new folder remains selected, which means it is active. If you create a new folder now, it will be a ***subfolder***—a folder stored in another folder.

If nothing happens when you type or if the computer beeps, you may not be in Rename mode. To change to Rename mode, click the folder name beneath the folder icon, or right-click the icon and select Rename from the shortcut menu.

4 Click in a blank area of the drive [A:] window.

This deselects the First Folder and makes the drive [A:] window active. Now, try creating another folder on the disk in drive A:.

Naming Folders

Folder names can be any length, and you can use all but nine of the characters on your keyboard, including spaces. The nine exceptions are: \/:*?"<> |.

continues ▶

To Work with Folders (continued)

5 **Open the File menu, move the mouse pointer to the New command, and choose Folder from the New nested menu.**
Windows creates another new folder on the disk in drive A.

6 **Type `Second Folder` and press ↵Enter.**
You now have two folders on your floppy disk in drive A—First Folder and Second Folder, as shown in Figure 5.15. The Second Folder is still selected. Now try moving a folder.

Figure 5.15
There are two folders on the disk in drive A.

7 **Move the mouse pointer to the Second Folder icon, press and hold the left mouse button, and drag the icon on top of the First Folder icon.**
The easiest way to move a folder or file in Windows is to drag it to its new location. Notice as you drag that the mouse pointer changes to display a folder icon.

8 **Release the left mouse button when the First Folder icon is highlighted.**
Windows moves the Second Folder into the First Folder. Second Folder is now a subfolder of First Folder.

> **Copying Folders**
> To copy a folder instead of moving it, you must press and hold Ctrl as you drag.

9 **Double-click the First Folder icon.**
This opens the First Folder window, as shown in Figure 5.16. The Second Folder icon appears in the window. Now, try deleting a folder.

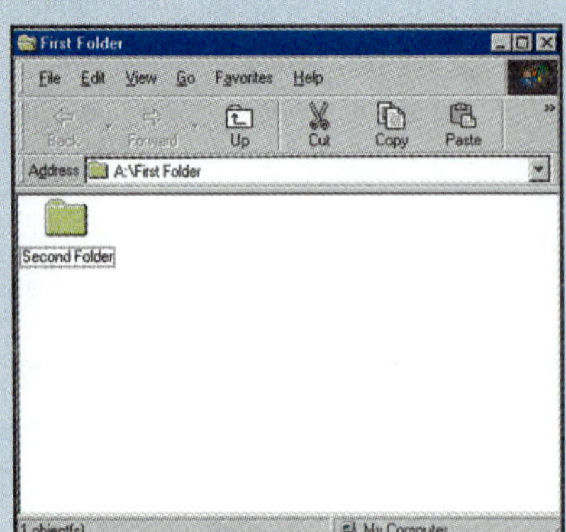

Figure 5.16
You can easily move folders from one location to another.

10 Click the Second Folder icon in the First Folder window.

This selects the folder you want to delete.

If the folder name changes to Rename mode, you clicked the folder name instead of the folder icon. Click the icon to select it.

Selecting Multiple Folders

To select more than one folder, press and hold Ctrl as you click. All the selected objects appear highlighted. You can also select a continuous list of objects. Simply click the first object in the list, and then press and hold ⇧Shift while you click the last object in the list.

---

11 Press Del on your keyboard.

The Confirm Folder Delete dialog box opens, as shown in Figure 5.17. Before Windows deletes an object, you must confirm the action.

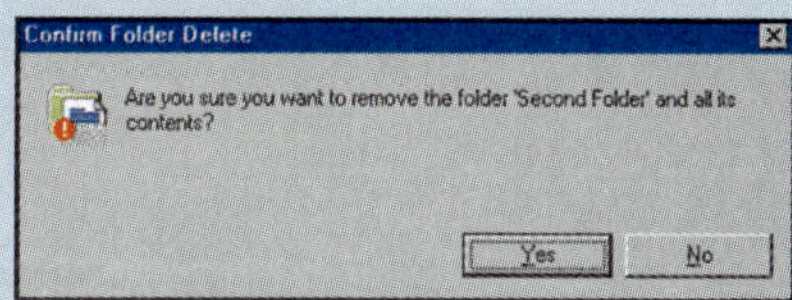

Figure 5.17
The Confirm Folder Delete dialog box.

12 Click the Yes button in the Confirm Folder Delete dialog box.

Windows removes the Second Folder from the First Folder window. If anything was stored in the deleted folder, it would be removed as well.

Items deleted from a floppy disk cannot be restored. Be sure you have the correct file selected before you click Yes in the Confirm Delete dialog box.

---

13 Click the Close button in the First Folder window, and then click Close in the drive [A:] window.

This closes first the First Folder window and then the drive A: window, leaving the My Computer window open on the desktop. Leave it open to use in the next lesson, when you learn how to work with files.

Using Undo

You can use the Undo command to undo a move, a renaming, and many other actions. Immediately after the action, open the Edit menu and choose Undo. You can even undo a deletion from a hard disk. You cannot, however, undo a deletion from a floppy disk.

Using Windows Explorer

You can create, copy, move, rename, and delete folders in Windows Explorer by using the same steps that you use in a folder window.

Lesson 5: Working with Files

Keeping your files organized so that you can find them when you need them is possibly the most basic and most important computer task. If you can't retrieve data stored in a file, what good is your computer?

Usually, you create files as you enter the data by using an application program. For example, when you write a letter using a word processing program, you save the letter as a file. When you set up a budget using a spreadsheet program, you save the budget as a file. You use Windows to make sure that the files are organized. For example, you can keep a file safe by backing it up from your hard disk to your floppy disk, or by moving it from one folder to another.

However, you can also use Windows to create some blank files. The methods used to create, name, move, copy, and delete files are very much the same as those you use for creating, naming, moving, copying, and deleting folders. In this lesson, you create a blank text file on drive C, copy it to a disk in drive A, delete it from the hard disk, and restore it. Try working with files now.

To Work with Files

1. **Open the drive [C:] window.**
This is the drive in which you want to create the new file.

2. **Open the drive [C:] window File menu, and move the mouse pointer to the New command.**
The New nested menu opens. Below the line on the menu is a list of file types that you can create.

3. **Click Text Document on the New nested menu.**
Windows creates a new blank text document file, as shown in Figure 5.18. The default filename is New Text Document. Unlike the new folders, it is not in Rename mode.

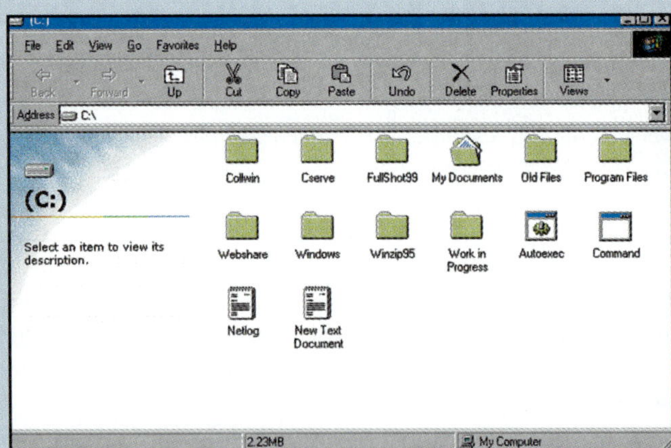

Figure 5.18
The new file appears in the active window.

4. **Right-click the new file icon and select Rename from the shortcut menu.**
Now, the filename is in Rename mode.

5 Type `File 1` and press ↵Enter.

The text document file is now named `File 1`. It is still selected. Try copying the file to a floppy disk now.

Naming Files

The same naming rules that apply to folders apply to files (you can use all characters except /\:*?"<>|). Filenames often include a ***filename extension***—a "dot" (.) followed by three characters. Filename extensions help identify different ***file types***. A file type is the kind of data contained in a file. For example, text files usually have the extension .TXT. Some application programs automatically add extensions to whatever name you give a file. For example, Microsoft Word adds the extension .DOC to filenames.

In Windows, you don't usually see extensions on your screen, but you can if you want to. Simply choose Folder Options from the View menu in the My Computer window, click the View page tab, click the Hide file extensions for known file types check box to deselect it, and then click OK.

---

6 Right-click the selected file.

A shortcut menu appears, listing commands that affect the file.

7 Move the mouse pointer to the Send To command on the shortcut menu.

This opens a nested menu of locations to which you can copy the selected file, as shown in Figure 5.19.

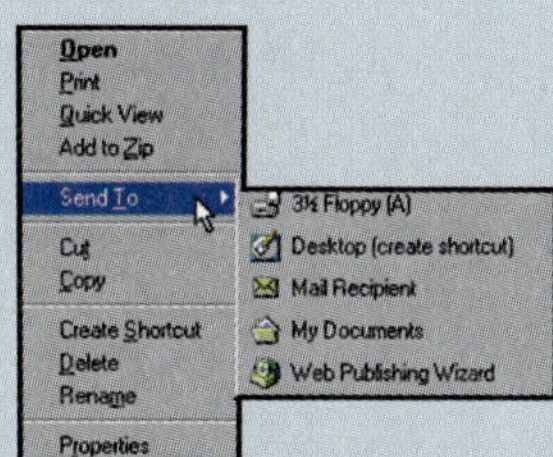

Figure 5.19
Use the shortcut menu to copy a file to a floppy disk.

8 Click 3 1/2 Floppy [A] on the Send To nested menu.

Windows copies File 1 to the disk in drive A. When the copy is finished, the drive [C:] window is still open. File 1 is now stored on both the hard disk (drive C) and the floppy disk in drive A. (To see the file on drive A, double-click the drive [A:] icon in the My Computer window.) Delete the file from your hard disk.

The Send To command on the shortcut menu copies files—it does *not* move them. To move a file, drag it from one location to another.

---

continues ▶

To Work with Files (continued)

Using the Windows Clipboard
You can also use the ***Windows Clipboard*** to copy or move files and folders. The Clipboard is a temporary storage area in your PC's memory. To copy an item, you first copy it to the Clipboard, and then paste it into its new location. To move an item, you first cut it to the Clipboard, and then paste it into its new location. The cut item is deleted from its original location.

To copy an item to the Clipboard, right-click it and choose Copy from the shortcut menu. To cut an item to the Clipboard, right-click it and choose Cut from the shortcut menu. To paste the item, right-click the destination—such as a disk icon or a folder icon—and click Paste on the shortcut menu.

9 **Click the file icon to select it, and then press Del.**
The Confirm File Delete dialog box appears. Before you delete a file, Windows asks you to confirm that you want to send the file to the Recycle Bin.

10 **Click Yes in the Confirm File Delete dialog box.**
Windows sends the file to the Recycle Bin. Now, try restoring the file.

11 **Double-click the Recycle Bin icon on the desktop.**
This opens the Recycle Bin window, as shown in Figure 5.20.

If you can't see the Recycle Bin window on the desktop, it's probably hidden behind an open window. To move a window, click and drag its title bar. To minimize an open window, click the Minimize button on the right end of the title bar. To minimize all open windows at once, right-click an empty spot on the Taskbar and choose Minimize all Windows from the shortcut menu.

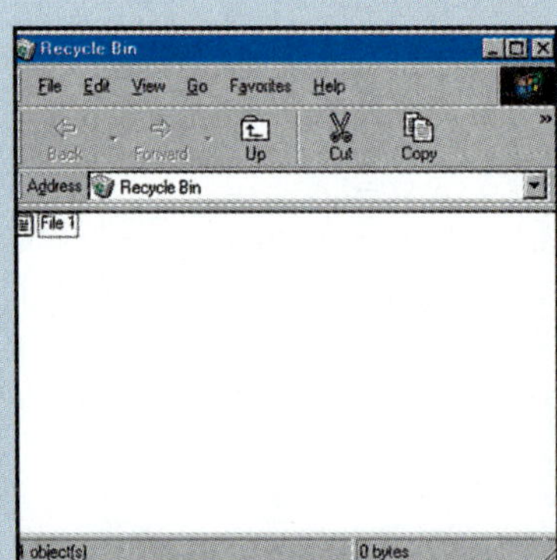

Figure 5.20
A list of deleted files appears in the Recycle Bin window.

12 **Right-click the File 1 file in the Recycle Bin file list, and then choose Restore from the shortcut menu.**

Empying the Recycle Bin

All files deleted from a hard disk remain in the Recycle Bin until you empty the bin. To empty the bin, open it, and then choose Empty Recycle Bin from the File menu. Deleted folders don't appear in the Recycle Bin window, but if you restore a file to a folder that has been deleted, the folder is restored as well.

The file is restored to its previous location on drive C. Close the Recycle Bin, as well as all other open windows.

Summary

This project covered the basics of storing data on your PC. You learned how to identify removable storage devices and how to format a floppy disk. You also learned how to use Windows to work with folders and files.

To expand on your knowledge, spend a few minutes checking your understanding of concepts and terms. Additionally, complete some of the Skill Drill and Challenge exercises.

Checking Concepts and Terms

True/False

For each of the following, check *T* or *F* to indicate whether the statement is true or false.

__T __F **1.** Most PCs have a 3 1/2-inch floppy disk drive. [L1]

__T __F **2.** You can't move a folder to another disk. [L4]

__T __F **3.** A disk must be formatted before you can store data on it. [L2]

__T __F **4.** High-density disks can store more data than double-density disks. [L1]

__T __F **5.** After you name a file or folder, you can never change the name. [L4, L5]

__T __F **6.** You cannot restore a file deleted from a floppy disk. [L4]

__T __F **7.** If you move a folder and then change your mind, you can use the Undo command to reverse the move. [L4]

__T __F **8.** Use the Windows Clipboard to rename folders. [L4]

__T __F **9.** All tape drives are installed inside the system unit. [L1]

__T __F **10.** When you view a window as a Web page, everyone accessing the Internet can view that window, too. [L3]

Multiple Choice

Circle the letter of the correct answer for each of the following.

1. To copy a folder to another location, you must press and hold which key while you drag? [L4]

a. Enter

b. F1

c. Ctrl

d. Shift

2. How much data can you store on a high-density 3 1/2-inch disk? [L1]

a. 720K

b. 1.44MB

c. 360K

d. 1.2MB

3. How long do deleted files remain in the Recycle Bin? [L5]

a. one week

b. one month

c. one year

d. until you empty the bin

4. Which of the following usually represents the first hard disk on your computer? [L1]

a. A:

b. B:

c. C:

d. D:

5. Which of the following options do you use to reformat a disk? [L2]

a. Fast Format

b. Quick Format

c. Reformat

d. Format Again

6. Which of the following characters is not allowed in a file or folder name? [L4, L5]

a. .

b. *

c. #

d. !

7. Which folder displays the components of your computer system? [L3]

a. My Computer

b. Recycle Bin

c. Windows

d. Control Panel

8. Which command can you use to copy a folder to a floppy disk? [L4]

a. Cut

b. Rename

c. Send To

d. Restore

9. Which of the following can help identify the contents of a disk? [L2]

a. Clipboard

b. properties

c. label

d. capacity

10. Which of the following procedures can help ensure that your data is kept safe? [L1]

a. formatting

b. backing up

c. cutting

d. maximizing

Screen ID

Locate the following items, shown in Figure 5.21.

Figure 5.21

A. Drive C window
B. Maximize button
C. Vertical scrollbar
D. My Computer window
E. Close button
F. Folder icon
G. File icon

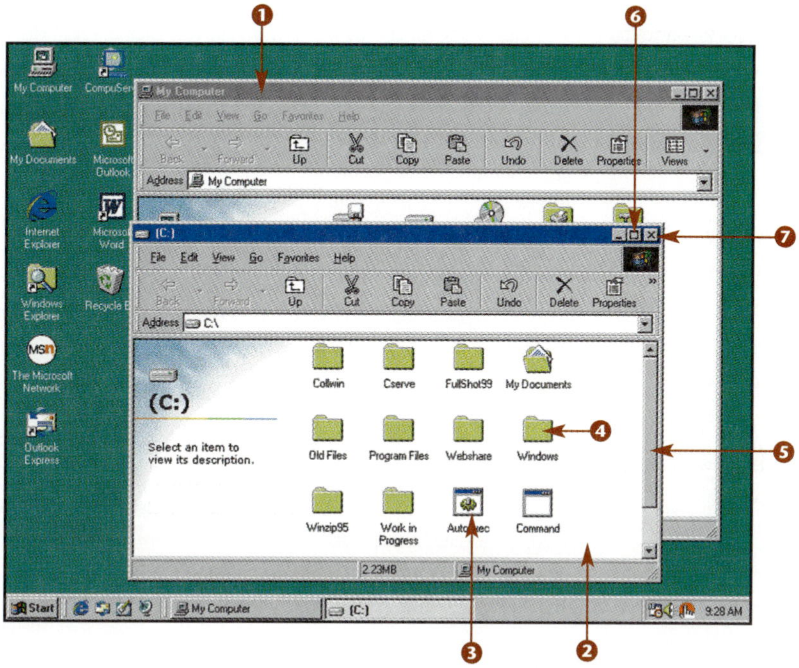

1. ____________ 4. ____________ 6. ____________
2. ____________ 5. ____________ 7. ____________
3. ____________

Discussion Questions

1. Consider the different types of removable storage devices available. What are the pros and cons of each type?
2. Compare the Windows filing system with a typical, non-electronic filing system. What part of a desk is equivalent to a disk? What is the equivalent of a folder? How about a file?
3. What is the importance of maintaining an organized filing system on your PC? Can you think of ways your filing system might put your data at risk? How about ways it helps protect your data?

Skill Drill

Skill Drill exercises reinforce project skills. Each skill reinforced is the same, or nearly the same, as a skill presented in the project. Detailed instructions are provided in a step-by-step format.

1. Exploring the Contents of Your Computer

Even if you have never created a file or folder, your computer is chock-full of information. Whenever a program is installed on your PC, new files and folders are installed to make the program work—and to make you work easier as well. You can explore your disks to see what files and folders you already have. To explore the contents of your computer, follow these steps:

1. Start your computer.
2. Double-click the My Computer icon to open the My Computer window.
3. Double-click the icon for your hard disk drive. See what folders and files are already stored on your hard disk drive.
4. Open some of the folders on your hard disk drive to see what they contain.
5. If you have another hard disk drive, see what it contains.
6. Insert a CD in your CD drive, or a used floppy in your floppy drive.
7. Click the My Computer button on the Taskbar.
8. Open the window for the CD drive or the floppy drive.
9. Click the Start button on the Taskbar.
10. Highlight the Programs command, and click Windows Explorer on the Programs menu.
11. Click the Windows folder in the left frame of Windows Explorer. This displays the contents of the Windows folder in the right frame of the window.
12. Close all open windows and shut down Windows.

2. Organizing Your Hard Disk

Now that you have learned the basics of how to keep a disk organized, you can set up a system of folders that will work for you. When you create folders, think about what types of files you work with and how you want to keep the files organized. Keep in mind that a disk is like a file cabinet, and the folders are like drawers in the cabinet. If you create and name folders so that you can tell what's in them, you will have no trouble keeping track of your important data. To organize your hard disk, follow these steps:

1. Start Windows
2. Double-click the My Computer icon to open the My Computer window.
3. Look at what is already stored on drive C.
4. Look for a My Documents icon in the drive C window. My Documents is a folder created by Windows and used for storing files that you create with Microsoft applications such as MS Word. If there is a My Documents folder, skip to step 10.
5. If there is no My Documents folder icon in the drive C window create it as follows:
6. Click File.
7. Click New.
8. Click Folder.
9. Type `My Documents`.
10. Double-click the My Documents folder icon.
11. In the My Documents window, create a folder in which you can store your word-processing documents.
12. Create subfolders in the word-processing folder in which you can store different kinds of documents, such as letters, memos, and reports.
13. If you plan to use another application, such as a spreadsheet or a database, create a folder for that type of document as well.
14. Click the Letters folder icon.
15. Click File.
16. Click New.
17. Click Text Document.
18. Type `Letter 1`.
19. Move the Letter 1 file into the Memos folder.
20. Copy the Letter 1 file back into the Letters folder.
21. Delete the Letter 1 file from the Memos folder.
22. Open the Recycle Bin.
23. Restore the Letter 1 file to the Memos folder.
24. Close all open windows and shut down Windows.

Challenge

Challenge exercises expand on or are somewhat related to skills presented in the lessons. Each exercise provides a brief narrative introduction, followed by instructions in a numbered-step format. The steps are not as detailed as those in the Skill Drill section.

1. Plan and Purchase Removable Storage Devices

It is important to have disks or tape cartridges on hand all the time, so you can be prepared to back up or copy your data on to removable media. In this exercise, determine the type of removable devices you need for your computer and how much they will cost.

1. Figure out what type of disks or tape cartridges you need.
2. Refer to magazines or contact a retail store to find out how much the devices cost. Ask if you can purchase floppy disks in bulk.
3. If possible, look at some actual floppy disk boxes and see if you can decipher the information written on them.
4. Use the Properties dialog box to determine how much data is already stored on your hard disk.
5. Based on the capacity of your floppy disks, determine how many you will need to back up your entire hard disk. How many tape cartridges would you need? How many Zip disks?

2. Formatting Floppy Disks

After you purchase floppy disks, you should always have a few ready for use. Format and label at least three floppy disks for use in your drive A. If you have preformatted blank disks, see if you can locate an old floppy that contains data you no longer need, and reformat that one.

1. Start your computer.
2. Insert a disk in drive A.
3. Open the drive A window to make sure that there is nothing you want to keep stored on the disk you are about to format.
4. Format the disk, including an electronic label.
5. Repeat the procedure to format the other disks.
6. Attach paper labels, with the correct names, to the formatted disks.
7. Close all open windows and shut down Windows 98.

Project 6

Project 6

Learning About PC Memory

Objectives

In this project, you learn how to

- ➤ **Identify Different Types of Memory**
- ➤ **Identify Memory Requirements**
- ➤ **Determine the Memory on Your Computer**

Key terms introduced in this project include

- cache memory
- conventional memory
- expanded memory
- extended memory
- memory
- memory requirement
- minimum requirements
- recommended requirements
- ROM
- system requirements
- upper memory
- video RAM
- virtual memory

Why Would I Do This?

Memory is the electronic circuitry in which the PC stores information, including programs and data, currently in use. All PCs use two basic types of memory: RAM and **ROM**. ROM stands for read only memory, and is the memory built into your computer's CPU by the manufacturer. You learned about RAM in Project 1, "Getting Started with Personal Computer Hardware." The amount of ROM on your computer is determined by the manufacturer, but you decide how much RAM you need.

For most applications, the more RAM you have installed, the faster your PC can process information. This is because the more memory you have, the more room there is to hold a lot of working information at any one time. Using RAM, the PC doesn't waste time reading and writing data from and to a disk. Also, the amount of RAM you have installed determines whether you can run large, complex programs and determines how many programs you can run at the same time under multitasking operating systems such as Windows and OS/2.

In this project, you learn what types of RAM exist, and what they do. You also learn how to determine how much memory you already have on your PC, as well as how much memory you should have.

Lesson 1: Identifying Different Types of Memory

Most PCs, no matter how much memory is installed, use only the first 640K (kilobytes) for running the operating system and application programs and for temporarily storing data. Ten years ago, 640K of memory was enough to run most available programs. Today, however, most programs are too large to fit into 640K at one time, so computer technicians figured out how to let some PCs use additional memory for storing information. This additional memory is classified into three basic categories.

In this lesson, you learn about the three categories of PC RAM.

Breaking the Memory Barrier
In theory, computers using Windows 98 (or another 32-bit operating system such as OS/2 or Windows NT) are not limited by the 640K conventional memory barrier. However, the way that application software programs running under these operating systems are written also affects their capability to access all available memory.

To Identify Different Types of Memory

The following list helps explain the three categories of memory:

- Every PC can access all available conventional memory.

  The first 640K (kilobytes) of RAM on a PC is called ***conventional memory***.

- All data is processed in conventional memory.

  All programs are run in conventional memory. The operating system is processed in conventional memory, and data that is being used is stored in conventional memory.

- The more programs that you have running, and the larger those programs are, the less conventional memory you have available for processing.

  If the computer doesn't have enough memory available, the PC can't execute commands and process data. You will see a message on your screen telling you that you don't have enough memory to load a program or to complete a calculation.

- PCs based on an 80286 or higher microprocessor can use ***upper memory***.

  Upper memory is all memory installed on the computer between conventional memory and 1024K (one megabyte).
- You can temporarily store the operating system and some utility programs in upper memory.

  Storing programs in upper memory leaves more conventional memory free for processing data. If your PC has more than 640K memory and has at least an 80286 microprocessor, it makes use of upper memory.
- Some PCs can also use ***extended memory***.

  Extended memory—sometimes called high memory—is all memory over 1MB (megabyte). PCs manufactured today can use 4GB (gigabytes) of memory or more.
- Windows 98 uses ***virtual memory*** to boost performance.

  Virtual memory is actually hard disk space that Windows reserves for use as extra memory. When actual memory becomes full, Windows can temporarily store data in virtual memory.
- Older-model PCs can sometimes benefit from ***expanded memory***.

  Expanded memory is a combination of hardware and software that lets PCs based on the 8088 microprocessor (and some 80286s) access upper memory. This type of memory is sometimes called LIM-compatible because it was developed by Lotus, Intel, and Microsoft.
- Most PCs now come with ***cache memory*** built into the CPU.

  Cache memory is made up of additional memory chips that can boost the PC's processing speed because commonly used instructions that are otherwise stored on disk drives or in RAM can be stored in cache. Cache is especially useful for large, complex programs such as spreadsheets and relational databases.
- To boost the performance of the display monitor, PCs also have ***video RAM*** (sometimes called graphics RAM).

  Video RAM is made up of additional memory chips that are built right into the video display adapter card that controls the monitor. The amount of video RAM determines how many colors can be displayed and how fast the images appear.

Temporary Storage
Remember that RAM is short-term memory—it isn't designed for permanent data storage. When you shut off your PC or close an application, you lose the data in RAM. To save information permanently, you must store it on disk or tape.

Lesson 2: Identifying Memory Requirements

Every software application has a ***memory requirement***, or a minimum amount of memory that it requires in order to run. For example, most new application programs need at least 8MB of memory. Your computer must meet the minimum memory requirement for you to use the program.

Adding Memory
Most new computers come with a minimum of 64M of RAM; some computers have less and others have more. If you do not have enough memory installed, you can upgrade most PCs by installing additional memory modules.

Every person using a personal computer has different memory requirements for it. The type of work you do and the kinds of software that you use determine your memory needs. You can, however, take certain steps to be sure that you have enough memory before you purchase a new software program.

To Identify Memory Requirements

1. **Read the back of any software package before you purchase it.**
   All software programs have ***system requirements*** listed on the back of the package. System requirements list the system components you need in order to use the software. Memory requirements are part of the system requirements.

2. **Look for the requirement that mentions memory.**
   First, most packages list the type of operating system (such as Apple, OS/2, Windows 95/98, or Windows NT) and microprocessor (such as Pentium II, Pentium III, and so on) that a program requires. The memory requirements are listed next.

3. **Look for the "recommended" requirements.**
   Manufacturers often list the ***minimum requirements*** as well as the ***recommended requirements***. The minimum requirements are requirements for getting the software up and running. The recommended requirements are the features you need in order to use the software to its fullest capabilities.

Lesson 3: Determining the Memory on Your Computer

You can easily find out how much memory you have installed on your PC. This is useful for determining whether you have enough to meet the requirements for running a new program, and also to determine whether your PC is making the best use of the memory that's available.

In this lesson, you use your computer's startup routine to find out how much memory you have installed, and then you use Windows 98 to analyze your computer's memory.

To Determine the Memory on Your Computer

1. **Shut down Windows and turn off your PC.**
   During startup, PCs count the amount of installed memory, and most PCs display it on the screen before starting the operating system. Before you shut off your PC, remember to save all data and close all open files and programs, including Windows.

2 Turn on your PC.

Watch the display screen carefully as the computer goes through its startup routine. The amount of memory installed should appear on the screen for a moment. If you miss it or it doesn't appear, do a warm reboot or check your system properties.

3 Right-click the My Computer icon on the desktop.

A shortcut menu appears, as shown in Figure 6.1.

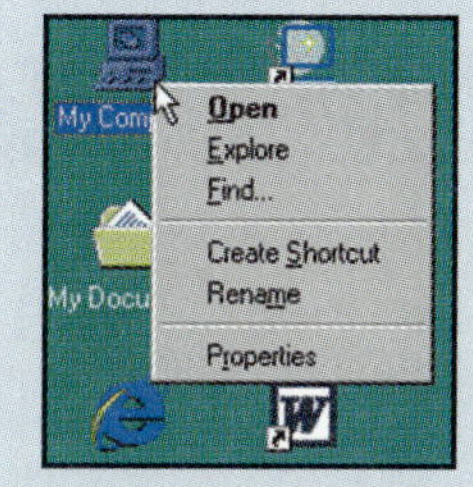

Figure 6.1
You can open the Properties dialog box from the My Computer shortcut menu.

4 Click Properties on the shortcut menu.

The System Properties dialog box appears. The amount of memory installed on your computer is displayed on the General page of this dialog box. To find out how much memory is being used and how much is free, you must look at the Performance page.

5 Click the Performance tab at the top of the dialog box.

The performance properties are displayed, as shown in Figure 6.2. You can see that many of the properties have to do with memory.

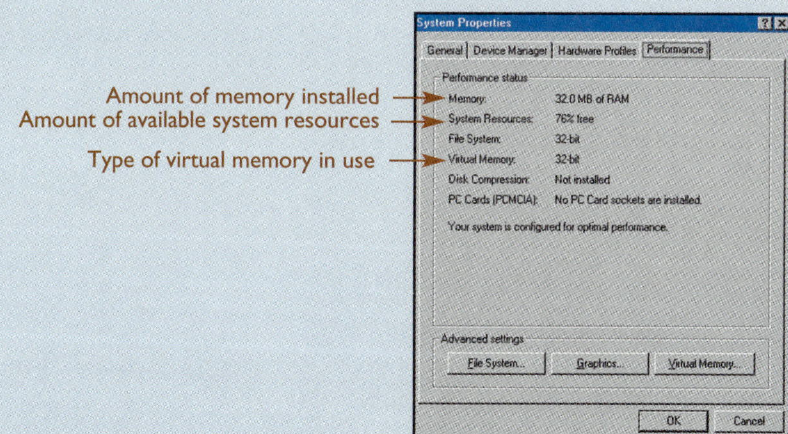

Figure 6.2
The Performance tab of the System Properties dialog box.

6 Click OK in the System Properties dialog box.

Windows' Memory Troubleshooter

Windows 98 automatically manages the way your PC uses memory. If you have problems, try using the Memory troubleshooter, which you can access from the Windows Help program. Click the Start button, and then click Help. Click the Contents page tab. Open the Troubleshooting topic. Open the Windows 98 Troubleshooters. Click Memory.

Summary

In this project, you learned about computer memory—specifically about RAM. You learned how your PC uses memory, and you learned how to determine the amount of memory you need to run software applications. Finally, you learned how to find out how much memory you already have installed on your PC.

To expand on your knowledge, spend a few minutes checking your understanding of concepts and terms. Additionally, complete some of the Skill Drill and Challenge exercises.

Checking Concepts and Terms

True/False

For each of the following, check *T* or *F* to indicate whether the statement is true or false.

__T __F **1.** You can make your computer smarter by installing more memory. [L1]

__T __F **2.** No matter how much memory you have installed, all PCs process data in conventional memory. [L1]

__T __F **3.** If you want to be able to display more colors on your monitor, you should increase the amount of video RAM you have installed. [L1]

__T __F **4.** To find out the memory requirements for a new program, open the software box and look on the program disks. [L2]

__T __F **5.** To find out how much memory you have installed, read the label on the back of your system unit. [L3]

__T __F **6.** The minimum requirements are enough to run an application to the best of its capabilities. [L2]

__T __F **7.** The amount of ROM installed in your PC is determined by the computer manufacturer. [L1]

__T __F **8.** Windows 98 manages your PC's memory. [L1]

__T __F **9.** Most new computers come with at least 8G of RAM installed. [L2]

__T __F **10.** Cache memory helps prevent your computer from crashing. [L2]

Multiple Choice

Circle the letter of the correct answer for each of the following.

1. To find out how much memory you have on your PC, which dialog box should you look in? [L3]

a. Memory Properties

b. System Memory

c. System Properties

d. Memory Performance

2. To help increase the processing speed of your PC, what type of memory should you add? [L1]

a. RAM

b. ROM

c. conventional

d. video RAM

3. How much memory is considered conventional? [L1]

a. up to 640K

b. between 640K and 1MB

c. between 1MB and 16MB

d. above 16MB

4. What is the minimum amount of memory that you need to run most new application programs? [L2]

a. 2MB

b. 4MB

c. 8MB

d. 32MB

5. What is memory over 1MB called? [L1]
   a. extended memory
   b. expanded memory
   c. upper memory
   d. conventional memory

6. What type of memory helps boost the performance of the display monitor? [L1]
   a. monitor RAM
   b. video RAM
   c. color RAM
   d. animation RAM

7. What screen shows the amount of memory installed? [L3]
   a. Shut down
   b. Reboot
   c. Startup
   d. Desktop

8. What should you check to be sure you can run software to its fullest capabilities? [L2]
   a. minimum memory requirements
   b. recommended memory requirements
   c. upgrade memory requirements
   d. base level memory requirements

9. How much memory should you have installed in your PC? [L2]
   a. 8MB
   b. 32MB
   c. 64MB
   d. every one has different memory requirements

10. Where should you store data you want to use again in the future? [L1]
   a. extended memory
   b. expanded memory
   c. on a disk
   d. conventional memory

Discussion Questions

1. How important is RAM to your PC? Can you list ways in which it improves your system's performance? How about ways it might impede performance?
2. RAM can be expensive. If you have a limited budget, you may have to decide between buying additional RAM or buying a different computer component, such as a faster processor or a larger-capacity hard drive. Discuss the trade-offs of buying more or less RAM.

Skill Drill

Skill Drill exercises reinforce project skills. Each skill reinforced is the same, or nearly the same, as a skill presented in the project. Detailed instructions are provided in a step-by-step format.

1. Finding Out How Much Memory You Have

Using the techniques described in this project, find out how much memory is installed on your computer.

1. Start your PC.
2. Watch your monitor to see whether the amount of memory is displayed.
3. In Windows 98, right-click the My Computer icon.
4. Click Properties on the shortcut menu.
5. Locate the amount of installed memory on the General page tab.
6. Click the Performance page tab.
7. Locate the amount of free system resources.
8. Click the close button to close the dialog box.
9. Shut down Windows before shutting off your computer.

2. Finding Out How Much Memory Application Programs Require

After you know how much memory you have installed, you can determine whether it's enough to run certain software applications. Take some time to find out the memory requirements of some popular programs.

1. Look in a magazine or catalog, and make a list of the memory requirements of five different software applications.
2. If possible, go to a retail store and look at the software packaging to find out memory requirements of the applications.
3. See if there is a difference between the minimum and recommended requirements.
4. Compare the memory requirements with the amount of memory installed on your PC to see whether you would be able to use the programs.

Challenge

Challenge exercises expand on or are somewhat related to skills presented in the lessons. Each exercise provides a brief narrative introduction, followed by instructions in a numbered-step format. The steps are not as detailed as those in the Skill Drill section.

1. Planning the Amount of Memory You Need for Your Computer System

You want to be able to run the most advanced software programs available on your PC. You also want to be prepared for future advancements in technology. Take some time now to plan how much memory you want on your computer, and how you want to manage it.

1. Check the minimum memory requirements for the software applications that you plan to use.
2. Compare the minimum memory requirements to the recommended memory requirements.
3. Visit or call a computer store, or read a catalog, to find out how much memory is included with a new computer.
4. Compare the price of a new computer with 96MB or more of memory to a new computer with 64MB or less of memory.
5. Find out which new computers can be upgraded with more memory. If you already own a computer, find out whether you can add memory to it.
6. Find out the current cost of memory chips, either from a local dealer or by phone order. This information changes daily, so don't be surprised by the answer.

2. Finding Out How Much Virtual Memory Windows Uses on Your PC

1. Start your PC.
2. Open the System Properties dialog box.
3. Display the Performace page tab.
4. Click the Virtual Memory button.
5. Write down the current settings. If they are dimmed so you can't see them, click the Let me manage my own virtual memory option button.
6. Cancel out of the dialog box without changing any settings.

Project 7

Project 7

Working with Windows Applications

Objectives

In this project, you learn how to

- **Use a Windows Application**
- **Use Multiple Windows Applications**
- **Use the Windows Clipboard**
- **Print a File**
- **Create a Program Shortcut**

Key terms introduced in this project include

- accessories
- cascades
- document
- drawing application
- graphics files
- insertion point
- print
- print queue
- spools
- word processing

Why Would I Do This?

Windows 98 makes it easy to control your PC through the use of menus, graphical elements, and plain English commands. One of the primary benefits of Windows 98 is that all applications that work with it use similar—sometimes identical—commands. This similarity means that once you learn to use Windows 98, you can quickly learn to use all Windows-based applications.

Versions of Windows

As mentioned earlier, this book teaches the use of Windows 98. However, there are other versions of Windows, including older versions such as Windows 95; the version for handheld devices, called Windows CE; Windows 2000; and a more powerful version called Windows NT, which is becoming more popular. All of these versions of Windows have similar features. You should be able to transfer your knowledge of one version to any of the others.

In this project, you learn how to use many of the features that you will find in all Windows 98 applications. You learn how to start and exit Windows-based applications, use more than one application at a time, create and print a file with a Windows-based application, and use the Windows Clipboard to share information among applications.

Lesson 1: Using a Windows Application

You use Windows 98 to manage your applications and files, but you use the applications themselves to get your work done. For example, although you copy, rename, and organize files with Windows 98 (refer to Project 5, "Learning about PC Storage"), you actually enter data to create files using an application.

Windows comes with a collection of applications called ***accessories***. You might also have other Windows applications installed on your computer, such as Microsoft Word or Intuit Quicken.

In this lesson, you use the accessories programs to learn how to start a Windows application, create a file with a Windows application, and exit a Windows application. Try using Windows applications now.

To Use a Windows Application

1. **With Windows 98 running on your computer, click the Start button on the taskbar, and then move the mouse pointer up to the Programs folder.**
   This action opens the Start menu and the Programs nested menu. The Accessories folder is on the Programs nested menu.

2. **Move the mouse pointer to the Accessories folder.**
   A menu of applications and subfolders stored in the Accessories folder opens, as shown in Figure 7.1.

Accessories folder

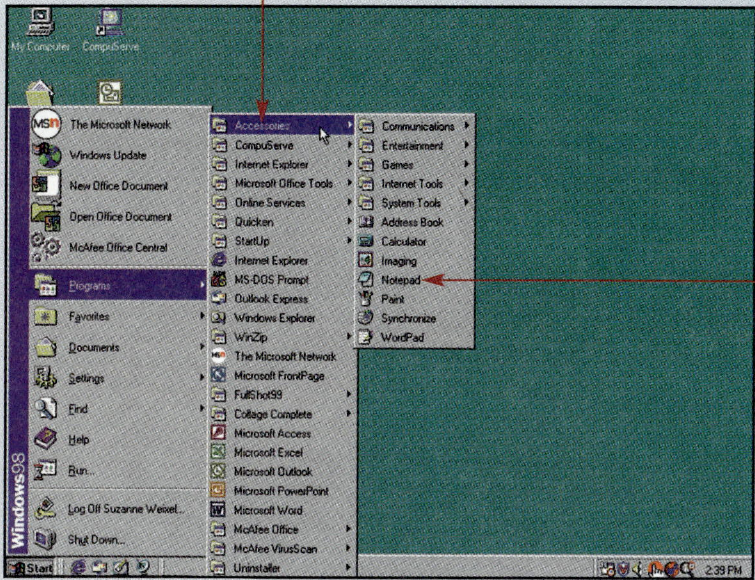

Notepad application

Figure 7.1
The Accessories folder contains many useful applications that come with Windows 98.

3 Click Notepad on the Accessories menu.
This starts the Notepad accessory program (see Figure 7.2). Notepad is a very simple ***word processing*** application. You use a word processing application to create text-based documents such as letters, memos, and reports. Notepad starts by displaying a new untitled document.

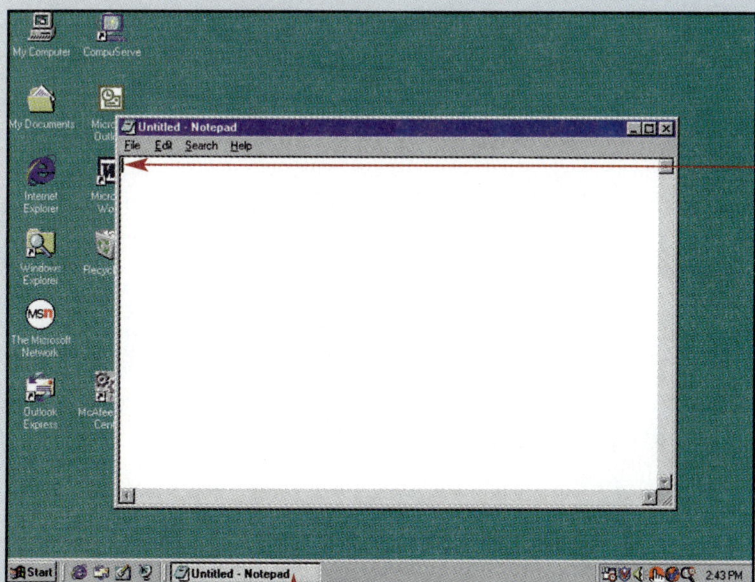

Insertion point

Notepad button on the taskbar

Figure 7.2
A blank document window in Notepad.

4 Type `I am using the Notepad word processing program.`
As you type, the characters are displayed onscreen to the left of the ***insertion point***. The insertion point is a flashing line that is displayed onscreen during editing. Now, save the text you have typed in a file.

continues ▶

To Use a Windows Application (continued)

5 Open the File menu, and choose Save.

The Save As dialog box opens (see Figure 7.3). You use this dialog box to name a file the first time you save it or to save an existing file with a new name. The Save As dialog box opens only the first time you choose File, Save to save a new file—or any time you choose File, Save As.

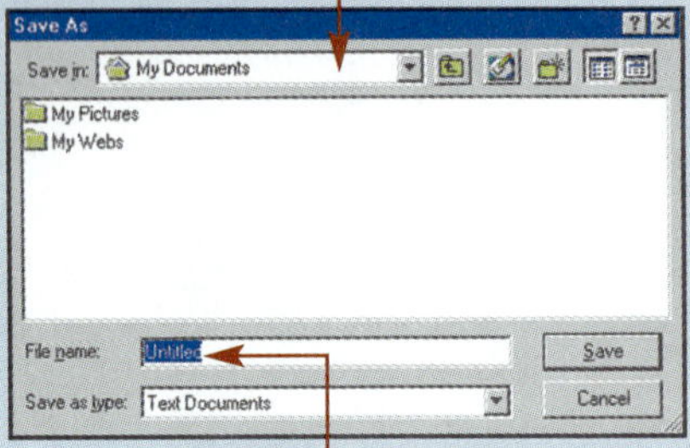

Figure 7.3
The Save As dialog box.

6 In the File name text box, type `My First File`.

This is the name you want to give your new file.

7 Choose Save.

Windows saves the file, and keeps it displayed onscreen (see Figure 7.4). By default, Windows saves the file in the My Documents folder on drive C. Your instructor may ask you to save the file on a different drive or in a different folder.

8 Open the File menu, and choose Exit.

This action closes Notepad and the My First File file. Don't worry, though, the file is safely stored on a disk, so you can open it again in the future. Leave Windows 98 running to use in the next lesson, in which you learn how to use more than one application at a time.

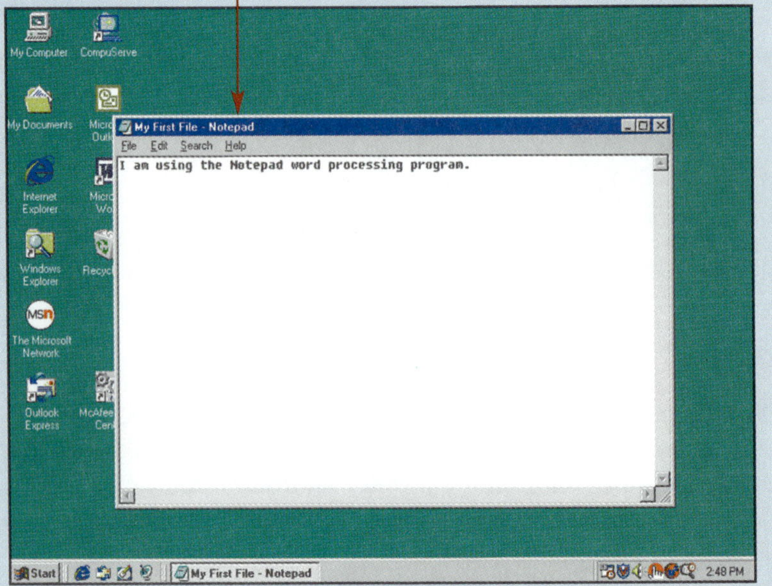

Figure 7.4
The file remains open onscreen, although you saved it on a disk.

More about Closing and Saving
You can quickly close an application window, thereby exiting the application, by clicking the window's Close button (the X in the upper-right corner. Refer to Project 4, "Getting to Know Your Operating System," for a refresher on using a window's Close button).

If you decide to exit an application before you save the changes you have made to a file, the application displays a message box, asking if you want to save the changes. Choose Yes to save the changes and exit, or choose No to exit without saving the changes.

To quickly save a file that you have already named, press Ctrl+S.

Lesson 2: Using Multiple Windows Applications

With Windows, you can have more than one application open on your computer at the same time. You can change back and forth from one application to another, and you can arrange the application windows on the desktop so that you can quickly access the one you need. The only limit to how many applications you can use at one time is the amount of memory you have installed in your computer.

Opening Multiple Documents
Most applications allow you to open more than one document at a time. Each document is represented by a button on the taskbar. The commands and actions for switching between open documents are the same as for switching between open applications.

In this lesson, you use the Windows accessories to learn how to open more than one application at a time, arrange open windows on the desktop, and switch between open windows.

To Use Multiple Windows Applications

1. **Click the Start button on the taskbar, move the mouse pointer to the Programs folder, and then move the mouse pointer to the Accessories folder on the Programs nested menu.**
   The Accessories menu opens.
2. **Click on Notepad in the Accessories menu.**
   This action starts Notepad, with a new untitled document displayed.
3. **Click the Start button on the taskbar, move the mouse pointer to the Programs command, and then move the mouse pointer to the Accessories folder in the Programs nested menu.**
   The Accessories menu opens again. Notice that the Notepad application window is still open on the desktop (see Figure 7.5).

continues ▶

To Use Multiple Windows Applications (continued)

Figure 7.5
You can use the Start menu to open additional applications without closing applications that are already running.

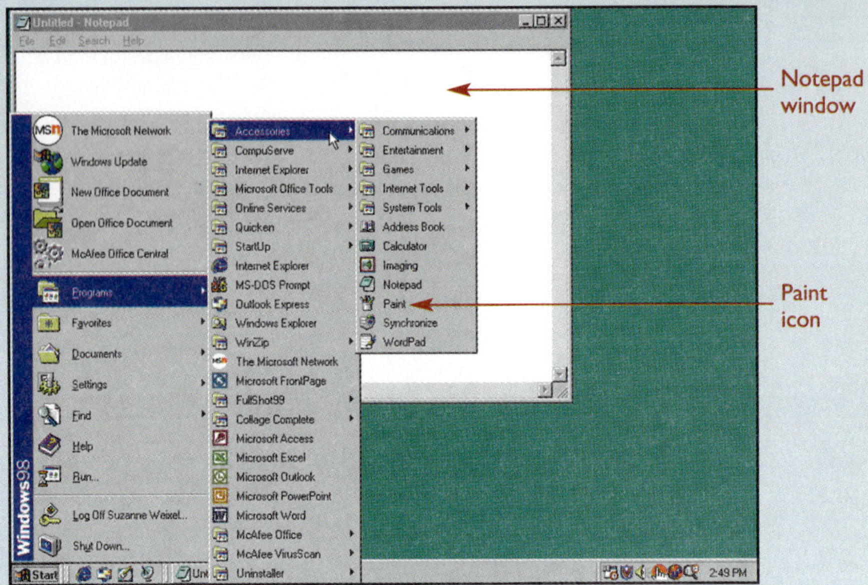

4 Click the Paint icon on the Accessories menu.

This action starts the Paint application (see Figure 7.6). Paint is a ***drawing application***, which you can use to create or edit pictures and other ***graphics files***. Notice on the taskbar that there are now buttons for both Notepad and Paint. The Paint button appears "depressed" because Paint is the active window.

Figure 7.6
An untitled document in Paint.

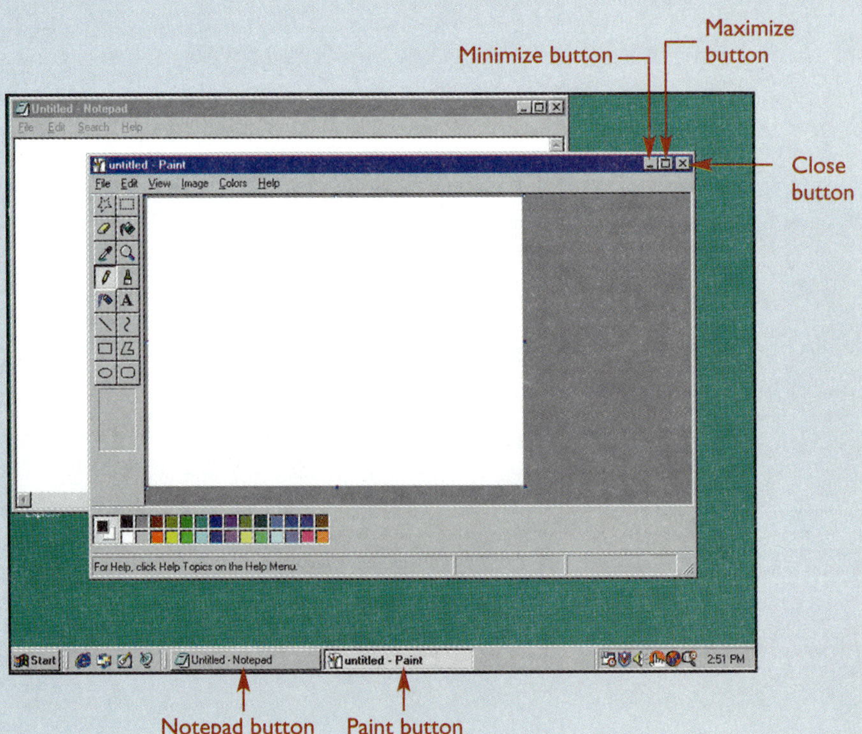

Identifying the Active Window
The active window (the window you are currently working in) is always on top of other open windows, and it always has a highlighted title bar. In addition, the taskbar button for the active window always appears depressed.

5 Click the Maximize button at the right end of the Paint title bar.
The Paint window increases in size to fill the desktop. You can't see the Notepad window, but it is still open. Notice the Notepad button, which is still visible on the taskbar.

If the Paint window is already maximized, you can skip Step 5; or you can click the Restore button, and then click the Maximize button.

Window Control Buttons
Every window has three buttons at the right end of its title bar: the Minimize button, the Maximize/Restore button, and the Close button.

6 Click the Notepad button on the taskbar.
The Notepad application window becomes active.

7 Right-click an empty area of the taskbar, and choose Tile Windows Vertically from the shortcut menu that opens.
This action ***tiles*** the windows, which means they are arranged side by side on the desktop so they don't overlap (see Figure 7.7). To tile them one above the other, choose Tile Windows Horizontally.

Figure 7.7
Two windows tiled vertically on the desktop.

continues ▶

To Use Multiple Windows Applications (continued)

When you work in tiled windows, the entire contents of each window probably won't fit onscreen. The active window has scrollbars that you can use to scroll up and down or left and right to access all the data you need.

8 **Right-click the taskbar again, and choose Cascade Windows from the shortcut menu.**

This action ***cascades*** the windows, which means all the open windows on the desktop are arranged so that they overlap evenly, leaving part of each window visible (see Figure 7.8).

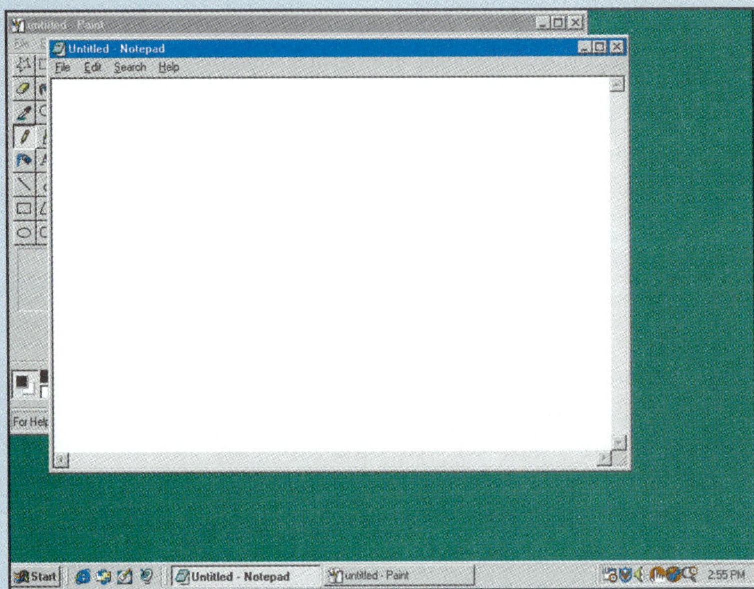

Figure 7.8
Two windows cascaded on the desktop.

9 **Click the Minimize button of the Notepad window.**

This action minimizes the Notepad window (see Figure 7.9). Notepad is still running, but, instead of being open in an application window, it is displayed only as a taskbar button.

10 **Click the Notepad button on the taskbar.**

Notepad is restored to its previous location on the desktop.

11 **Click the Paint taskbar button, and then click the Close button in the Paint window.**

This makes the Paint window active, and then closes the Paint application. Leave Notepad open to use in the next lesson, in which you learn how to copy and move information from one application window to another.

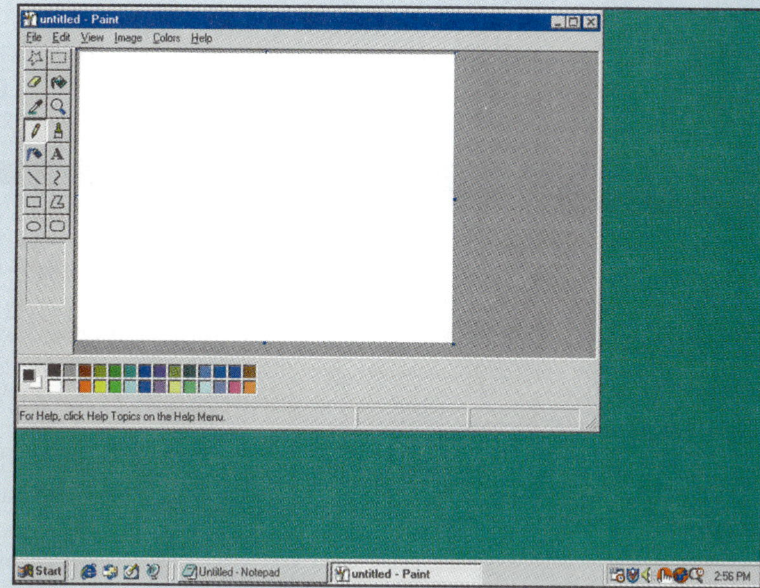

Figure 7.9
Notepad is minimized, but Paint is still open on the desktop.

Moving and Resizing Windows

You can move and resize windows on the desktop. To move the entire window to a new location on the desktop, simply click and drag the window's title bar. This is useful if a portion of a window is covering something that you need to see. You can drag the border or corner of a window to change the window's size or shape. Resize a window when you want to make it larger or smaller.

Other Ways to Change the Active Window

If you can see an open window on the desktop behind the active window, you can switch to that window by clicking inside it.

You can use the Alt+Tab key combination as another fast way to switch between open applications. Press and hold down Alt, and then press Tab. Each time you press Tab, the name of another open application appears in a gray box onscreen. When you see the name of the application you want to use, release Alt; you instantly switch to it.

If you have a 104-key Windows keyboard, you can use the Windows logo key in combination with Tab (in place of Alt) to scroll through the open windows.

Lesson 3: Using the Windows Clipboard

One of the most useful features of Windows applications is the Windows Clipboard. In Project 5, "Learning about PC Data Storage," you learned that you can use the Clipboard to copy or move entire files and folders; you can also use it to copy or move data from one location in a Windows application file to another location. You can copy and move data within a file, between files in the same application, and even between files in different applications.

In this lesson, you learn how to use the Clipboard to copy text from a Notepad word processing ***document***—or file—into a document created with the WordPad word processing application. To complete the steps in this lesson, Notepad should be open. Try copying the data now.

To Use the Windows Clipboard

1 Click the Maximize button in the Notepad window, open the File menu, and choose Open.

The Open dialog box displays (see Figure 7.10). You use the Open dialog box in Windows applications to open files that have been saved and closed.

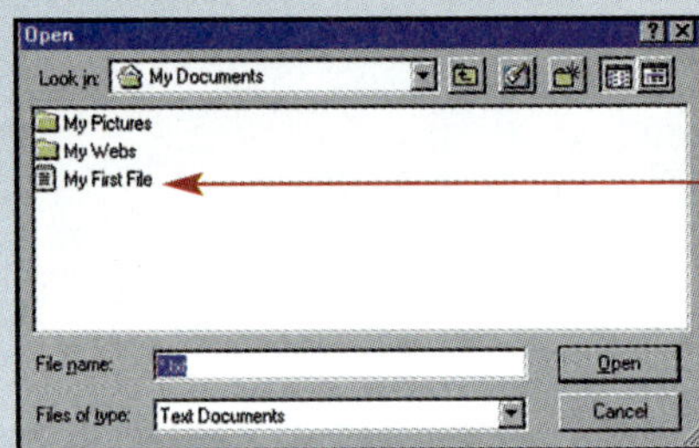

Figure 7.10
The Open dialog box.

2 In the list of files, select `My First File`, and then choose Open.

This action opens the file that you created and saved in Lesson 1.

Using the Open Dialog Box

By default, the Open dialog box displays a list of files stored in the My Documents folder. The displayed files are in the file format used by the current application. You can change the list to display files stored in any folder on any disk in your PC, and you can change the file type to display different file formats.

To display different file types, click the drop-down arrow next to the Files of type box, and then click the file type you want.

To change disks or folders, click the drop-down arrow next to the Look in box, and then click the disk or folder you want. You may have to repeat this step to locate the correct folder.

If there are a lot of files or folders in the list, use the scrollbar to scroll up or down to find the item you want.

3 In the My First File document, drag the mouse pointer across the complete line of text.

This action selects the line of text. The selected text appears highlighted (see Figure 7.11).

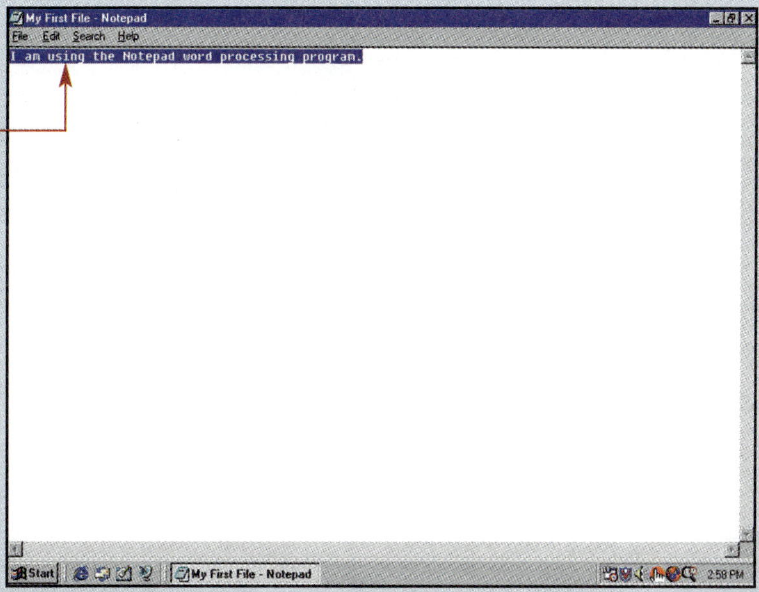

Figure 7.11
Before you can copy text to the Clipboard, you must select it.

4 **Open the Edit menu and choose Copy.**
This command copies the selected text to the Windows Clipboard. Now, open a document in another application.

5 **Click the Start button, move the mouse pointer to the Programs folder, and then move the mouse pointer to the Accessories folder.**
The Accessories menu opens.

6 **Click the WordPad accessory.**
WordPad opens as the active application, and Notepad moves to the background (see Figure 7.12). Notice the toolbars and the ruler in the WordPad window. WordPad is a more sophisticated word processing program that comes as a Windows 98 accessory. You can use Notepad to quickly jot down a few lines of text, but if you want to make the text look good, or if you are creating a document with more than just a few lines of text, you need a word processing application with more features.

About Word Processors
Although more sophisticated than NotePad, WordPad is still a fairly simple application with limited features. Chances are, you have a full-featured word processing application such as Microsoft Word installed on your computer. For more about word processing applications, see Project 9, "Getting Started with PC Applications."

7 **In the WordPad application window, open the Edit menu, and choose Paste.**
The text from the Clipboard is pasted into the WordPad document at the insertion point location (see Figure 7.13).

8 **Click the Notepad button on the taskbar.**
This makes Notepad active.

continues ▶

To Use the Windows Clipboard (continued)

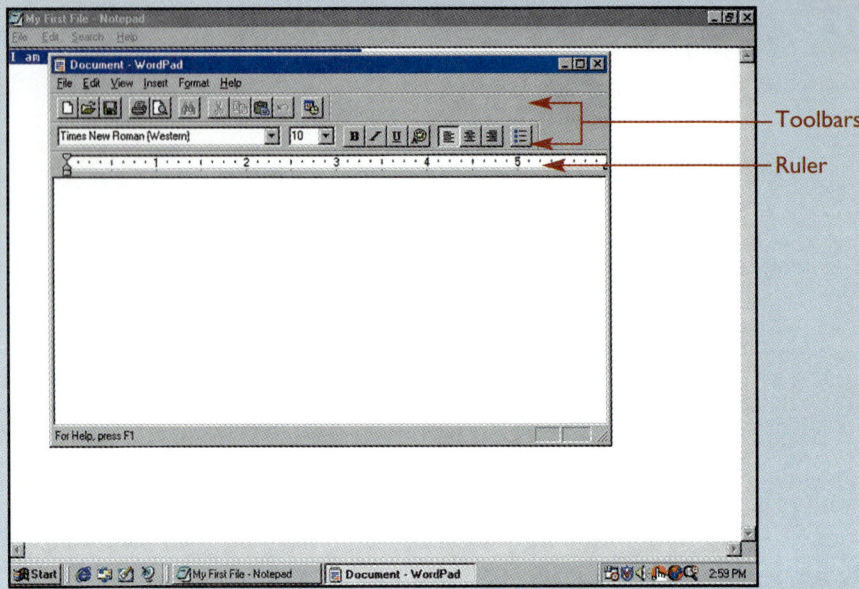

Figure 7.12
An untitled document in WordPad.

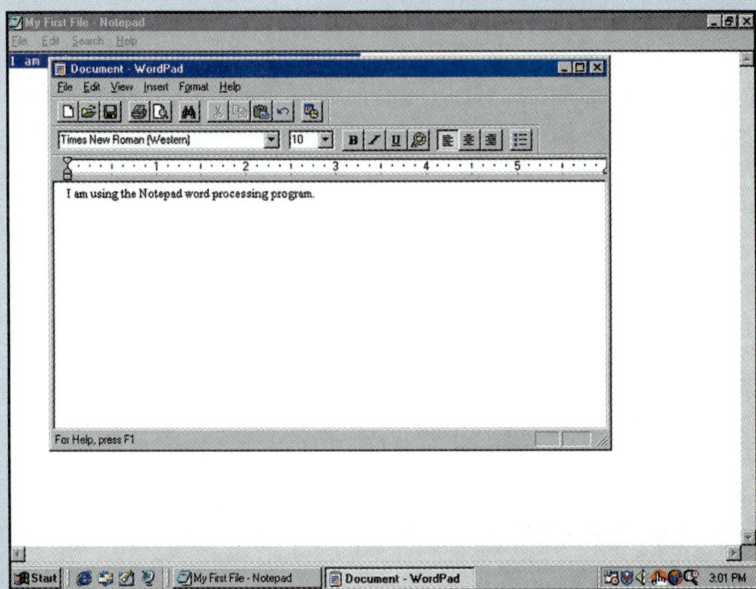

Figure 7.13
The copied text is pasted into the WordPad document.

9 In Notepad, open the File menu, and choose Exit.
Notepad closes, but WordPad is still open onscreen. Leave it open so that you can use it in the next lesson, in which you learn how to print a file in a Windows application.

Moving Data with the Clipboard
You can use the Clipboard to move data from one location to another, as well as to copy data. First, select the data; then choose Edit, Cut to delete the selection from its current location and place it on the Clipboard. Then, move the insertion point to the new location, and finally choose Edit, Paste.

Other Ways to Cut, Copy, and Paste
Shortcut key combinations let you perform the Copy, Cut, and Paste commands even more quickly. Press Ctrl+C to copy a selection to the Clipboard; press Ctrl+X to cut a selection and place it on the Clipboard; press Ctrl+V to paste a selection from the Clipboard to the insertion-point location.

In many Windows applications, including all of the Microsoft Office applications, you can use toolbar buttons and shortcut menus to cut, copy, and paste.

Lesson 4: Printing a File

After you create a file in a Windows application, you will probably want to ***print*** it. Printing a file creates a hard copy version of the file. The file, however, remains saved on disk.

Windows handles all the printing tasks for Windows applications. After you have selected to print a file, you can continue working in an application, which means that you don't have to sit around waiting for a file to print before you can get additional work done. You can select to print many files at a time—even files from different applications. Windows ***spools*** them: it stores them in memory, and then prints them in order as soon as the selected printer is available.

In this lesson, you learn how to print a file and also how to open a printer folder to check to see which files are waiting to be printed. Although you don't have to open a printer folder window before printing a file, you do so in this lesson to see how files sent to the printer are listed while they wait to print.

Try printing a file now.

To Print a File

1. **Click the Start button on the taskbar, move the mouse pointer to the Settings command, and click Printers on the Settings nested menu.**
The Printers folder window opens, as shown in Figure 7.14. If your computer system is connected to a printer, there should be at least two icons in the Printers folder window: the Add Printer icon, which you use to set up a new printer for use with your PC, and the icon representing your printer. If your PC is connected to more than one printer, there is an icon for each printer.

Selecting the Correct Printer
If there is more than one printer icon in your Printers folder, ask your instructor which printer you should use.

continues ▶

To Print a File

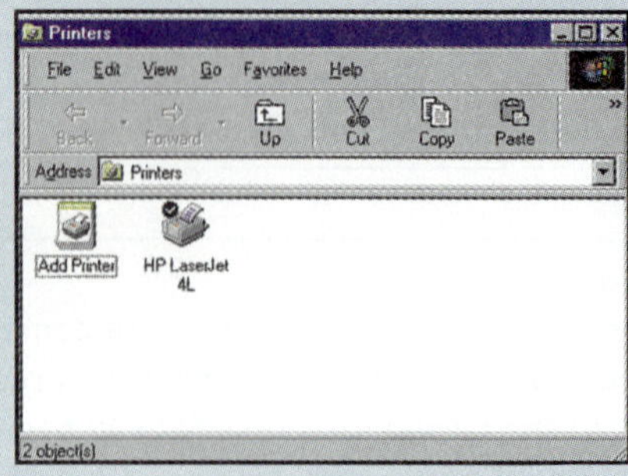

Figure 7.14
At least two icons should appear in the Printers window.

2 Double-click the icon representing your printer.
This opens the printer window for your printer (see Figure 7.15). If any documents were sent to be printed, the document names and status are listed in this window.

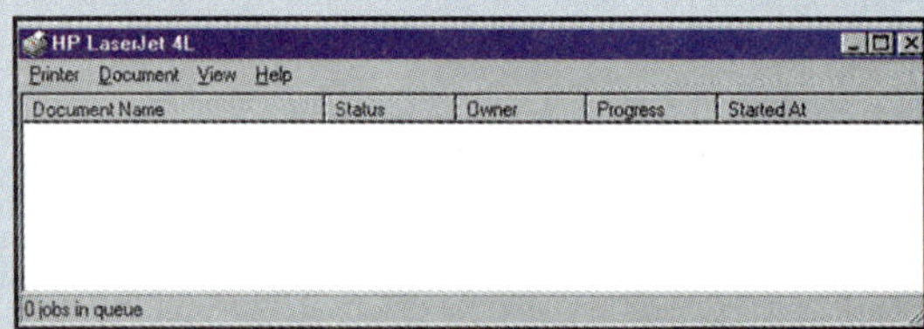

Figure 7.15
Your printer window should look similar to this one, which is for an HP LaserJet 4L printer.

3 Open the Printer menu and choose Pause Printing.
This command tells Windows to suspend printing temporarily. When a printer is paused, you can send a file to be printed, but it won't print until you give the command to make the printer active again. In real life, this is useful if you decide to change paper or if you need to leave the room and want to be present when the document prints. During this lesson, you will use this technique to see how files are spooled and listed in the printer window.

If you have no printers set up to print Windows documents, check with your instructor about what to do next.

4 Click the WordPad button on the taskbar.
WordPad becomes active again. The text you copied should still display in the document window.

5 Open the File menu, and choose Print.
The Print dialog box opens (see Figure 7.16). You use the dialog box to set printing options, such as how many copies to print and which pages to print.

6 Choose OK.
WordPad sends the document to the printer. Because the printer is paused, the document is kept in the ***print queue***, waiting until you give the command to make the printer active. The print queue is simply a list of files waiting to print. If the printer were not paused, and if there were no other documents waiting to print, the document would print immediately.

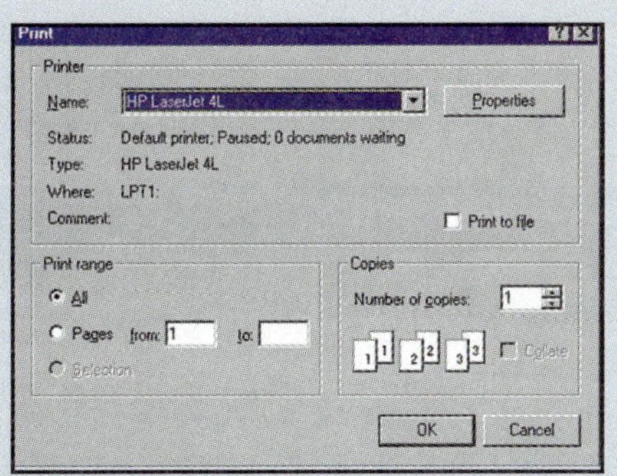

Figure 7.16
The Print dialog box.

❼ **Click the button representing your printer window on the taskbar.**
Your printer window becomes active (see Figure 7.17). You can see the document listed and waiting to print.

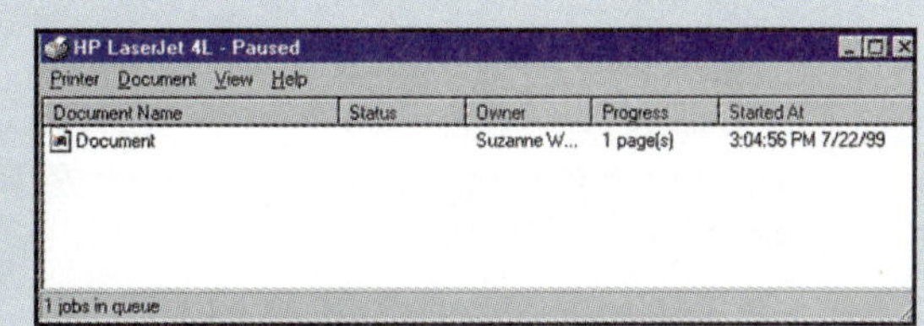

Figure 7.17
Documents waiting to print are listed in the printer window.

❽ **Open the Printer menu and choose Pause Printing again.**
The printer becomes active again, and the file prints.

If an error message displays, telling you that the printer is offline or is not ready to print, check your printer to be sure it is online. You can't print if the printer is off, if the printer doesn't have any paper, or if the printer is not online. Printers often have a light that indicates whether the printer is online and ready to receive commands from the computer.

---

❾ **Switch back to WordPad, and choose File, Exit.**
This action closes the WordPad program. Because you did not save the file before exiting, WordPad displays a message, asking you if you want to save the changes to the document.

❿ **Choose No.**
You don't have to save the untitled document. If you choose Yes, the Save As dialog box opens so that you can name the file. Close all open windows, but leave Windows open to use in the next lesson, in which you learn how to create a program shortcut.

Lesson 5: Creating a Program Shortcut

The Start menu provides an easy way to start programs in Windows, but you may have to wade through several layers of nested menus to find the application you want. If you use an application frequently, you can create a program shortcut icon on the desktop. Then, to start the application, you simply double-click the shortcut icon. Windows comes with some program shortcuts already on the desktop.

To create a shortcut, locate the file that starts the program for which you want to create a shortcut, and then drag it onto the desktop. In this lesson, you learn how to create a shortcut to the WordPad application.

To Create a Program Shortcut

1. **Double-click the My Computer icon on the desktop.**
   The My Computer window opens.

2. **Double-click the drive [C:] icon in the My Computer window.**
   The drive [C:] window opens.

3. **Double-click the Program Files folder icon in the drive [C:] window.**
   The Program Files window opens.

4. **Double-click the Accessories folder icon in the Program Files window.**
   The Accessories window opens, as shown in Figure 7.18. Notice the WordPad program icon in the Accessories window. The file that starts the WordPad program is stored in the Accessories folder, which is stored in the Program Files folder, which in turn is stored on drive C of your computer.

Figure 7.18
You will find the WordPad file in the Accessories window.

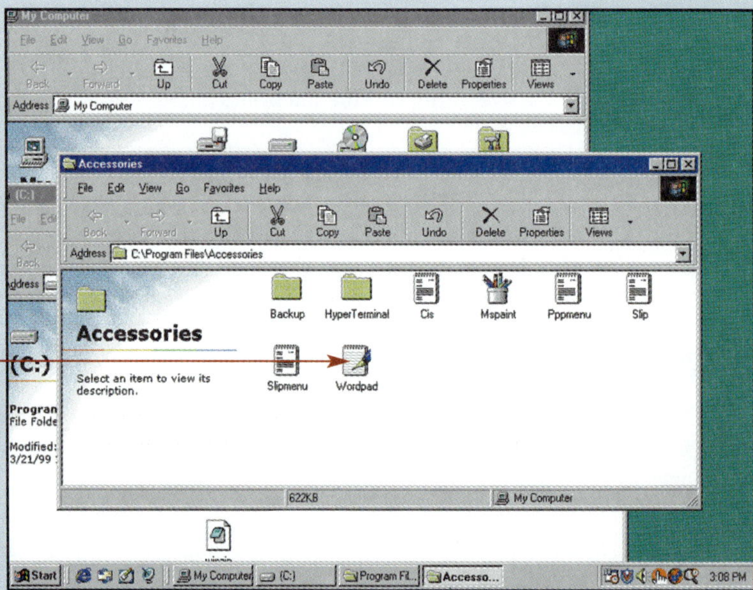

Locating Application Files

It's not always easy to figure out where the file that starts an application is stored. If the application is listed on the Programs menu or a nested menu, you can right-click it and choose Properties. The location where the file is stored is listed in the Properties dialog box.

Often, you'll find the file in a folder with the same name as the application. For example, you would look in the Quicken folder on drive C to find the Quicken application file. Also, you can identify an application file from its icon. Folder icons look like folders; document file icons look like pieces of paper. Application files are usually little pictures that are somehow related to the program. For example, that Quicken program file looks just like the picture on the Quicken box.

If all else fails, try reading the documentation that came with the application.

5 Drag the WordPad file out of the Accessories folder window and onto any blank area of the desktop.

When you release the left mouse button, the shortcut icon is displays on the desktop, as shown in Figure 7.19. Windows automatically names the icon, but you can edit the name if you want. The WordPad file is still stored in the Accessories folder.

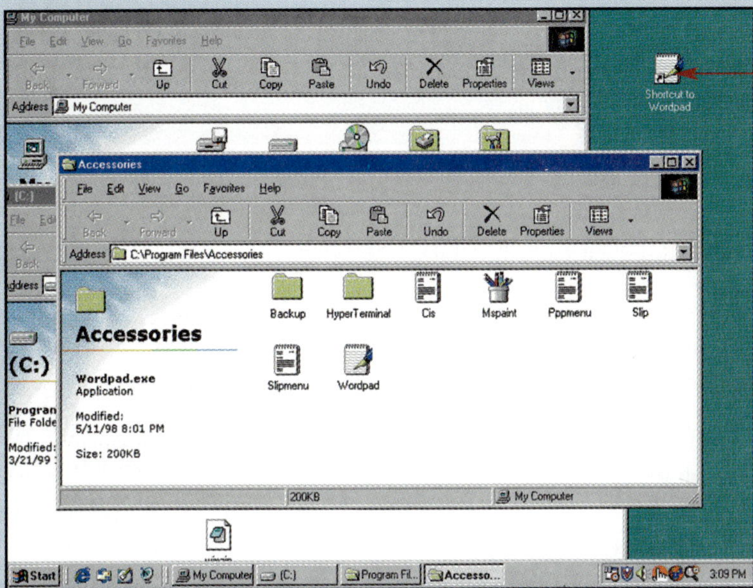

Figure 7.19
You can drag a file onto the desktop to create a shortcut.

The WordPad shortcut icon

If you can't see any blank area of the desktop because there are too many open windows, close or minimize some of them. Simply use the taskbar to make a window active, and then click the window's Close or Minimize button.

6 Double-click the shortcut icon.

WordPad starts.

7 Open the File menu and choose Exit.

WordPad closes.

Other Types of Shortcuts

You can create shortcuts to folders and document files, too. Use the same steps you learned for creating a program shortcut—just locate and drag the folder or document file icon onto the desktop.

Summary

In this lesson, you had the opportunity to use Windows applications to create, edit, and print files. You learned how to open applications and arrange application windows on the desktop, how to use the Clipboard to copy text from one document to another, and how to create a shortcut to quickly start an application.

Take a few minutes to check your skills and to complete some of the Skill Drill and Challenge exercises.

Checking Concepts and Terms

True/False

For each of the following, check *T* or *F* to indicate whether the statement is true or false.

__T __F **1.** You can run only one application at a time in Windows 98. [L2]

__T __F **2.** You can see buttons for all open windows on the Windows taskbar. [L1]

__T __F **3.** You can move windows around on the desktop. [L2]

__T __F **4.** To change to another open window, click in it. [L2]

__T __F **5.** Use the Windows Clipboard to copy or move data from one file to another. [L3]

__T __F **6.** After you send a file to a printer, there is no way to suspend printing. [L4]

__T __F **7.** Windows automatically closes one window when you make a different window active. [L2]

__T __F **8.** Put a shortcut on the desktop so you can quickly start an application. [L5]

__T __F **9.** Notepad is a good application to use when you just want to jot down a few quick notes. [L1]

__T __F **10.** Paint is a good application to use when you want to create a complex word processing document. [L2]

Multiple Choice

Circle the letter of the correct answer for each of the following.

1. Which of the following is *not* a way to switch between open applications? [L2]

a. Click the taskbar button.

b. Press Alt+Tab.

c. Click inside another window.

d. Use the Clipboard.

2. What is the shortcut key for copying information to the Clipboard? [L3]

a. Ctrl+Y

b. Ctrl+O

c. Ctrl+P

d. Ctrl+C

3. What does Windows 98 do to files sent to be printed? [L4]

a. It wraps them.

b. It spools them.

c. It packages them.

d. It clips them.

4. In which folder can you find the collection of programs that come with Windows 98? [L1]

a. Applications

b. Attachments

c. Accessories

d. Add-Ins

5. Which menu commands let you place a selection on the Clipboard? [L3]
   a. Edit, Copy
   b. File, Copy
   c. Edit, Paste
   d. File, Paste

6. To move a window, what should you drag? [L2]
   a. its taskbar button
   b. its title bar
   c. its corner
   d. its menu bar

7. What is the name of the folder in which documents created with Windows applications are saved, by default? [L1]
   a. My Documents
   b. Windows Documents
   c. Notepad Documents
   d. WordPad Documents

8. On which nested menu do you find the Printers folder? [L4]
   a. Programs
   b. Accessories
   c. Favorites
   d. Settings

9. What arrangement should you use when you want all open windows to overlap evenly on the desktop? [L2]
   a. tile vertically
   b. cascade
   c. tile horizontally
   d. line up overlapping

10. What button should you click to display a window only as a taskbar button? [L2]
   a. Start
   b. Maximize
   c. Minimize
   d. Help

Screen ID

Identify each of the items shown in Figure 7.20.

Figure 7.20

A. Start button
B. Active window
C. Wordpad Program shortcut icon
D. Insertion point
E. Inactive window
F. Active window close button
G. Active taskbar button
H. Inactive taskbar button

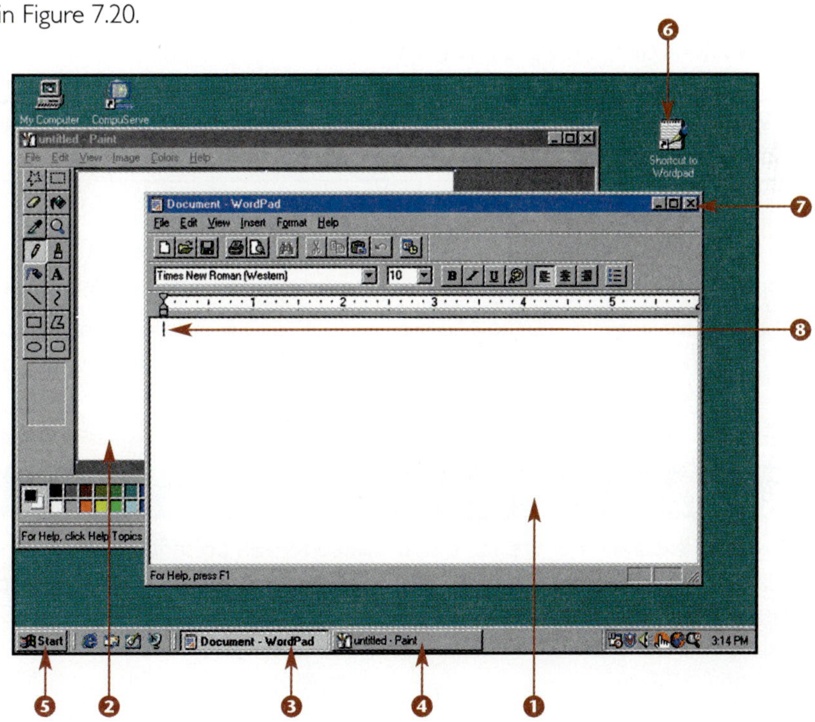

1. ____________ 4. ____________ 7. ____________
2. ____________ 5. ____________ 8. ____________
3. ____________ 6. ____________

Discussion Questions

1. Windows lets you have more than one application open at the same time. Why is it useful to be able to use more than one application at once?
2. One of the benefits of using Windows is that many commands are the same in different applications. Discuss the commands you have already used that are the same in different applications. Have you come across any commands that are not the same? Can you imagine some commands that might be different, depending on the application you are using?
3. Windows makes it easy to integrate data from one application with another application. Think about what it means to be able to integrate data. Why is it important? List circumstances in which you might need to use the Clipboard.

Skill Drill

Skill Drill exercises reinforce project skills. Each skill reinforced is the same, or nearly the same, as a skill presented in the project. Detailed instructions are provided in a step-by-step format.

1. Practicing Managing Windows

To practice managing windows, follow these steps:

1. Open the Paint, Notepad, and Calculator windows.
2. Tile the open windows.
3. Cascade the windows.
4. Maximize, and then restore the Paint window.
5. Minimize, and then restore the Notepad window.
6. Close all open windows.

2. Try Some Windows Games

To try some Windows games, follow these steps:

The Windows games may not have been installed on your PC during setup. Run Windows setup again to add them to your Accessories folder.

1. From the Accessories menu, point at Games to see what's on the Games menu.
2. Start Solitaire or the first game on the list.
3. Use the Help menu to find out how to play.
4. Minimize the game, and open Minesweeper or Freecell.
5. Use the Help menu to find out how to play.
6. Close all open applications, including games, before shutting down Windows.

Challenge

Challenge exercises expand on or are somewhat related to skills presented in the lessons. Each exercise provides a brief narrative introduction, followed by instructions in a numbered-step format. The steps are not as detailed as those in the Skill Drill section.

1. Using Accessories

You may be able to use Windows accessories to improve efficiency at work, school, or home. Now that you have experience using common features of Windows applications, explore some Windows accessories to find out which ones will be of use to you.

1. Open the Accessories menu to see what programs are available.
2. Open Notepad and create a simple file. Type a note to remind yourself about an appointment.
3. Open the Calculator and try tallying some figures, such as one day's receipts.
4. Start Paint, and maximize the window.
5. Test some of the Paint tools. Create a logo or picture.
6. Close all open applications before shutting down Windows.

2. Creating and Printing a File

Practice using a Windows application to create and print a file.

1. Start the WordPad application, and then create a file containing a list of other people in your class.
2. Save the file with the name `Class`.
3. Use the Clipboard to copy the list to another location in the same document.
4. Start Notepad, and then copy the list from the WordPad file into a Notepad file.
5. Save the Notepad file with the name Another Class.
6. Print both the WordPad file and the Notepad file.
7. Close all open applications before shutting down Windows. If prompted, save the changes to the two files.

Project 8

Project 8

Getting Started with the Internet

Objectives

In this project, you learn how to

- **Understand the Internet**
- **Establish an Internet Access Account**
- **Start Internet Explorer**
- **Navigate a Web Site and Search the Internet**
- **Print a Web Page**
- **Disconnect from the Internet**

Key terms introduced in this project include

- chat rooms
- domain
- email
- forums
- home page
- HTML (Hypertext Markup Language)
- HTTP (Hypertext Transfer Protocol)
- hyperlink target
- Internet
- Internet Service Provider (ISP)
- offline
- online
- online services
- search engine
- server
- uniform resource locator (URL)
- Web browser
- Web pages
- Web site
- World Wide Web

Why Would I Do This?

The ***Internet***, a global network of computers that are connected to each other via cables, satellites, and telephone lines, is a powerful and exciting part of everyday life.

Most Internet users primarily take advantage of the sites and pages contained on the ***World Wide Web***, or Web for short. The Web is a subset of the Internet and is comprised of ***Web pages***, or graphical documents stored on the Web. Businesses, organizations, and private individuals all can post Web pages for Internet users worldwide to access. Many of these pages are changed and updated frequently, so what you see today could easily change by tomorrow.

Using the Internet and the Web, you can access information and services stored on computers all over the world.

Some of the things you can do while connected to the Internet include the following:

- Research topics from astronomy to zoology
- Conduct banking
- Purchase airline tickets
- Browse—and shop!—at virtual malls
- Check the weather around the globe
- Monitor stock prices
- Send and receive ***email***, electronic messages transmitted between people using networked computers
- Play games

In this project, you learn the basics of how to use your PC to access the Internet and locate information ***online*** (while you are actively connected to the Internet). You learn what the Internet is and how to start Internet Explorer, a popular ***Web browser***. Web browsers are software programs that provide the tools you need to locate and display information stored on the Internet or World Wide Web. You also learn how to use a search engine to find specific information, move through a ***Web site***, a series of linked Web pages, and print a Web page.

Lesson 1: Understanding the Internet

The Internet was originally developed as a means of sharing information among government agencies and universities around the world. Advances in technology, such as more powerful PCs and faster modem connections, made the Internet accessible to basically anyone with a PC, a modem, and a telephone line. If you are considering using the Internet, it is important that you understand what it is.

In this lesson, you learn information that will help you understand more about the Internet.

To Understand the Internet

Following are important facts you need to know about the Internet:

1. **The Internet is a collection of interconnected networks.**
   Each network is comprised of a group of computers connected to the same ***server***, which is the computer that controls resources, stores data, and manages access for the network. To create the Internet, the servers are connected. When you access the Internet to locate information, you are accessing one of the Internet servers. Servers are located all over the world—in businesses, universities, and government facilities.

2. **The World Wide Web is a subset of the Internet.**
   To make the Internet more appealing to the general population, businesses realized that it had to be easier to use and more fun to look at. As a result, the World Wide Web was developed. The Web is comprised of Internet servers that use ***HTTP (Hypertext Transfer Protocol)***—defined as a transfer standard for data—to transmit documents formatted in ***HTML (HyperText Markup Language)***. HTML is the file format that supports graphics, formatted text, and other elements used to make up the graphical pages of the Web.

   Not all Internet servers support HTTP, so although the Web is part of the Internet, the Internet is not the same thing as the Web.

3. **HTTP enables servers to transmit a formatted page over the text-based Internet.**
   Web pages are formatted with graphics images, borders and lines, animations, and other interesting elements using HTML. Because most Web browsers support HTML, anyone accessing the Internet can display an HTML-formatted page on his or her PC.

   Creating Your Own Web Pages
   Using HTML to format a Web page used to be complicated. If you wanted to create a Web page, you had to hire someone who knew HTML to do it for you. Now, there are many applications available for creating HTML documents, and there are applications that make it easy to store existing documents in HTML format. For example, Microsoft Word 2000 makes creating a document to store on the Web as easy as creating any word processing document.

   Just creating a Web page is only the first step, however. You must be able to store the page on a Web server so people can access it from the Internet. Many ISPs provide a small amount of storage space on a server as part of your monthly subscription fee, or you can purchase space on a commercial Web server.

4. **Web pages are interconnected to other Web pages by using hyperlinks.**
   Hyperlinks are text or graphics linked to related information in the same page, or in a different page. Onscreen, hyperlinks appear underlined and in a different color from surrounding text. When the mouse pointer touches a hyperlink, the pointer resembles a hand with a pointing finger. When you click a hyperlink, the linked page displays. That's why it's easy to surf—or navigate—through the Web.

continues ▶

To Understand the Internet (continued)

5 **You access the Internet via a company or organization called an *Internet Service Provider (ISP)*. The ISP provides access to the Internet, usually for a fee.**

When you subscribe to an ISP, you receive communications software that enables your PC to access the Internet and an email address. Depending on your ISP, you may also receive other amenities, such as access to technical support, subscribers-only ***forums*** (Web sites devoted to a particular topic), ***chat rooms*** (Web sites where you can communicate in real time), and personal Web page storage space.

6 **The Internet also makes it possible to link the world via email.**

Anyone who subscribes to an ISP receives an email address; you can send and receive email worldwide to anyone else with an email address on the Internet.

Addressing Email

You use email to send and receive messages to other computer users on a network. To send an email message, you must address it to the person you want to receive it. On a company intranet, that may be as simple as typing the person's name or ID.

When you send mail to someone via the Internet, you need to include the individual's ID name or number (assigned by the ISP) followed by the address of the ISP—called a ***domain***—that administers his or her email account. The ID is separated from the domain by an "at" sign (@).

The last three letters of an address identify the type of domain. For example, .com (the most common domain) indicates a commercial business, .edu indicates a university or educational institution, .org indicates an organization, and .gov indicates a government agency.

Each email address on the Internet must be unique so that the correct person receives the mail. That's why some email addresses are filled with letters, numbers, and symbols such as a dot (.) and an underscore (_).

Lesson 2: Establishing an Internet Access Account

Before you can log on to the Internet, you must have an account with an ISP. If your employer or educational institution provides Internet access, you need to request an identification name or number, and a password in order to log in. If you want Internet access from your PC at home, you need to subscribe to an ISP.

In this lesson, you learn how to establish an account with an ISP.

To Establish an Internet Access Account

1 **Decide which ISP you want to use.**

Many business and organizations offer Internet access. You have to consider whether you want additional services, such as access to private forums and chat rooms; or only basic services, such as email and Internet access. Other considerations include cost, whether cable or telephone companies in your area offer service, and ease of use.

Types of Internet Service Providers
Some common types of ISPs include the following:

- **Online services**. America Online, Microsoft Network, and Compuserve are ***online services***. They usually offer numerous services and options in addition to Internet access.
- **Access-only services**. These companies abound all over the world, and offer basic Internet access—usually for a slightly lower or comparable fee to an online service.
- **Cable providers**. Companies that once offered only television cable service now also provide access to the Internet via the same cables. Cable modem connections are faster than modems that use standard telephone lines, but they may be more expensive.
- **Telephone companies**. Many local telephone companies offer Internet access via fiber-optic ISDN cables. An ISDN line is also more expensive than online or access-only services, but it provides a much faster connection.

2 Install software for the selected ISP on your PC.

You may already have the software available. Windows comes with software for a few online services, including America Online, Compuserve, and Microsoft Network. You may have received software for an ISP when you purchased your PC, or you may have CDs that came in the mail. If you do not already have the software, you have to call the company and request it. They will probably mail you a CD, although cable and telephone providers have to actually come to your house to set up the connection.

Installing the ISP Software
If you have an installation CD, insert it in your CD drive. To use software that came with Windows, locate and double-click the icon for the ISP you selected. (It should be in the Online Services folder on your desktop. If it isn't, run Windows setup and add the ISP you want by using the Online Services component.) The installation procedure should start automatically. For more information on installing software, refer to Project 9, Lesson 9, "Installing Software."

3 Log on to the ISP and establish the account online.

This probably happens automatically during the software installation. You have to supply billing information, such as a credit card number, and you have to select an ID and password. There may be a short waiting period while the account is processed, during which you will have only limited access to services. For example, you may not be able to use email immediately.

4 Write your ID and password down, and store them in a secure location.

You may forget your ID or password, and then be unable to log on to your ISP. Keep them safe so you can find them, if necessary.

Security Online

The Internet is a very public place. Keep in mind that it may be possible for anyone with Internet access (which is pretty much everyone at this point) to access private information entered on the Internet. Here are a few rules to follow in order to safeguard yourself and your personal information:

- Never give anyone your password or user ID. The only time you should be asked for your password is when you are logging on to your ISP.
- Enter credit card information on secure sites only. The site should be able to provide you with security assurances.
- Never give out your home address to strangers you meet online.
- Run a virus-detection software program on your PC to guard against downloaded viruses.
- Monitor the use of the Internet by children and teenagers.

Lesson 3: Starting Internet Explorer

Internet Explorer is the Web browser that comes bundled with Windows. You use it to locate information on the Internet or Web, to save or print that information, to keep track of the sites you have visited, and to access your email software.

In this lesson, you learn how to start Internet Explorer and go to a specific Internet address.

To Start Internet Explorer

If you have a different Web browser installed on your PC, such as Netscape Navigator, you will probably be able to follow the steps in this exercise. The programs offer similar features and work in a similar manner. Ask your instructor for more information.

1. **With Windows running on your PC, locate the Internet Explorer icon on your desktop.**

   When you install Windows on your PC, Internet Explorer is installed as well. The icon is a blue letter E (see Figure 8.1).

   Internet Explorer on the Programs Menu

   If the Internet Explorer is not on your desktop, you can access it from the Programs menu. Click the Start button and highlight Programs. You'll see Internet Explorer listed with the other installed programs.

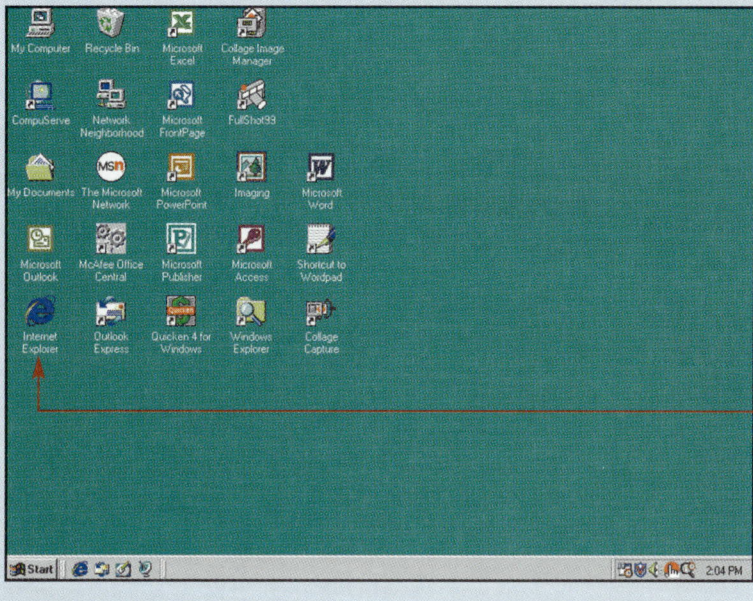

Figure 8.1
The Internet Explorer icon can be found on your Windows desktop.

2 **Right-click the Internet Explorer icon and click Properties on the shortcut menu.**
The Internet Properties dialog box displays (see Figure 8.2). In this dialog box, you can set properties for the way you want your Web browser to work. By default, Internet Explorer is set to access the home page for your ISP. A ***home page*** is the main Web page for a Web site. You can set Internet Explorer to access any Web page when it first starts. For this lesson, set Internet Explorer to access a blank page.

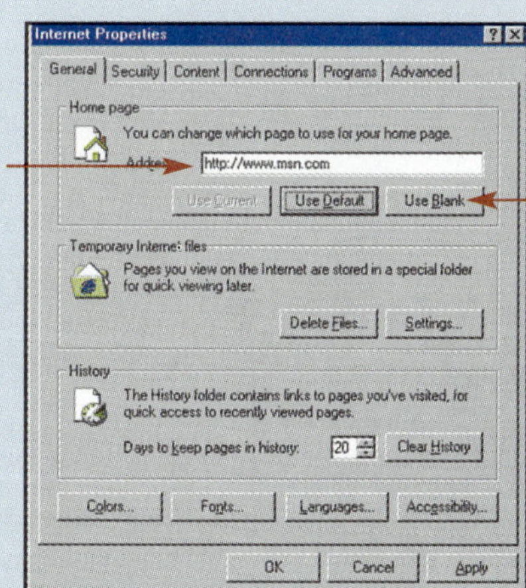

Figure 8.2
The Internet Properties dialog box.

3 **Click the Use Blank button in the Internet Properties dialog box.**
The address `About:Blank` is entered in the Address text box. This sets Internet Explorer to open to a blank page and remain ***offline*** (not connected to the Internet), instead of automatically dialing in to your ISP.

4 **Click OK.**
This closes the Internet Properties dialog box. You do not need to change any of the other default settings. Now, start Internet Explorer.

continues ▶

To Start Internet Explorer (continued)

5 Double-click the Internet Explorer icon on the desktop.

Internet Explorer starts, and displays a blank page, as shown in Figure 8.3. Table 8.1 describes the elements found in the Internet Explorer window.

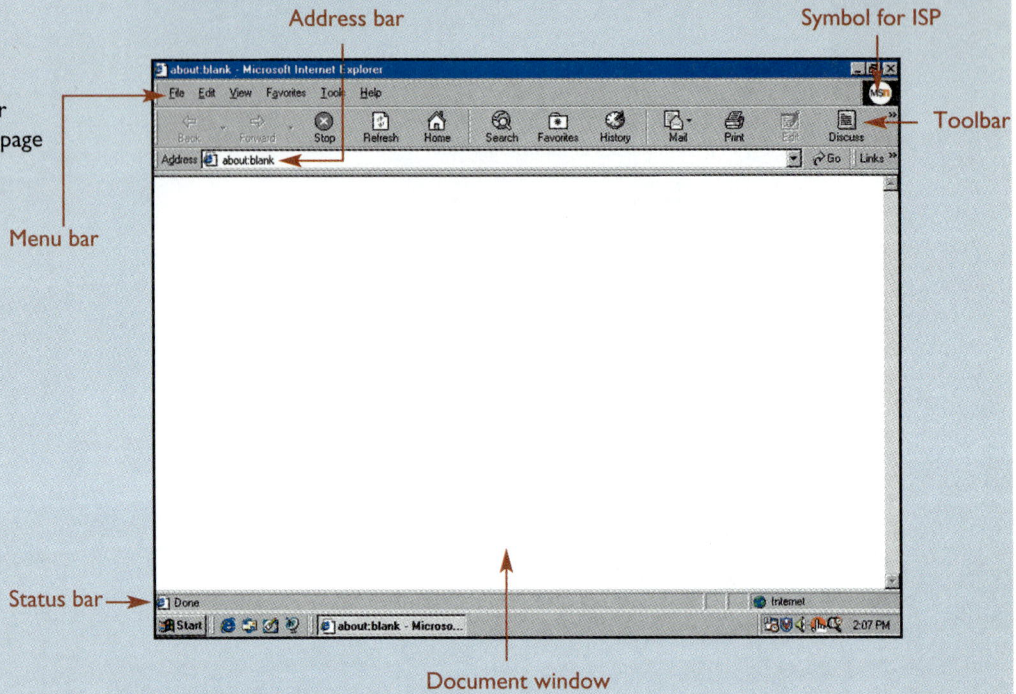

Figure 8.3
The Internet Explorer window with a blank page displayed.

Table 8.1. Elements of the Internet Explorer Window

Element	Description
Menu bar	A menu bar similar to menu bars in other Windows applications. Click a menu item to open a drop-down menu of commands.
Toolbar	A collection of buttons for accessing commonly used commands (see Table 8.2 for a description of the buttons).
Address bar	A textbox in which you type the ***uniform resource locator (URL)***, or Internet address, of the site that you want to display.
Document area	An area where a Web page is displayed. May be split into two frames (see Figure 8.4).
Status bar	A bar across the bottom of the window in which information about the status of the current page is displayed.
Explorer bar	A frame that opens on the left side of the document window when certain features are accessed, including the Features folder, the History folder, and search (see Figure 8.4).

6 Click the Favorites button on the toolbar.

The Favorites folder opens in the Explorer bar on the left side of the Internet Explorer window (see Figure 8.4). You use the Favorites folder to store the addresses of pages and files you access frequently. Descriptions of the other toolbar buttons can be found in Table 8.2.

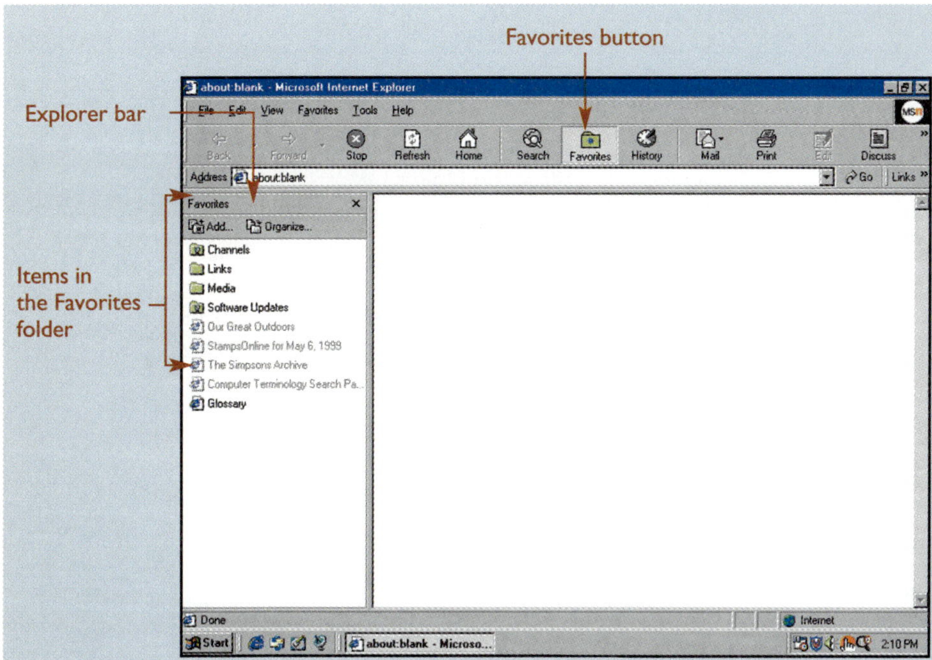

Figure 8.4
The contents of the Favorites folder are displayed in the Explorer bar. Some items are dimmed when you are working offline.

Table 8.2 Internet Explorer Toolbar Buttons

Button	Description
Back	Displays the page shown previously.
Forward	Displays the page shown before you clicked the Back button.
Stop	Interrupts the current action.
Refresh	Redisplays the current page.
Home	Displays the default home page, as set in the Internet Properties dialog box.
Search	Displays a ***search engine,*** which is a Web site used for locating information on the Internet.
Favorites	Opens the Favorites folder, in which you can store the addresses for sites you visit frequently.
History	Opens the History folder, which displays a list of sites you have visited in the past.
Mail	Displays a drop-down list of options you can use to create or retrieve email.
Print	Prints the current page.
Discuss	Starts an online discussion. You must have access to a discussion server to use this service.
Edit	Opens the document in your default Web page editor so you can make changes.
Full Screen	Displays the Web page in full screen view, without toolbars or the status bar.

continues ▶

To Start Internet Explorer (continued)

Using the Favorites Folder

The Favorites folder is created when you install Windows. By default, it includes a few addresses and subfolders containing other addresses that Microsoft thinks you may want to access frequently.

You can easily add a page to your Favorites folder. First, display the page, and then click Favorites on the Internet Explorer menu bar. Click Add to Favorites on the drop-down Favorites menu, and then click OK. The URL for the displayed page will be added to your Favorites folder.

You can also access the Favorites folder directly from the Start menu. Click Start, Favorites. A nested menu of pages and folders stored in the Favorites folder is displayed. Click a page to start Internet Explorer and display that page.

7 Click the Favorites button again.

The Explorer bar closes.

8 Click the Address bar and type the URL `http://www.rockhall.com`.

This is the URL of the Rock and Roll Hall of Fame Web site. If you know the URL of the Web site you want to visit, simply type it in the Address bar, and then press ↵Enter. Displaying a Web site is much quicker and easier when you know its URL; if you have to search for a site, you may find yourself wading through many unrelated Web sites.

9 Press ↵Enter.

Internet Explorer starts your communications software and logs on to your ISP. It may prompt you to enter your ID and password. Once connected to your ISP, it locates and displays the Web page (see Figure 8.5). Notice the network icon in the systray area on the Windows taskbar. This icon is displayed whenever your PC is online. Leave Internet Explorer open to use in the next lesson, in which you learn how to navigate a Web site and search the Internet.

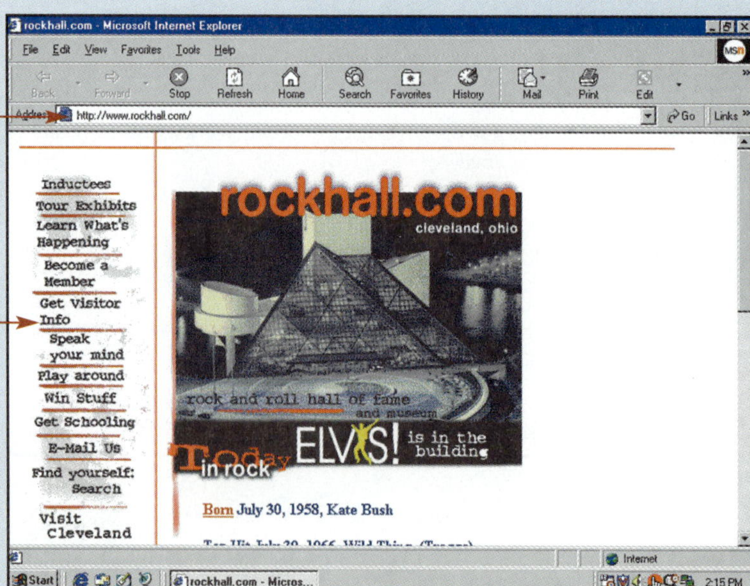

Figure 8.5 The Rock and Roll Hall of Fame Home page displayed in Internet Explorer.

If you do not have an account with an ISP, you will not be able to work online. Ask your instructor how to proceed.

Change Your Default Home Page
To change your default home page back from `About:Blank` to the default, right-click the Internet Explorer icon on the desktop and choose Properties. Click the Use Default button, and then click OK.

Lesson 4: Navigating a Web Site and Searching the Internet

Once you are working online, you move from page to page by using hyperlinks and the buttons on your Web browser's toolbar. You can also enter a different URL to jump quickly to a new site. If you don't know exactly which site you are looking for, you can use one of the Internet's many search engines to try to find it.

In this lesson, you learn how to navigate around a Web site and how to use a search engine to locate information on the Internet.

To Navigate a Web Site and Search the Internet

1. **In the Rock and Roll Hall of Fame Home Page Index, click the Tour Exhibits link.**
Internet Explorer displays the ***hyperlink target***, which is the destination page. In this case, it's the Web page listing the current exhibits at the Rock and Roll Hall of Fame, as shown in Figure 8.6. Many Web sites have indexes of links on one side of the page or across the top. The links are designed to help you navigate through a site to find the information you need.

A Hyperlink Reminder
To identify a hyperlink, rest your mouse pointer on it. The pointer should change to a hand with a pointing finger. Sometimes, a ScreenTip describing the hyperlink target displays as well. After you click a hyperlink, it usually displays in a different color.

Don't worry if the Web page displayed on your screen doesn't look the same as the Web page shown in the figures. Web pages are constantly being changed and updated. If the links used in the steps are not available, ask your instructor which links to use.

2. **Use the vertical scrollbar to scroll down the page.**
Most Web pages contain more information than can fit on one screen. You use the scrollbars to scroll up and down to view the rest of the page.

continues ▶

To Navigate a Web Site and Search the Internet (continued)

Figure 8.6
The Exhibits page in the Rock and Roll Hall of Fame Web site.

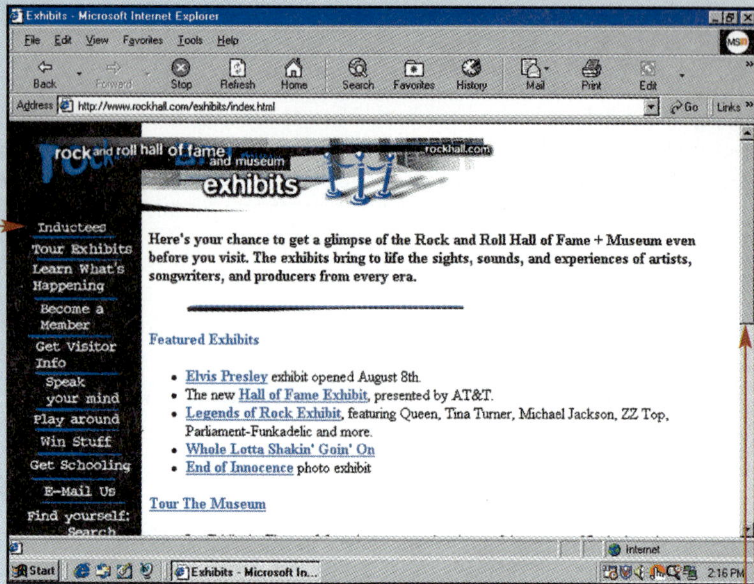

3 **Click the Museum Facts link.**
Internet Explorer displays the Museum Facts page, as shown in Figure 8.7.

Figure 8.7
Use the toolbar buttons in your Web browser to move forward and back through pages you have already displayed.

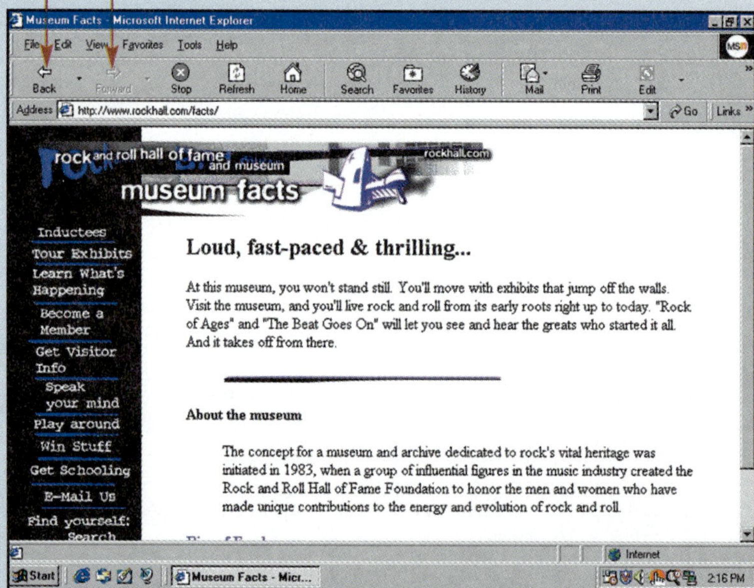

4 **Click the Back button on the Internet Explorer toolbar.**
The previous page—in this case, the Exhibits page—displays. You can click the Back button to continue moving backward through all of the pages you have opened this session.

5 Click the Forward button on the Internet Explorer toolbar.
The Museum facts page displays again. The Forward button is not available until you click the Back button. Use it to move forward to the page that displayed before you clicked Back. Now, try using a search engine to locate information on the Internet.

6 Click the Search button on the Internet Explorer toolbar.
The Explorer bar opens, displaying the search engine recommended by your ISP, as shown in Figure 8.8. Notice that the current Web page still displays; however, it is shown only in the right frame of the window.

The figures in this book use the AltaVista search engine, but you may use any search engine that you want or one suggested by your instructor. Keep in mind that the search results will vary, depending on the search engine that you use.

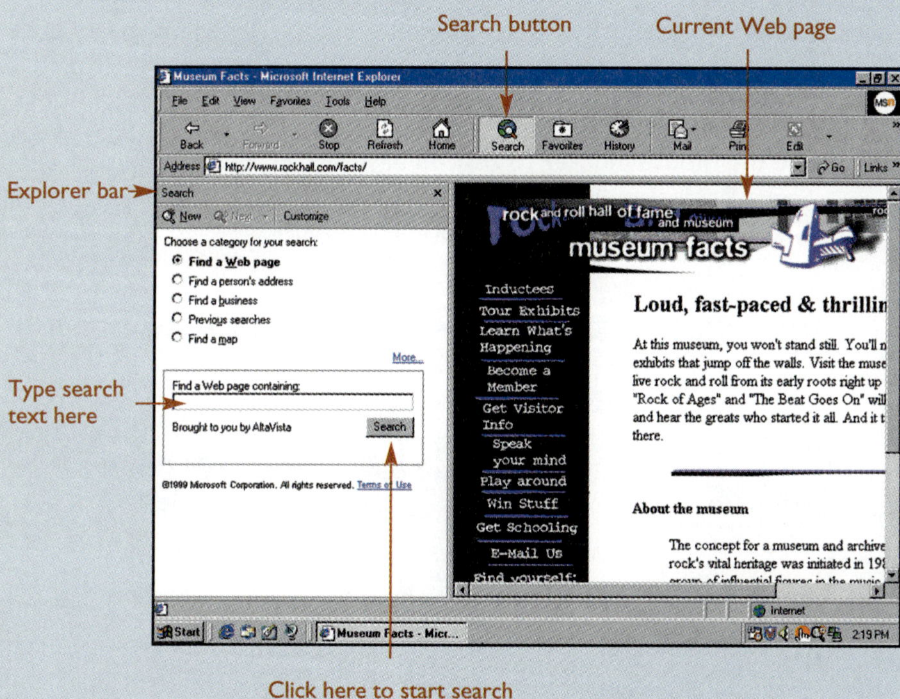

Figure 8.8
A search engine opened in the Explorer bar.

Search Engines
There are numerous search engines available on the Internet. Some are general search engines designed to search the entire Internet for any page that mentions the keyword or phrase that you enter. Others are tailored to search certain servers for specific categories, industries, or content. Some of the general search engines available include AltaVista, Yahoo!, Excite, and HotBot.

If you want to use a different search engine than the one displayed when you click the Search button in the Internet Explorer toolbar, you can type its URL in the Address bar. For example, AltaVista is the search engine used in the figures for the book. To use the AltaVista search engine, type `www.Altavista.com` in the Address bar, and then press ↵Enter. Internet Explorer will display the AltaVista search page in the full window instead of in the Explorer bar.

continues ▶

To Navigate a Web Site and Search the Internet (continued)

7 In the search text box, type `The Titanic`, and then click the Search button.

The search engine starts looking for pages that contain the text you entered in the search box. It compiles a list and displays the first set of matches onscreen, along with a Next button, which you can click to show the next set of matches (refer to Figure 8.9). It also displays the number of total matches found, which can be overwhelming. Notice that in Figure 8.9, 543,870 matches were found!

The items listed in the search frame may not match the items displayed in Figure 8.9, even if you are using the same search engine. The Internet changes frequently; there is no guarantee that a site you visit one day will be there the next, let alone that it will contain the same information. If the links used in this lesson do not display in the first list of matches, click the Next button to see if you can locate them. If you cannot find the same links, simply select a different site.

8 Move the mouse pointer to rest on any item in the search list.

A ScreenTip displays information about the hyperlink target (see Figure 8.9). This information can help you decide whether you want to go to that site or not.

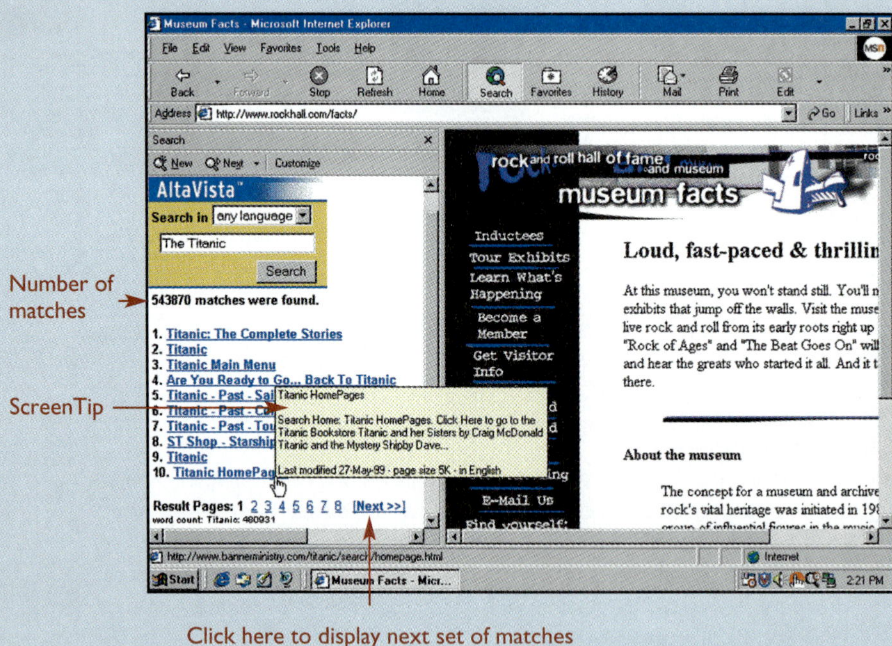

Figure 8.9
The search results.

9 Click the link to `RMS Titanic, Inc. Titanic Gallery Main Hall.`

Internet Explorer displays the page in the right frame of the window, leaving the search list displayed in the Exlporer bar. If you don't like the page, you can select a different one from the search list or start a new search.

You may have to scroll down the list of links in the Explorer bar to locate the link you need. If you still don't see it, click the Next button. It may be in the next set of matches.

10. **Click the link to `Encyclopedia Smithsonian: The Titanic.`**
Internet Explorer displays the page in the right frame of the window, replacing the previously displayed page.

11. **Click the Search button on the Internet Explorer toolbar.**
Internet Explorer closes the Explorer bar and expands the current Web page to fill the window. Leave Internet Explorer running with the Titanic page displayed to use in the next lesson, in which you learn how to print a Web page.

Lesson 5: Printing a Web Page

To preserve information that you locate on the Internet for future reference, you can print the Web page. For example, you may want to print a recipe you located online, or directions to a hotel where you'll stay while traveling on business. Printing a Web page is very similar to printing any document (refer to Project 7, Lesson 4, "Printing a File").

In this lesson, you learn how to print a Web page. Before you start, you should make sure that your printer is online and loaded with paper.

To Print a Web Page

1. **Click the picture of the Titanic on the Web page.**
Internet Explorer displays the hyperlink target, which is a black and white photographic image of the ship. Remember that graphics can be hyperlinks, too.

2. **Click the Print button on the Internet Explorer toolbar.**
Internet Explorer prints a copy of the current page.

3. **Click the Back button on the Internet Explorer toolbar.**
Internet Explorer displays the previous page. Try printing more than one copy of the displayed page.

4. **Click File, Print.**
The Print dialog box displays, as shown in Figure 8.10.

5. **Type `2` in the Number of copies text box.**
This tells Internet Explorer that you want to print two copies of the current page. You could set other print options in the Print dialog box, too. For example, you can select to print all pages that are linked to the current page.

6. **Click OK.**
Internet Explorer prints two copies of the page. Leave Internet Explorer open. In the next lesson, you learn how to close Internet Explorer and disconnect from the Internet.

continues ▶

To Print a Web Page (continued)

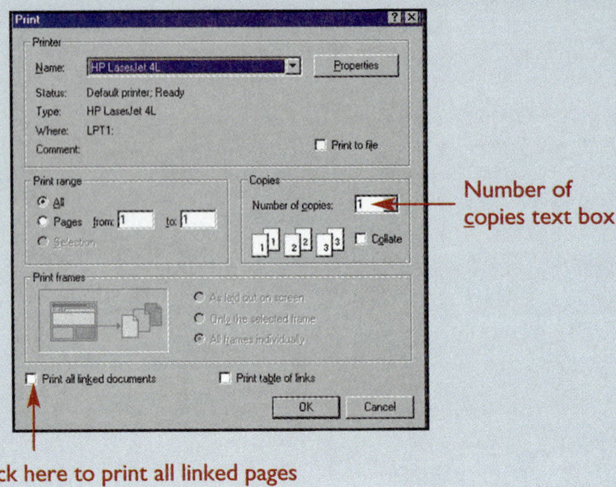

Figure 8.10
The Print dialog box.

Saving a Web Page
You can also save a Web page as a document on your PC. Use the File, Save As command as you learned in Project 7, Lesson 1, "Using a Windows Application." By default, the file is saved in HTML format. You can open it with any application that supports HTML, including Internet Explorer or Microsoft Word (versions 97 and 2000).

Lesson 6: Disconnecting from the Internet

When you complete your session on the Internet, you can disconnect. Reasons for disconnecting include the following:

- You have a limited amount of access time, which would be wasted by leaving the modem online.
- You may incur additional charges if you stay connected for too long.
- Unless you have a phone line dedicated to your modem for Internet access, staying online means that you cannot receive incoming calls.

In this lesson, you learn how to close Internet Explorer and disconnect from the Internet.

To Disconnect from the Internet

1 Click File, Close.

This closes Internet Explorer; however, your modem is still online. A dialog box similar to the one shown in Figure 8.11 displays. You must disconnect to end the session.

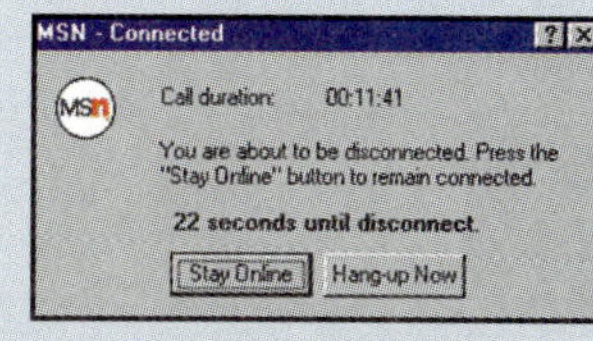

Figure 8.11
The Microsoft Network's Connected dialog box.

2 Click Hang-up Now.

Your modem disconnects from your ISP, ending the session. Your ISP may have a different button for disconnecting.

If you do not see a dialog box asking if you want to hang up, you still have to be sure to disconnect. Otherwise, your computer remains online, using connect time and possibly incurring additional charges. To disconnect directly from Windows, right-click the network icon in the systray area and click Disconnect on the shortcut menu (see Figure 8.12).

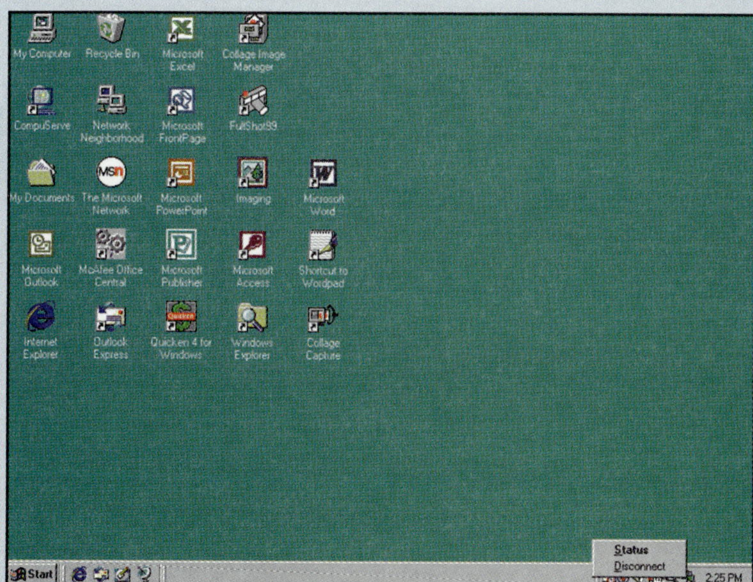

Figure 8.12
Use the network shortcut menu to disconnect from the Internet.

Summary

In this lesson, you learned the basics of using Internet Explorer to access the Internet. You learned about the Internet and how to establish Internet access. You started Internet Explorer and learned how to enter an Internet address to display a specific Web page. You also learned how to navigate through a Web site and how to use a search engine to locate information when you don't know a specific site's address. Finally, you learned how to print information off the Internet and how to disconnect from the Internet.

Take a few minutes to check your skills and to complete some of the Skill Drill and Challenge exercises.

Checking Concepts and Terms

True/False

For each of the following, check *T* or *F* to indicate whether the statement is true or false.

__T __F **1.** The Internet and the World Wide Web are the same thing. [L1]

__T __F **2.** Most Web browsers support HTML. [L1]

__T __F **3.** Internet Explorer is the only Web browser that works with Windows. [L3]

__T __F **4.** You need to remember your ISP password because you may have to submit it when you purchase merchandise online. [L2]

__T __F **5.** The Forward button is not displayed on the Internet Explorer toolbar until you click the Back button. [L3]

__T __F **6.** AltaVista is the only search engine available for searching the Internet. [L3]

__T __F **7.** You cannot print the graphics images displayed on a Web page. [L4]

__T __F **8.** As soon as you close Internet Explorer, your modem disconnects from the Internet. [L5]

__T __F **9.** The Favorites folder is created when you install Windows. [L3].

__T __F **10.** You can send email only to someone who uses the same ISP as yours. [L1]

Multiple Choice

Circle the letter of the correct answer for each of the following.

1. What do you need before you can log in to the Internet? [L2]

a. an email address

b. an account with an ISP

c. a home page

d. cable television

2. What is the name of the protocol used to transmit data on the Web? [L1]

a. URL

b. WWW

c. HTTP

d. HRPL

3. What is the main page of a Web site called? [L3]

a. main page

b. first page

c. title page

d. home page

4. What is the abbreviation for an Internet address? [L3]

a. URL

b. DUK

c. ADD

d. HTM

5. Which folder should you use to store the addresses of sites you visit frequently? [L3]

a. History

b. Favorites

c. Frequents

d. Best

6. What does the mouse pointer look like when it rests on a hyperlink? [L3]

a. arrow

b. palm of a hand

c. hand with a pointing finger

d. question mark

7. What type of Web site can you use to locate information on the Internet? [L3]

a. search engine

b. chat room

c. home page

d. email address

8. Where on the desktop can you find a network icon? [L5]

a. scrollbar

b. menu bar

c. Start menu

d. systray

9. What do you call a group of linked Web pages? [L3]

a. search engine

b. ISP

c. Web site

d. Web browser

10. What type of software do you use to access, locate, and display Web pages? [L1]

a. Web browser

b. word processor

c. operating system

d. utility

Screen ID

Label each of the following elements shown in Figure 8.13.

Figure 8.13

A Current Web page

B Index of links

C Forward button

D Address of current Web page

E Back button

F Network icon

G Scrollbar

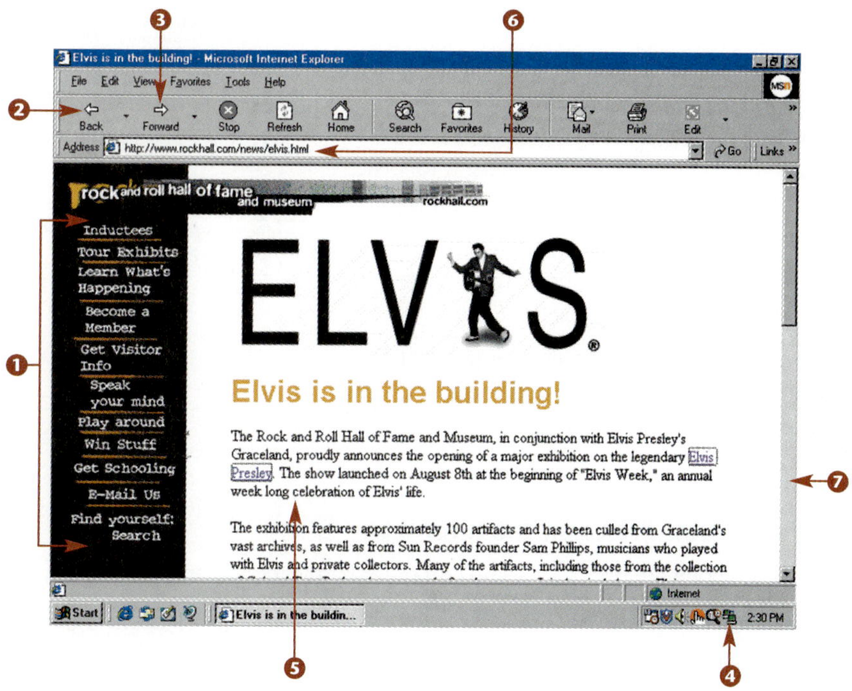

1. ______________ **4.** ______________ **6.** ______________

2. ______________ **5.** ______________ **7.** ______________

3. ______________

Discussion Questions

1. The Internet is one of the most exciting technologies to develop in the past decade, capturing the imagination of people from all walks of life. What are some reasons for its popularity?

2. One activity that is gaining in popularity on the Internet is shopping. What are the pros and cons of online shopping?

3. The Internet is changing the way some companies do business. Can you think of ways that the Internet can help companies increase business? How about businesses that might be hurt by the Internet?

Skill Drill

Skill Drill exercises reinforce project skills. Each skill reinforced is the same, or nearly the same, as a skill presented in the project. Detailed instructions are provided in a step-by-step format.

Because information on the Internet changes all the time, the links used in the two Skill Drill exercises may not be available. You can use different links.

1. Using Windows to Access Help on the Internet

To use Windows to access Help on the Internet, follow these steps:

1. Start your PC.
2. Click the Start button.
3. Click Help.
4. Click the Web Help button on the Help toolbar.
5. Click the Support Online hyperlink at the bottom of the Web Help help page.

   Internet Explorer starts, logs in to your ISP, and displays the Highlights for Windows 98 Web page, which is part of Microsoft's Personal Online Support Web site. You can use the links in this site to locate information about Microsoft products, including Windows and Internet Explorer.
6. Click the Frequently Asked Questions link in the Index on the left side of the window.
7. Click the Select a Microsoft consumer product drop-down arrow, and then click Internet Explorer 5 (you have to scroll down the list to get to it)
8. Click the Go button.

   Internet Explorer displays the home page.
9. Click the Browsing link.

   Internet Explorer displays a list of questions.
10. Click the question `I receive the error "Internet Explorer could not open the search page." Why?`
11. Print the page that displays.
12. Click the Back button.
13. Click the Forward button.
14. Close Internet Explorer.
15. Disconnect from the Internet.

2. Locating Computer Prices on the Internet

In this exercise, you compare prices for some computer hardware you are dying to buy.

1. Start your PC.
2. Double-click the Internet Explorer icon on your desktop.

   Internet Explorer starts and displays the page you have designated as the home page in your Internet Properties dialog box. If necessary, it logs in to your ISP first.
3. In the Address bar, type `http://cnet.com`.
4. Press ←Enter.

   Internet Explorer locates and displays the home page for CNET.COM, a Web site that offers products and information about computer and technology.
5. Scroll down the page.
6. Click the Hardware link.

   Internet Explorer displays the target page.
7. Click the Compare Prices link in the Index across the top of the page (it's on the right).

   Internet Explorer displays the target page.
8. Under the Computer Systems heading, click the Top Ten link.

   Internet Explorer displays the target page, listing the top ten best-selling systems.

9. Click the first system in the list.

   Internet Explorer displays the target page that includes a table of retail outlets and prices for the selected system.

10. Print the page.
11. Close Internet Explorer.
12. Disconnect from the Internet.

Challenge

Challenge exercises expand on or are somewhat related to skills presented in the lessons. Each exercise provides a brief narrative introduction, followed by instructions in a numbered-step format. The steps are not as detailed as those in the Skill Drill section.

1. Using a Search Engine to Research a Topic

You can research any topic on the Internet. This is useful for many reasons, including preparing reports for business or school, finding product prices, locating real estate, or checking the weather if you are traveling. Try using a search engine to locate information about a topic that interests you.

1. Start Internet Explorer and open a search engine.
2. Type a key word in the search text box.

   For example, if you want to research elephants, type `elephants` in the text box.
3. Explore some of the pages displayed in the Search Results list.
4. If you like a site, try adding it to your Favorites folder.
5. If you find a page with useful information, print it.
6. When you finish, close Internet Explorer and disconnect from the Internet.
7. Close all open applications before shutting down Windows.

2. Getting Information About Microsoft Products and Services Online

Microsoft maintains a vast amount of information and technical support for its products on the Internet. You can start at the Microsoft home page and explore from there, or go directly to the page for a specific product or problem.

1. Start Internet Explorer.
2. Go to the site `http://www.Microsoft.com`.
3. Explore the links available from Microsoft's home page.
4. Try to locate information about Windows.
5. Try to locate information about Microsoft Network, the online service.
6. If you find a page that provides useful information, add it to your Favorites folder.
7. When you finish, close Internet Explorer and disconnect from the Internet.

Project 9

Project 9

Getting Started with PC Applications

Objectives

In this project, you learn how to

- **Identify Features of a Word Processing Application**
- **Identify Features of a Spreadsheet Application**
- **Identify Features of a Database Application**
- **Identify Features of a Graphics Application**
- **Identify Features of a Desktop Publishing Application**
- **Identify Other Types of Applications**
- **Choose Applications**
- **Install Software**

Key terms introduced in this project include

- database applications
- desktop publishing applications
- financial applications
- install
- integrated applications
- multimedia applications
- presentation applications
- software
- spreadsheet applications
- utilities

Why Would I Do This?

The only way to benefit from having a computer is to run ***software*** on it. Software is the coded instructions that run on your PC and tell the hardware how to process information. Without software, your computer is just a hunk of expensive metal and plastic, taking up valuable desk space. Think of your PC as a stereo system and software as a CD. No matter how fancy the stereo is, it can't play music until you insert the CD into it.

Some software comes with your PC. For example, Windows is usually installed before you bring your computer home. The software applications that you use to accomplish most of your work don't come with the PC. You must purchase them separately, and then ***install*** the programs. Installing sets up the software to run on your computer so you can use it.

In this project, you learn about the most common types of applications available and how to decide which programs will work best for you. You also learn how to install software on your PC.

Lesson 1: Identifying the Features of a Word Processing Application

You use a word processing application to enter, edit, arrange, and print text. You can also use this type of program to create memos, letters, reports, and any other text-based document. In this lesson, you learn what features to look for in a word processing application.

- **A word processing application is like a computerized typewriter.**

  You benefit from using a word processing application if you spend a lot of time typing, sending out bulk mailings, or preparing documents of any kind.

- **Word processing applications come in different levels of sophistication.**

  Some word processing applications, such as NotePad, one of the Windows 98 accessory applications, provide only very basic text entry and editing capabilities (see Figure 9.1).

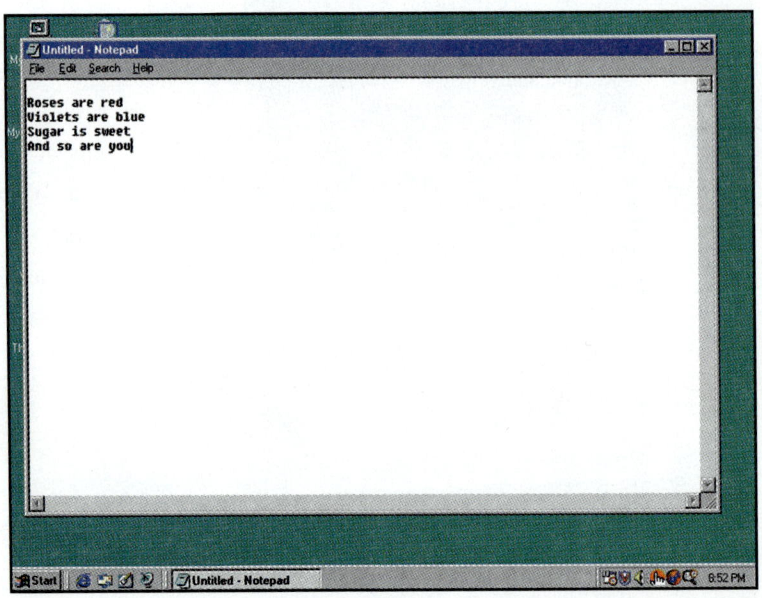

Figure 9.1
You can use NotePad to create simple word processing documents.

Some word processing applications are quite complex. You can use them to format and design newsletters, brochures, and other materials that incorporate graphics, drawings, tables, and charts. Some word processing applications include features for managing long documents, such as indexing and automatic creation of tables of contents. Microsoft Word, Lotus Word Pro, and Corel WordPerfect are three examples of a more complex word processing application (see Figure 9.2). Table 9.1 describes some common features of word processing applications.

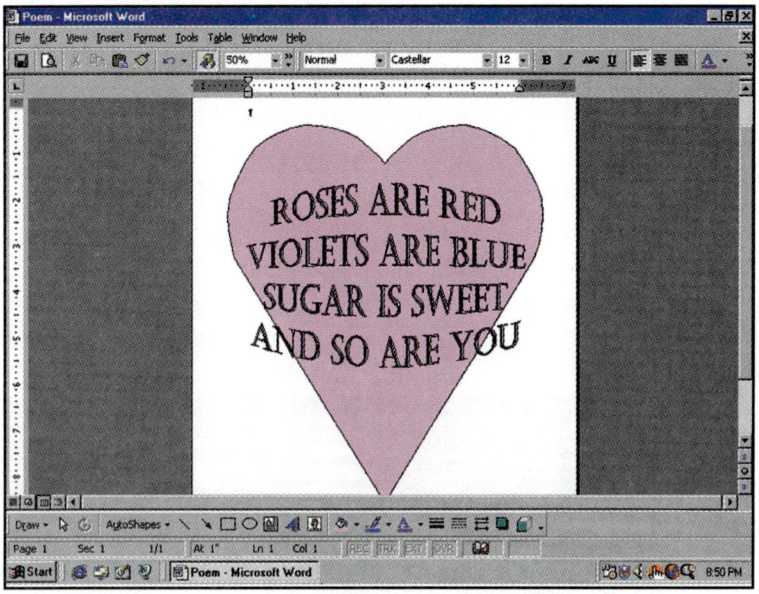

Figure 9.2
With Microsoft Word, you can create complex word processing documents.

Table 9.1. Word Processing Features

Feature	Purpose
Word wrap	To automatically wrap text from the end of one line to the beginning of the next line.
Copy and move	To easily rearrange text in a document.
Search and replace	To easily find a word or phrase in a document, and to replace it with another word or phrase, if necessary.
Formatting	To enhance the appearance of a document by changing typefaces, adding visual effects such as boldface or italics, and positioning text on the page.
WYSIWYG editing	To display a document on the computer screen exactly as it will print on paper. (WYSIWYG stands for "What You See Is What You Get.")
Spelling checker	To examine the text in a document for spelling errors.
Grammar checker	To examine the text in a document for grammatical errors.
Merge	To combine two documents to create a single document. Usually used for combining a mailing list and a form letter to create a mass mailing.
Outlining	To organize a document by creating an outline.
Tables	To organize information in columns and rows.
Graphics	To enhance a document with pictures, drawings, and photographs.

Lesson 2: Identifying Features of a Spreadsheet Application

Spreadsheet applications enable you to manipulate numbers and compute mathematical equations. You can use this type of application to set up budgets, prepare long-range forecasts, and create other financial reports. In this lesson, you learn what features to look for in a spreadsheet application.

- **You can add, subtract, multiply, divide, and perform advanced calculations on numbers entered in a spreadsheet.**

  You benefit from using a spreadsheet if you spend a great deal of time using a calculator or an adding machine, preparing financial reports, or creating tables and charts of any kind.

- **Spreadsheets come in different levels of sophistication.**

  Some spreadsheets provide basic mathematical capabilities; others include complex functions, what-if analyses, and charting capabilities. Microsoft Excel and Lotus 1-2-3 are two examples of complex spreadsheets (see Figure 9.3). Table 9.2 describes some common features of spreadsheet applications.

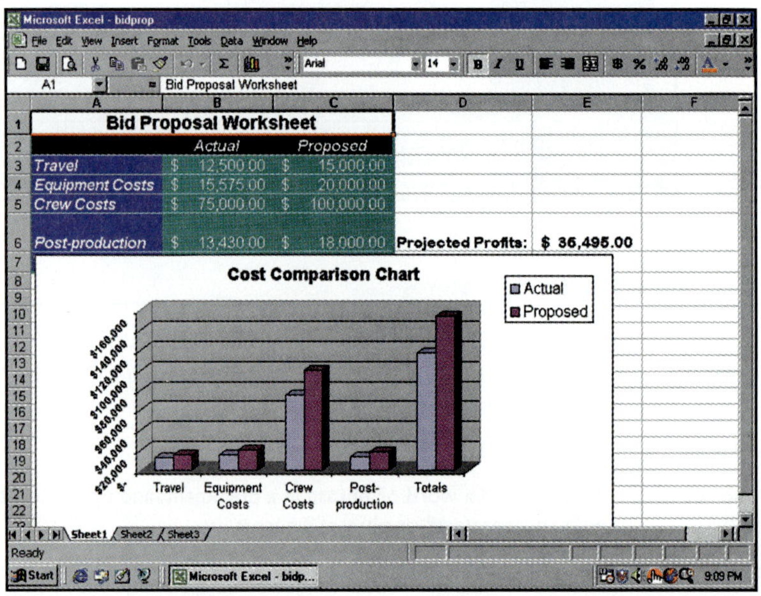

Figure 9.3
Microsoft Excel provides sophisticated spreadsheet capabilities.

Table 9.2. Spreadsheet Application Features

Feature	Purpose
Formulas	To set up and perform calculations on data that has been entered in a spreadsheet.
Built-in functions	To automatically enter commonly used formulas, such as totaling a column of numbers or calculating a loan payment.
Automatic updating	To automatically update calculations when data in the spreadsheet changes.
What-if analyses	To calculate the possible results of different scenarios, such as what would happen to profits if the product price were raised by 10 percent.
Graphing and charting	To create a visual image to depict trends and relationships between numbers.
Formatting	To automatically display numbers as currency, dates, or percentages; and to improve the appearance of a printed spreadsheet by adding effects such as boldface and italics, as well as borders and shading.

Lesson 3: Identifying Features of a Database Application

Database applications enable you to store, track, and manage records of any kind of information. Most databases have two parts—one part is like a giant rotary file file that you can fill with electronic index cards. The other part is like a research assistant you can tell to search through the records to sort them and generate reports about them.

In this lesson, you learn what features to look for in a database application.

- **You can use a database application to collect, organize, and analyze any information (for example, mailing lists, recipes, employees, and CD titles).**

  You benefit from using a database application if you keep records of any kind, and if you use records to assemble lists or reports.

- **Database applications come in different levels of sophistication.**

  Some database applications are straightforward and easy to use, yet they provide strong data management and analysis capabilities. Some database applications are very difficult to use and rival programming languages in their complexity. Microsoft Access, Lotus Approach, and Filemaker Pro are some examples of common database applications (see Figure 9.4). Table 9.3 describes typical database application features.

Figure 9.4
Databases such as Access let you store data in many file formats, including photos, sounds, and videos, as well as text.

Table 9.3. Database Application Features

Feature	Purpose
Search	To scan through records to find the information you need.
Sort	To organize and arrange the records so that you can find the information you need.
Forms	To enter and edit data, one record at a time.
Query functions	To instruct the database to display only the specified information.
Reports	To generate printed records of database information.
Relational capabilities	To combine, or relate, data from one file with data from another file.
Formatting	To enhance the appearance of a database file onscreen, or to enhance data in a printed report.

Lesson 4: Identifying Features of a Graphics Application

Graphics applications enable you to create artwork that you can print or incorporate in other applications. In this lesson, you learn what features to look for in a graphics application.

- **You can use graphics applications to create and edit images such as logos for stationery.**

  You benefit from using a graphics application if you want to improve the appearance of documents by adding pictures, if you create artwork for reproduction on any medium, if you design models, or if you want to create animated effects.

- **Different kinds of graphics applications have different purposes.**

  You can use clip art applications to insert predrawn artwork into any document. Draw and paint applications let you create your own artwork. Computer-aided design (CAD) applications enable you to create detailed images, such as schematics and blueprints. Photo editing applications let you edit scanned photographs. Microsoft Draw, Corel Graphics II, Lotus Freelance Graphics, Software Publishing's Harvard Graphics, and Kodak Imaging are examples of graphics applications (see Figure 9.5). Table 9.4 describes some features to look for in graphics applications.

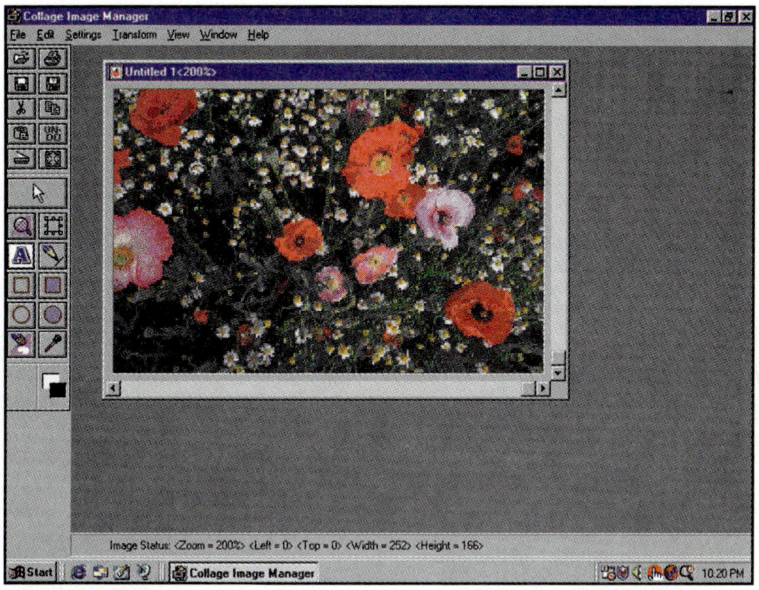

Figure 9.5
You use graphics applications to generate and edit images and pictures.

Table 9.4 Graphics Application Features

Feature	Purpose
Drawing tools	To create different effects in an image, such as adding geometric or freeform shapes, rotating objects, or incorporating text.
Editing	To change or modify an existing or original image.
Three-dimensional imaging	To display an image onscreen from different angles.
Compatibility	To share data with other applications, such as word processing applications, spreadsheet applications, or database applications.

Lesson 5: Identifying Features of a Desktop Publishing Application

Desktop publishing applications generally combine data from other applications, such as text from a word processing application and artwork from a graphics application, to create professional documents that you can print for distribution. In this lesson, you learn what features to look for in a desktop publishing application.

- **Desktop publishing applications are used to create documents, such as newsletters, reports, books, and annual reports, which require sophisticated page layout.**

  You benefit from using a desktop publishing application if you produce any kind of document for reprinting or publication, if you want to incorporate graphics into your documents, or if you find word processing applications too limited in their page layout and document-design features. Adobe PageMaker, Microsoft Publisher, QuarkXpress, and Corel Ventura are examples of desktop publishing applications (see Figure 9.6). Table 9.5 describes some common features of desktop publishing applications.

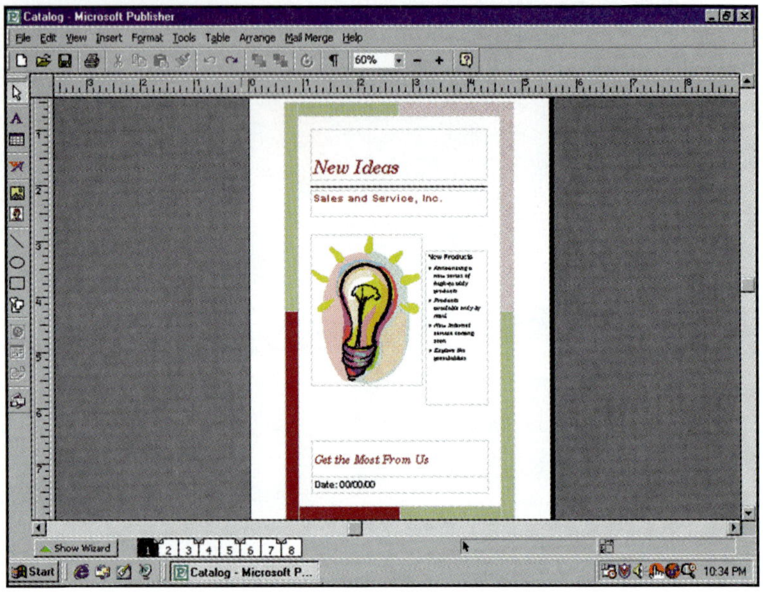

Figure 9.6
You can create printer-ready documents with desktop publishing applications.

Table 9.5 Desktop Publishing Features

Feature	Purpose
Page formatting	To set margins, headers, footers, columns, and other page layout characteristics.
Template	To save a page design for use in other documents.
Text editing	To make changes to text and to add visual enhancements to text, such as boldface and italics.
Graphics	To create and edit artwork, and to position images on a page.
Font	To enhance the appearance of text on a page by changing the typeface style.

Lesson 6: Identifying Other Types of Applications

Application software programs exist for almost every imaginable purpose on earth. If you can think of it, someone has probably written a program for it. The following list provides additional types of software applications:

- ***Financial applications***, such as Intuit Quicken and Microsoft Money enable users to track home and small business finances, prepare tax returns, balance checkbooks, and set up budgets (see Figure 9.7).

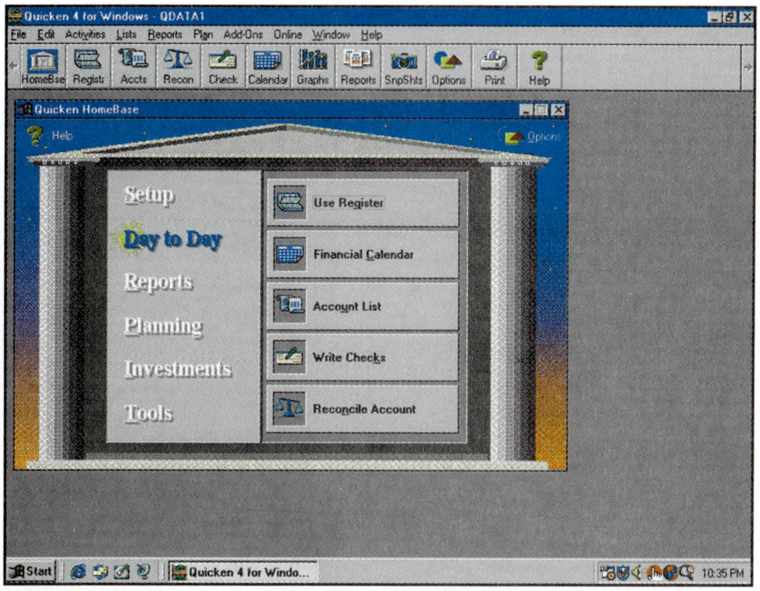

Figure 9.7
Quicken is a popular home finance application.

- Games provide entertainment.
- Educational applications teach all subjects, at all levels, from preschool ABCs to to typing to foreign languages to how to play chess or golf.
- ***Multimedia applications***, such as Microsoft Encarta, incorporate text, sound, and graphics for a variety of applications, including education and games (see Figure 9.8). They require a computer equipped for multimedia, which usually includes a CD drive for running the applications, and a sound board and speakers for outputting the sound portion of the applications.
- Communications applications enable you to communicate with other computers, online services, bulletin boards, and the Internet via a modem and a telephone line. Communications applications control the way data is transmitted and received between computers.

Communications Software and Online Services
It's important to note that online services and the Internet are not technically applications. They are services that you can access using your computer, a modem, and a communications application. Often, however, when you subscribe to an online service such as CompuServe or America Online, you are provided with a communications application that is specifically designed to connect to that service.

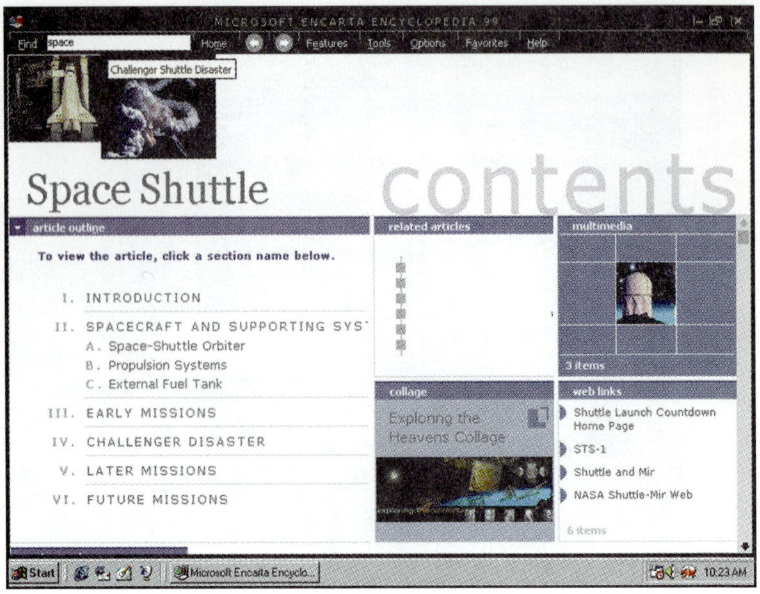

Figure 9.8
Multimedia applications incorporate text, sound, video, and graphics.

- ***Presentation applications*** enable you to create slides using text and graphics. You can run the slides as a slide show, or print them on overhead transparencies or other media. Microsoft PowerPoint is an example of a presentation application.
- Electronic mail, or email, lets you send public or private messages to other computer users on a network, an online service, or a bulletin board. You can also transmit files and documents by attaching them to email messages. Email support may be built into communications software, or built into other applications designed for use on a network.
- Internet browser applications such as Internet Explorer and Netscape Navigator provide features for accessing the Internet and locating online information.
- Web site design applications are used to design, create, and manage Web pages and Web sites. Microsoft FrontPage is an example of a Web site design application.
- ***Integrated applications***, or suites, combine more than one application into one product. Most include a word processing application, a spreadsheet, and a database, and may include other applications as well. Microsoft Works, Microsoft Office, and Lotus SmartSuite are examples of integrated applications.
- ***Utilities*** help make your computer and your applications more efficient. Some come built into your operating system or into Windows; and you can purchase thousands of utilities separately. Some of the functions of utilities are to help manage memory, back up data files, check for software viruses that can damage your computer, help you manage your files more efficiently, and recover or restore damaged files. PC Tools, Norton Utilities, and McAfee Office are examples of utility packages.

Lesson 7: Choosing Applications

You should take the time to decide which software programs you will need. Make sure that you consider the tasks you will use the application for, as well as what kind of computer the application will run on.

The single biggest mistake you can make is to purchase an application that doesn't perform to its full potential, or even run at all, on your computer. The following is a list of steps you can take to help determine what kind of applications you should purchase:

- Make a list of the things you want to do with your computer.
- Make a list of the things you might want to do in the future.
- Plan a budget—software can be expensive.
- Shop around. Read ads, visit stores, surf the Web, and talk to friends about the applications they use.

The following list provides other factors to consider when you are ready to purchase software applications:

- Check the system requirements on the back of the software package.
- Make sure that the software is compatible with the microprocessor you have in your computer.
- Make sure that you have enough memory on your computer to run the application effectively.
- Make sure that you have a large enough disk drive to run the application.
- If the program comes on a floppy disk(s) or CD, make sure that you have the correct drive to run it.
- Make sure that the application runs under the operating system you have on your computer. If you have a PC running Windows, but you buy software for an Apple Macintosh, you're out of luck.
- If the application requires a mouse, make sure that you have a mouse.

After you purchase an application, send in the registration card immediately. Becoming a registered user ensures you certain rights, including access to upgrades and improvements, as well as access to technical support from the manufacturer.

Lesson 8: Installing Software

You can't use a software application until you install it on your computer. You can't just put the original program disk into a disk drive and start the program, and you can't just copy the data from the program disk onto your hard drive and start the program. Often, program files are compressed on the program disks and are decompressed during installation.

This lesson provides some basic guidelines for installing a Windows-based application on a PC.

To Install Software

1. **Read the instructions carefully before you start.**
   Most programs come on CDs, although some may come on floppy disks. They all include information about how to correctly install the program.

continues ▶

To Install Software (continued)

Buying the Right Software
Read the box to make sure that you purchased the correct software for your computer before you remove the wrapping from the package. Check the system requirements to be sure that you will be able to install the software on your PC. Most retailers do not take software back if the package has been opened.

2. **Start your PC.**
   You must install Windows applications with Windows running.

3. **Insert the CD labeled Disc #1 or Setup in your CD drive.**
   Most software setup programs will start automatically when you insert the Setup CD. If it does, skip to Step 7; if it doesn't, continue with Step 4.

   Many applications come with more than one disc and you must start with Disk #1: the Setup disc. The installation program prompts you about when to insert the next disc until the entire program has been installed. This can take anywhere from a few minutes to almost an hour, depending on the size of the application program.

Installing from Floppy Disks
If an application comes on floppy disks, make copies of each of the original program disks before installing the software.

If you use the original disks to install the program, you run the risk of damaging the disks. You should copy the disks and use the copies to install the program. Keep all original disks in a safe location.When you are ready to begin, insert Disk #1 into your floppy drive A. Most applications that come on floppy disks have many disks, and you must start with Disk #1. As with CDs, Disk #1 may be labeled Setup. You will have to swap disks in and out of the disk drive until the entire program is installed.

4. **Open the Start menu, click the Settings command, and choose Control Panel from the nested Settings menu.**
   The Control Panel window opens.

5. **Double-click the Add/Remove Programs icon.**
   The Add/Remove Programs Properties dialog box is displayed, as shown in Figure 9.9.

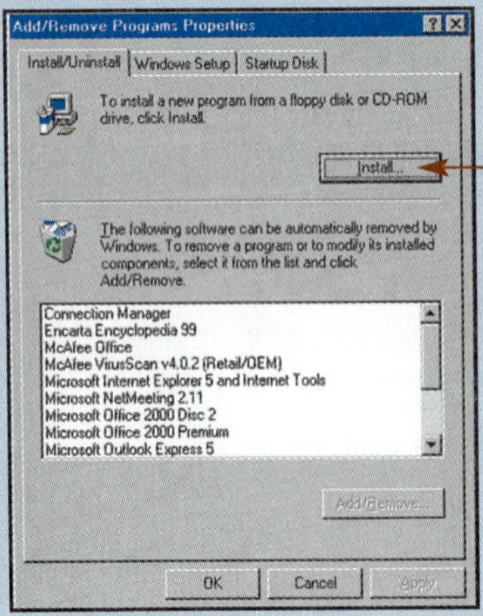

Figure 9.9
The Add/Remove Programs Properties dialog box.

6 Click the Install button near the top of the dialog box.
This starts the installation utility program that comes with Windows.

7 Click Next and follow the instructions that appear in the dialog box until the installation is complete.
When you finish, you can start the application. Read the user's guide to find out how.

If you have completed your session on the computer, close all applications and shut down Windows before shutting off your computer. You may also keep your computer running to finish the end-of-chapter exercises.

Entering Information During Installation
During installation, you will probably have to type in certain information, such as your name and product authorization numbers. You may also have to select certain options, such as in which directory or program group you want to install the program.

Remember, it's illegal to install software that you obtain from an unauthorized source—including friends and coworkers.

Summary

In this final project, you learned about the software applications that make your computer more than just a pile of plastic and metal. You had the opportunity to read about different ways you can use software, and you discovered the different features to look for in a program. Finally, you learned how to install new software on your computer.

Take a few minutes to check your skills and to complete some of the Skill Drill and Challenge exercises.

Checking Concepts and Terms

True/False

For each of the following, check *T* or *F* to indicate whether the statement is true or false.

__T __F **1.** WordPad is a word processing application that comes with Windows. [L1]

__T __F **2.** You can install a software program only by using a floppy disk that fits into drive A. [L8]

__T __F **3.** An application with a merge feature is suitable for creating mass mailings. [L1]

__T __F **4.** It is illegal to install software that you obtain from an unauthorized source. [L8]

__T __F **5.** Most software retailers will not accept a returned software package if it has been opened. [L8]

__T __F **6.** WYSIWYG editing means you can see on your screen the way a document will appear when printed. [L1]

__T __F **7.** You must never make copies of original software disks. [L8]

__T __F **8.** Most software setup programs will start automatically when you insert the program CD. [L8]

__T __F **9.** The easiest way to install an application is to just copy the data from the program disk onto your hard drive. [L8]

__T __F **10.** Integrated applications combine more than one program into one product. [L6]

Multiple Choice

Circle the letter of the correct answer for each of the following.

1. Which type of application would be useful for creating original artwork to transfer onto T-shirts? [L4]

a. word processing

b. spreadsheet

c. graphics

d. communications

2. If you are the membership coordinator for a club or association, which type of software would be best suited for storing information about members? [L3]

a. desktop publishing

b. database

c. communications

d. financial

3. If you often need to prepare monthly expense reports, which type of application should you use? [L2]

a. word processing

b. communications

c. spreadsheet

d. graphics

4. Which type of application should you buy if you spend a great deal of time typing reports and papers? [L1]

a. graphics

b. spreadsheet

c. word processing

d. desktop publishing

5. Which type of application should you use to prepare an advertising brochure? [L5]

a. communications

b. spreadsheet

c. database

d. desktop publishing

6. What type of database can combine associated data between files? [L4]

a. integrated

b. multimedia

c. relational

d. graphical

7. Which of the following steps can help you determine what kind of applications you should purchase? [L7]

a. Shop around.

b. Surf the Web.

c. Talk to friends.

d. all of the above

8. Which of the following is an important factor to consider when you are ready to purchase a software application? [L7]

a. Is it compatible with your electrical source?

b. What are the memory requirements?

c. How much time does it take to install?

d. Will it fit on your desktop?

9. In which folder will you find the Add/Remove Programs icon? [L8]

a. Accessories

b. My Computer

c. Control Panel

d. Windows

10. Which of the following information are you likely to be prompted to enter during software installation? [L8]

a. your home address

b. a product authorization number

c. the name of the store where you purchased the software

d. the name of the manufacturer of your monitor

Discussion Questions

1. There are thousands of different applications available. Which applications do you think are the most popular, and why? Are the most popular applications also the most useful?
2. Do you think you can install an unlimited number of software applications? What are some aspects of your computer system that might limit the number or type of applications you can install?
3. If you could have only one type of application installed on your computer, which would it be? Why?

Skill Drill

Skill Drill exercises reinforce project skills. Each skill reinforced is the same, or nearly the same, as a skill presented in the project. Detailed instructions are provided in a step-by-step format.

1. Compiling a Wish List of Application

To compile a wish list of applications, follow these steps:

1. Write down the types of tasks you want to accomplish using your computer.
2. Write down the types of applications you could use to accomplish those tasks.
3. Shop around for pricing information about the different applications.
4. Look for information about specific products, including product reviews, advertisements, and sales promotions.
5. Set up a budget to determine which applications you can buy now and which you can buy in the future.

2. Installing Software

To install software, follow these steps:

If you do not have a new software application to install on your PC, see whether you can locate installation instructions for software that you already have installed. Instead of installing the software, read the instructions.

1. Start your computer.
2. Decide which drive you will be using to install the software.
3. Insert Disc #1 into the drive.
4. Open Control Panel and use the Install/Remove Programs utility to add the software.
5. When the installation is complete, put the program disc(s) away in a safe place.

Challenge

Challenge exercises expand on or are somewhat related to skills presented in the lessons. Each exercise provides a brief narrative introduction, followed by instructions in a numbered-step format. The steps are not as detailed as those in the Skill Drill section.

1. Make Software Purchasing Decisions

Compile a list of applications that you want to own; then research the cost, system requirements, and other pertinent information.

1. Write down the tasks you need to accomplish with your PC.
2. Write down the type of applications you can use to perform these tasks.
3. Use magazines and contact retail outlets to determine the brand names of applications you might want to buy.
4. If you have access to the Internet, look up feature lists for each application online, so you can compare the different products.
5. Don't forget to check compatibility and system requirements to make sure your computer can handle the applications.

2. Setting Up a Budget for Purchasing Applications

Make a purchasing plan for the next three months that takes into consideration the applications you need, the importance of each task, and whether the hardware you have already planned to acquire will meet the system requirements needed to run the selected applications.

1. Using the list you compiled in the previous exercise, prioritize the applications in order of importance.
2. Research pricing information for the applications you decide to purchase.
3. Set up a budget for the next three months, setting spending limits for both hardware and software.

Task Guide

A book in the *Essentials* series is designed to be kept as a handy reference beside your computer, even after you complete all the projects and exercises. Any time you have difficulty recalling the sequence of steps or a shortcut needed to achieve a result, look up the general category in the following alphabetized list, and then quickly home in on your task at hand. For your convenience, some tasks have been duplicated under more than one category. If you have difficulty performing a task, turn to the page number listed in the third column to locate the step-by-step exercise or other detailed description. If a task does not include a page reference, it is a bonus task from the author that was not within the scope of the book. For the greatest efficiency in using this Task Guide, take a few minutes to familiarize yourself with the main categories and keywords before you begin your search.

To	Do This	Page Number
Windows Operating System		
Display a ScreenTip	Rest the mouse pointer on an element.	56
Move an icon on the desktop	Drag the icon to a new location.	57
Open the Start menu	Click the Start button.	56
Open My Computer	Double-click the My Computer icon.	59
Select a menu command	Click the command.	60
Open a shortcut menu	Right-click an element.	59
Close a window	Click the Close button or press Alt+F4.	57 and 60
Open the Date/Time Properties dialog box	Right-click the time in the Systray. Click Adjust Date/Time.	60
Open the Display Properties dialog box	Right-click the desktop. Click Properties.	64
Start Windows Help	Click the Start button. Choose Help.	68
Select a Help topic	Click the Contents tab. Click a main topic (Book icon). Click the desired subtopic (page icon).	68
Browse the Help index for a topic	Click the Index tab. Type the topic in the text box. Double-click the desired topic.	68
Data Storage		
Format a disk	Insert disk in drive A. Select drive A. Click File, Format. Then click Start. When formatting is finished, click Close.	81

continues ▶

To	Do This	Page Number
Reformat a disk	Insert disk in drive A. Select drive A. Click File, Format. Select Quick option. Click Start. When formatting is finished, click Close.	81
Display the contents of drive or folder	Double-click the My Computer icon. Double-click the drive icon.	84
Change the way icons display	Open the window. Click View. Click desired view option.	84
File/Folder Options		
Create a new folder	Click File, New. Click Folder. Type a new folder name.	88
Create a new file	Click File, New. Click the desired file type. Type a new file name.	92
Move a file or folder	Drag to a new location.	92
Copy a file or folder	Press and hold Ctrl. Drag to a new location.	92
Delete a file or folder	Click the desired item. Press Del. Click Yes.	92
Restore a deleted file	Double-click the Recycle Bin icon. Right-click the desired item. Click Restore.	92
Save a file the first time	Click File, Save As. Type the filename. If necessary, select a new storage location from the Save in drop-down list. Click Save.	92
Save a file again	Click File, Save.	92
Close a file	Click File, Close.	92
PC Memory		
Determine software memory requirements	Read the software package.	103
Determine installed memory	Watch the screen during startup or right-click My Computer; then click Properties. Click the Performance page tab. Click OK.	104
Windows Applications		
Start a Windows accessory	Click the Start button. Choose Programs, Accessories. Click the desired accessory.	110
Save a file the first time	Click File, Save As. Type a filename. If necessary, select a new storage location from the Save in drop-down list. Click Save.	110
Save a file again	Click File, Save.	110
Close a file	Click File, Close.	110
Exit an application	Click File, Exit.	110
Arrange open windows	Right-click the taskbar. Click Tile Horizontally or Tile Vertically, or Cascade.	113
Make a window active	Click the window's taskbar button.	113

To	Do This	Page Number
Create a program shortcut	Open My Computer. Open the folder containing the program file. Drag the program file onto the desktop.	123
The Internet		
Start Internet Explorer	Double-click the Internet Explorer icon on the desktop.	136
Display the contents of the Favorites folder	Click the Favorites button on the Internet Explorer toolbar.	136
Start a search	Click the Search button on the Internet Explorer toolbar.	141
Go to a Web page	Type the URL in the Address page; then press ↵Enter.	141
Use a hyperlink	Click the hyperlink.	141
Display the previous page	Click the Back button on the Internet Explorer toolbar.	141
Display the next page	Click the Forward button on the Internet Explorer toolbar.	141
Print a Web page	Display the Web page; then click the Print button on the Internet Explorer toolbar.	145
Close Internet Explorer	Click File, Close.	146
Disconnect from the Internet	Right-click the Network icon in the Systray. Click Disconnect.	146
Software Installation		
Determine software memory requirements	Read the software package.	163
Install the software	Insert the program CD in the CD drive, or insert program disk #1 in drive A. If Setup does not start automatically, click Start, Settings. Click Control Panel. Double-click the Add/Remove Programs icon. Click Install. Follow the onscreen instructions.	163
Help		
Start Windows Help	Click the Start button. Choose Help.	68
Select a Help topic	Click the Contents tab. Click a main topic (Book icon). Click the desired subtopic (page icon).	68
Browse the Help index for a topic	Click the Index tab. Type the topic in the text box. Double-click the desired topic.	68

Glossary

All key terms appearing in this book (in bold italic) are listed alphabetically in this Glossary for easy reference. If you want to learn more about the feature or concept, turn to the page reference shown after the definition. You can also use the Index to find the term's other significant occurrences.

accessories Software programs used for common tasks, included with the Windows operating system. Also the name of the folder in which the accessory programs are stored. [p. 110]

active Currently in use. [p. 82]

applications A software program designed for a specific purpose, such as a word processing program or an electronic mail program. [p. 53]

back up Copy data from one storage device to another for safekeeping. [p. 78]

bit The smallest unit of computer data. Eight bits equal one byte. [p. 11]

boot The process of starting a computer. The term comes from the expression "to pull yourself up by your bootstraps." [p. 36]

bus The set of wires or conductors that expansion cards and peripherals use to communicate with the CPU. [p. 7]

bytes A measure of the information stored on a disk or in memory. One byte represents one typed character. [p. 7]

cable modem A modem that transfers data over a cable instead of over telephone lines. For example, it may use ISDN, Ethernet, or coaxial cable. [p. 24]

cache memory Additional memory chips, built in to the motherboard, which can boost the PC's processing speed because commonly used instructions that are otherwise stored on disk drives or in RAM can be stored in cache. [p. 103]

cascades Arranges in an evenly overlapping fashion. [p. 116]

CDs (compact discs) Storage devices that are used in CD drives. Some are designated CD-ROM, which means that a PC can read data from them, but cannot write data on them. CDs that can be written on one time as well as read from are designated CD-R. CDs that can be rewritten are called CD-RW. You must have a CD drive that can write as well as read in order to store data on a CD-RW or CD-R. [p. 3]

central processing unit (CPU) The main microprocessor chip that controls the computer. [p. 6]

chat rooms Web sites where you can communicate in real time with other people logged in to the same site. [p. 133]

check boxes Square boxes that you click to select or deselect a setting in a dialog box. A selected check box has as check mark or X in it. [p. 63]

chips Tiny integrated circuits that either control computer functions or store information. [p. 4]

click To press and release the left mouse button. [p. 53]

cold boot To start your computer when the power is off. [p. 42]

color palette A selection of available colors. [p. 67]

command-line interface An interface that requires you to type specific commands to communicate with the PC. [p. 52]

commands Instructions given to the computer by a user or by a program. [p. 52]

compact disc (CD) drives Used to read and sometimes write data to and from compact discs (CDs). [p. 3]

context-sensitive Pertaining to the current topic or the current command being attempted. [p. 68]

Control Panel A Windows system folder that contains utility programs you can use to check and change the settings that control most of your system components. [p. 60]

controller board A printed circuit board that attaches to an expansion slot inside the system unit and controls the operation of peripherals. [p. 4]

conventional memory The first 640K of RAM. [p. 102]

data Any kind of information processed or stored by your computer. [p. 3]

database applications Applications designed for the storage and retrieval of any type of data. [p. 157]

dedicated outlet An electrical outlet installed specifically for plugging in the computer and computer components. [p. 19]

default The way an option is set before you change or customize it. [p. 45]

desktop publishing applications Applications designed for creating published documents. [p. 159]

dialog box An onscreen window displayed by Windows or a Windows application, in which you must make a choice or enter additional information to complete a command. [p. 43]

digital pen A device used to write information on a digitizing tablet. [p. 9]

digital video disc (DVD) A disk that stores data in digital format, which can be played using a DVD drive. DVD drives are faster and store more data than CD drives. They can also read regualr CDs. [p. 3]

digitizing tablet A device that translates written data into digital data that a computer can understand. [p. 9]

disk capacity The amount of data you can store on a disk. [p. 79]

disk density How tightly packed data can be on the disk. [p. 79]

disk drives Hardware storage devices that read information and sometimes write information to magnetic storage disks. [p. 2]

document A file created with a word processing application. Often used as a synonym for any data file created with an application. [p. 118]

domain The address of an Internet server. [p. 134]

double-click The action of clicking the left mouse button twice in rapid succession. [p. 55]

dragging The action of pressing and holding the left mouse button, and then moving the mouse pointer. [p. 57]

drawing application An application used to create and edit drawings and other graphics files. [p. 114]

drops The action of releasing the left mouse button after dragging. [p. 58]

drop-down arrow An arrowhead pointing down next to a button on a toolbar or in a dialog box. Click the arrow to open a list of options. [p. 62]

email Electronic messages transmitted to other computer users on a network. [p. 132]

ergonomic Designed for comfort. [p. 20]

expanded memory A combination of hardware and software that lets older PCs, based on the 8088 microprocessor, and some 80286s access upper memory. This type of memory is sometimes called LIM-compatible, because it was developed by Lotus, Intel, and Microsoft. [p. 103]

expansion slots Slots inside the system unit, in which controller boards can be inserted. [p. 7]

extended memory All memory over 1MB. It is sometimes called high memory. [p. 103]

female connector A connector that has sockets sticking in. [p. 22]

file server A computer that controls files, programs, and access to data on a network. [p. 13]

file types The kinds of data contained in the file. [p. 93]

filename extension A dot (or period) followed by three or four characters, added to the end of a filename in order to identify the file type. [p. 93]

files The data you enter and save using application programs. [p. 53]

financial applications Software designed to help manage finances. [p. 162]

folder A group of related files. [p. 54]

format To prepare a disk for use. [p. 81]

forums Web sites devoted to a particular topic, in which you can find information about that topic and communicate with others about that topic. [p. 133]

graphical user interface (GUI) Pronounced "gooey"—An interface that combines graphics, menus, and plain English commands to let you communicate with the PC. [p. 52]

graphics files Files used to store pictures and other images such as photographs and drawings. [p. 114]

handheld device A PC designed to be carried in one's hand. [p. 8]

hardware The electronic components, boards, peripherals, and equipment that make up your computer. [p. 2]

home page The main page for a Web site, usually the first page displayed when you access the site. [p. 137]

hotkey The underlined letter in a menu or command name, used to access the menu or command with a keyboard. [p. 60]

HTML (Hypertext Markup Language) A file format that supports graphics, formatted text, and other elements that make the data nice to look at and easy to use. [p. 133]

HTTP (Hypertext Transfer Protocol) A standard for transmitting data that supports the HTML file format. [p. 133]

hyperlinks Text or graphics linked to related information in the same program, in a different program, or on the Internet. Often shortened to link. Onscreen, hyperlinks appear underlined and in a different color from surrounding text. When the mouse pointer touches a hyperlink, the pointer resembles a hand with a pointing finger. [p. 68]

hyperlink target The destination document displayed when a hyperlink is clicked. [p. 141]

icons Small pictures that represent applications, files, or folders. [p. 52]

increment arrows Small arrowheads pointing up and down that are used to change a number setting in increments. For example, increment arrows can be used to set a size value, change the date, or select a percentage. [p. 62]

inkjet printer Produces an image by spraying ink through a matrix. [p. 11]

input To enter data into a computer. As a noun, input means the data itself. [p. 8]

insertion point The flashing line that displays onscreen in a document or file during editing that indicates where data will be inserted. Sometimes called a cursor. [p. 111]

install To set up software to run or work on your computer. [p. 156]

integrated applications (also called a **suite**) A group of applications packaged together as one product, and designed to share data and features. [p. 162]

Internet A global network of computers that are connected to each other via cables, satellites, and telephone lines. [p. 132]

Internet Service Provider (ISP) A company or organization that provides access to the Internet, usually for a fee. [p. 133]

intuitive Understanding and responsive. In the case of software programs, it means flexible and easy to use. [p. 53]

joystick An input device often used with games. Joysticks connect to a game port on the system unit. [p. 9]

key combinations Pressing more than one key at the same time. [p. 43]

keyboard An input device attached to a computer, used to type characters and commands. [p. 2]

label A name given to a disk to help identify its contents. [p. 81]

laser printer Uses light and toner to create an image. [p. 11]

laptop A portable computer that is sized to be easily carried and designed to be used while away from one's desk. [p. 8]

list boxes A list of options displayed in a dialog box. You click an option in the list to select it. [p. 63]

log off To disconnect from a network. [p. 45]

log on To sign in to use a network. [p. 45]

male connector A connector that has pins sticking out. [p. 22]

maximizing Increasing the size of a window so that it fills the desktop. [p. 54]

megahertz (MHz) One million cycles per second—a measure of the speed of a microprocessor. [p. 6]

memory The electronic circuitry in which the PC stores information that it is currently using, including programs and data. [p. 102]

memory requirement The amount of memory you must have installed to run an application program on your PC. [p. 103]

menu A list of choices from which you can select commands. [p. 52]

menu bar A row of menu names, usually located under the title bar of a window. [p. 52]

minimizing Reducing a window to a button on the taskbar or to an icon on the desktop. [p. 54]

minimum requirements The requirements for getting a software program up and running. [p. 104]

modems Modems (short for modulator/demodulator) enable you to exchange information with other computers via telephone lines or cables. [p. 2]

monitor The hardware device that displays computer data in a format that you can understand. Also called a display or screen. [p. 2]

motherboard The main printed circuit board inside a system unit, to which all other devices are attached. [p. 6]

mouse An input device used to select commands on a PC screen. [p. 2]

multimedia applications Programs that use a combination of media such as graphics, text, sound, and video. [p. 161]

nested menus Menus that open when you point at a command on a different menu. Sometimes called a submenu. [p. 56]

network A group of computers linked together by cables to share data and resources. [p. 7]

offline Not connected. Used in reference to a peripheral device linked to a computer, or to a computer linked to a network. [p. 137]

online Actively connected and exchanging data. Used in reference to a peripheral device connected to a computer or to a computer connected to a network. [p. 132]

on/off switch The electrical switch on a hardware device that turns the device on and off. [p. 3]

online services Internet Service Providers that offer additional services such as private forums and chat rooms. [p. 134]

operating system A collection of software programs that controls the input and output of data, manages the way files are stored and retrieved, and processes commands that you enter. Most PCs run a version of Windows—either Windows 95, Windows 98, or Windows NT. Handheld devices run Windows CE. [p. 36]

option buttons Round buttons that you click to select or deselect an option in a dialog box. A selected option button has a dot in it. [p. 63]

output Data produced by the computer in a form that the user can understand. [p. 9]

parallel port A type of connection that sends data through eight wires simultaneously. They are called LPT ports and are usually used for connecting printers. [p. 25]

peripherals Another term for hardware devices. Any piece of hardware attached to your PC is a peripheral. [p. 2]

personal computer (PC) A stand-alone computer equipped with all the system, utility, and application software, and input/output devices needed to perform one or more tasks. [p. 2]

pointing The action of resting the mouse pointer on a particular element onscreen. [p. 56]

ports Electrical sockets on the outside of system units that are used to connect external peripherals to controller boards on the inside of system units. [p. 4]

power-on self-test (POST) A series of diagnostic tests that your computer runs when it first starts. It uses the POST to make sure that every component connected to the system unit is working the way it should. [p. 36]

presentation applications Software designed for creating slides and slide shows using text and graphics. [p. 164]

print To create a hard copy version of a file or document on paper using a printer. [p. 121]

print queue A list of documents or files waiting to be printed. [p. 122]

prompt A message displayed by Windows, telling you what action you should take next. [p. 41]

properties The settings that control the way a Windows element functions. [p. 61]

random access memory (RAM) The electronic memory in which the computer processes information until the information can be used or stored on disk. RAM is temporary, or volatile, memory—when you shut off the computer, everything stored in RAM disappears. [p. 6]

recommended requirements The recommended requirements are the features you need to use a software program to its fullest capabilities. [p. 104]

Rename mode A mode of operation in which you can edit the names of files and folders in Windows. [p. 89]

resolution A measurement of the sharpness of an image generated by an output device such as a monitor or a printer. [p. 11]

restoring Returning a window to its previous size and location on the desktop. [p. 54]

right-clicking The action of clicking the right mouse button. [p. 59]

ROM The memory chips built into your computer by the manufacturer that are used to start the system. [p. 102]

scanner A device used to input data that has already been printed on a page, such as a letter or a picture. Scanners are similar to copy machines, except that instead of copying the data from one piece of paper to another, they copy the data from a piece of paper into the computer's memory. [p. 9]

screen saver A program that moves images across your display screen. A screen saver prevents damage from screen burn-in, which occurs when your screen is idle for a long time and light leaves a permanent mark on the screen. [p. 64]

ScreenTip A line of text that identifies the button to which the mouse is currently pointing. [p. 56]

scrollbar An element used to shift the current display up and down (vertical scrollbar) or left and right (horizontal scrollbar). [p. 65]

SCSI (small computer system interface) Pronounced "scuzzy"—A data transfer standard which means that all SCSI devices transfer data the same way. Up to eight SCSI devices can use one SCSI port to transfer data at high speeds. SCSI devices are more expensive than devices that use other transfer standards. [p. 24]

search engine A Web site designed to locate information on the Internet by searching for key terms or phrases. [p. 141]

serial A type of connection that sends data through one wire. They are sometimes called RS-232 ports, or COM ports. Serial ports are commonly used for attaching serial printers, modems, and mice. [p. 23]

server A computer that manages other computers on a network. [p. 135]

shortcut An icon used to quickly access a program, file, or folder. [p. 88]

shortcut menu A menu that is displayed in response to a right-click, offering a short list of commonly used commands. [p. 59]

sleep mode (also called **standby mode**) An energy-saving setting used when you will be away from your computer for awhile but do not want to shut it down. [p. 45]

software Programs composed of coded instructions that run on the computer to tell the hardware how to process information. [p. 154]

spools Prepares for printing and stores in memory until the printer is available. [p. 121]

spreadsheet applications Software programs designed for creating documents, in which data can be entered in columns and rows. Usually used for performing calculations and data analyses. [p. 156]

standby mode See **sleep mode**.

status lights Light-emitting diodes (LEDs) on hardware devices that appear illuminated when the device is active and does not appear illuminated when the device is inactive. [p. 3]

subfolder A folder stored within another folder. [p. 89]

suite See **integrated applications**.

surge suppressor A device designed to moderate the flow of electricity in order to eliminate sudden surges. [p. 25]

system requirements The type of hardware that you need to run a software application. [p. 104]

system unit The main case that houses your personal computer components. [p. 2]

Systray The name of the system tray area at the end of the taskbar in Windows. The Systray displays icons for system settings, such as the clock/calendar, volume control, and the Task Scheduler. [p. 53]

tape drives Hardware storage devices used to read and write data onto tape cassettes. [p. 2]

task lighting Lighting concentrated on a specific location, such as the top of a desk. [p. 19]

taskbar An area displayed on the Windows desktop that contains buttons representing open applications, as well as buttons used to open menus or access commands. [p. 53]

text box An area in which you type data in a dialog box or on a toolbar. [p. 62]

tiled Arranged side by side. For example, windows can be tiled on the desktop or an image can be tiled as wallpaper. [p. 64]

title bar A row across the top of an open window that displays the name of the contents of the window. [p. 52]

toner Ink powder used in laser printers. [p. 10]

toolbars A collection of buttons, or tools, used to perform common tasks, such as starting a program or saving a file. [p. 55]

trackball An input device that you use like a mouse to move a pointer around the screen. Trackballs don't require a flat area the way a mouse does, so they are often built into portable PCs in place of a mouse. [p. 9]

uniform resource locator (URL) Pronounced "earl"—An address on the Internet. [p. 138]

uninterruptible power supply (UPS) A device that contains a backup power supply, usually a battery, so that attached electrical devices continue to operate in the event of a power failure. [p. 25]

upper memory All memory installed on the computer between conventional memory and 1024K (one megabyte). [p. 103]

utilities Software programs used for system maintenance, protection, or repair. [p. 162]

video RAM Additional memory chips that are built into the video display adapter card that controls the monitor. The amount of video RAM determines how many colors can be displayed and how fast images appear. [p. 103]

virtual memory Hard disk space that Windows reserves for use as extra memory. [p. 103]

virus A software program that, when executed, damages software and/or hardware devices on the computer system. [p. 28]

wallpaper A decorative image displayed on your desktop background. Wallpaper can be centered, which means that a single image is displayed in the middle of the desktop; tiled, which means the image is repeated evenly to cover the entire desktop in a pattern; or stretched, which means that a single image is enlarged to fill the desktop. [p. 44]

warm boot To restart the computer without shutting off the power; some of the startup routine procedures are skipped. [p. 42]

Web browser Software that makes it easy to locate and view information stored on the Internet. Common browsers include Internet Explorer and Netscape Navigator. [p. 132]

Web pages Documents stored on the World Wide Web. [p. 132]

Web site A set of linked Web pages. [p. 132]

windows Rectangular areas on the desktop in which information is displayed. Some windows display application programs, whereas some windows display dialog boxes. Don't confuse windows (lowercase "w") with Windows (uppercase "W"). [p. 52]

Windows Clipboard A temporary storage area that is used for copying and moving files, folders, and data from one location to another. [p. 94]

Windows desktop The main screen of the Windows operating system. It appears when you first start Windows and when no other programs are open on your screen. [p. 40]

word processing The act of using a word processing application to create, edit, format, and print text-based documents. [p. 111]

World Wide Web A system for finding information on the Internet through the use of linked documents. [p. 132]

Index

D

E

F

P

Q-R